Strategies for Success

NELSON / EDUCATION

NELSON EDUCATION

COPYRIGHT © 2010 by
Nelson Education Limited.

Printed and bound in Canada
1 2 3 4   12 11 10 09

For more information contact
Nelson Education Limited
1120 Birchmount Road,
Toronto, Ontario, M1K 5G4.
Or you can visit our internet site
at http://www.nelson.com

ALL RIGHTS RESERVED.
No part of this work covered by the copyright hereon may be reproduced, transcribed, or used in any form or by any means – graphic, electronic, or mechanical, including photocopying, recording, taping, web distribution or information storage and retrieval systems – without the written permission of the publisher.

For permission to use material from this text or product, submit all requests online at www.cengage.com/permissions.

Further questions about permissions can be emailed to permissionrequest@cengage.com.

Every effort has been made to trace ownership of all copyrighted material and to secure permission from copyright holders. In the event of any question arising as to the use of any material, we will be pleased to make the necessary corrections in future printings.

This textbook is a Nelson custom publication. Because your instructor has chosen to produce a custom publication, you pay only for material that you will use in your course.

ISBN-13: 978-0-17-649239-7
ISBN-10: 0-17-649239-9

Consists of Selections from:

Investing in Your College Education: Learning Strategies with Readings
Stewart, Hartman
ISBN 10: 0-618-38223-2, © 2006

FOCUS on College Success, First Edition
Staley
ISBN 10: 0-534-63865-1, © 2009

Becoming a Master Student Twelfth Edition
Toft, Mancina, McMurray
ISBN 10: 0-618-95029-X, © 2009

Looking Out/Looking In, Third Canadian Edition Authors
Adler, Proctor III, Towne, Rolls
ISBN 10: 0-17-642412-1, © 2008

Becoming a Master Student Fourth Canadian Edition
Toft, Swartz, Mancina, McMurray
ISBN 10: 0-618-49328-X, © 2006

Contents

Chapter 1   **Making the Initial Investment in Higher Education**
Selected from: Investing in Your College Education: Learning Strategies with Readings
Chapter One: Making the Initial Investment
Understanding What It Means to Be a College Student	page 2
What to Expect from Your Professors and What They Expect of You	page 3
Personal Responsibilities	page 4
Getting Critical: Switching to College-Level Thinking	page 5
Finding Your Place on Campus: Diversity and New Experiences in College	page 7
Finding and Using Campus Resources	page 9
Finding a Mentor	page 11
A Major Decision: Thinking Early and Often About Majors and Careers	page 12
A Quick Overview of Which Majors Lead to Which Careers	page 13

Chapter 2   **Learning Styles**
Selected from: FOCUS on College Success, First Edition
Chapter Two: Learning About Learning
You're about to Discover	page 33
FOCUS Challenge Case: Tammy Ko	page 34
What Do You Think?	page 35
Readiness Check	page 36
Go to the HEAD of the Class: Learning and the Brain	page 36
Use It or Lose It	page 37
Ask Questions and Hardwire Your Connections	page 37
Take Charge and Create the Best Conditions for Learning	page 38
Cultivate Your Curiosity: Can You Build a Better Brain?	page 39
Control Your Learning: Your Top-Ten List	page 43
Multiple Intelligences: How Are You Smart?	page 44
Translate Content into Your Own Intelligences	page 47
Use Intelligence-Oriented Study Techniques	page 48
Choose a Major and Career That Fit Your Intelligences	page 48
Develop Your Weaker Intelligences	page 50
How Do You Perceive and Process Information?	page 50
Exercise 2.1 VARK Learning Styles Assessment	page 52
Using Your Sensory Preferences	page 54
FOCUS on Careers: Neil Fleming, University Professor, Creator of the VARK	page 56
Create a Career Outlook: College Professor	page 57
What Role Does Your Personality Play?	page 58
Exercise 2.2 The SuccessTypes Learning Style Type Indicator	page 60
Interpreting Your SuccessTypes Learning Style Type Profile	page 62
Using Your SuccessTypes Learning Style Type Profile	page 64
Exercise 2.3 VARK Activity	page 65
Now What Do You Think?	page 66
Reality Check	page 66

Chapter 3	**Project Management**		
	Selected from: Becoming a Master Student, Twelfth Edition		
	Chapter Two: Time		
	Master Student Map	page	60
	You've got the time	page	61
	Journal Entry #6: Discovery/Intention Statement	page	61
	Exercise #6: The Time Monitor/Time Plan process	page	62
	Setting and achieving goals	page	67
	Journal Entry #7: Discovery Statement	page	67
	Exercise #7: Get real with your goals	page	69
	The ABC daily to-do list	page	70
	Exercise #8: Create a lifeline	page	72
	Mastering Technology: High-tech ways to manage time	page	72
	Stop procrastination now	page	75
	The seven-day antiprocrastination plan	page	76
	Quiz	page	95
Chapter 4	**Business Writing**		
	Selected from: Becoming a Master Student, Twelfth Edition		
	Chapter Eight: Communicating		
	Three phases of effective writing	page	251
	Phase 1: Getting ready to write	page	251
	Journal Entry #25: Discovery Statement	page	252
	Phase 2: Writing a first draft	page	253
	Phase 3: Revising your draft	page	255
	Mastering Technology: Write e-mail that gets results	page	257
Chapter 5	**Reading and Studying**		
	Selected from: Becoming a Master Student, Twelfth Edition		
	Chapter Four: Reading		
	Journal Entry #10: Discovery/Intention Statement	page	123
	How Muscle Reading works	page	124
	Phase one: Before you read	page	125
	Phase two: While you read	page	126
	Five smart ways to highlight a text	page	126
	Phase three: After you read	page	128
	Muscle Reading—a leaner approach	page	128
	Journal Entry #11: Discovery Statement	page	129
	When reading is tough	page	130
	Mastering Technology: Find what you want on the Internet	page	131
	Quiz	page	145

Chapter 6   Note-Taking
Selected from: Becoming a Master Student, Twelfth Edition
Chapter Five: Notes

Master Student Map	page	148
The note-taking process flows	page	149
Journal Entry #12: Discovery/Intention Statement	page	149
Observe	page	150
Journal Entry #13: Discovery/Intention Statement	page	152
What to do when you miss a class	page	152
Record	page	153
Review	page	158
Journal Entry #14: Discovery Statement	page	159
Quiz	page	173

Chapter 7   Listening and Memory
Selected from: Looking Out/Looking In, Third Canadian Edition
Chapter Seven: Listening: More Than Meets the Ear

Elements in the Listening Process	page	304
Hearing	page	304
Attending	page	305
Understanding	page	305
Responding	page	305
Remembering	page	306
The Challenge of Listening	page	309
Types of Ineffective Listening	page	309
Why We Don't Listen Better	page	312

Selected from: Becoming a Master Student, Twelfth Edition
Chapter Three: Memory

20 memory techniques	page	102
Quiz	page	119

Chapter 8   Test-Taking
Selected from: Becoming a Master Student, Twelfth Edition
Chapter Six: Tests

What to do before the test	page	178
How to cram (even though you shouldn't)	page	179
Ways to predict test questions	page	180
Cooperative learning: Working in groups	page	181
Journal Entry #16: Intention Statement	page	182
What to do during the test	page	183
F is for feedback, not failure	page	184

Words to watch for in essay questions	page 185
The test isn't over until...	page 186
The high costs of cheating	page 187
Mastering Technology: Perils of high-tech cheating	page 187
Let go of test anxiety	page 188
Have some FUN!	page 190
Exercise #18: Twenty things I like to do	page 190
Journal Entry #17: Discovery/Intention Statement	page 191
Journal Entry #18: Discovery Statement	page 191
Getting ready for math tests	page 192
Succeeding in science courses	page 193
Journal Entry #19: Discovery/Intention Statement	page 195
Quiz	page 201

Chapter 9 — Critical and Creative Thinking
Selected from: Becoming a Master Student, Twelfth Edition
Chapter Seven: Thinking

Becoming a critical thinker	page 207
Attitudes of a critical thinker	page 210
Finding "aha!" Creativity fuels critical thinking	page 211
Tangram	page 211
Ways to create ideas	page 212
Create on your feet	page 215
Quiz	page 231

Chapter 10 — Diversity
Selected from: Becoming a Master Student, Canadian Fourth Edition
Chapter Nine: Diversity

Diversity is real—and valuable	page 282
Communicating across cultures	page 284
Overcome stereotypes with critical thinking	page 288

Chapter 11 — Making Presentations and Public Speaking
Selected from: Becoming a Master Student, Twelfth Edition
Chapter Eight: Communicating

Mastering public speaking	page 259
Making the grade in group presentations	page 262
Quiz	page 267

Chapter 12 — Financial Planning
Selected from: Becoming a Master Student, Canadian Fourth Edition
Chapter Two: Planning

Financial planning: Meeting your money goals	page 95
Places to find money for your post-secondary education	page 98
Take charge of your credit card	page 99
Exercise #10: Education by the hour	page 100

Chapter 1

Making the Initial Investment in Higher Education

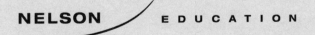

Chapter 1
Making the Initial Investment

This chapter will cover the following topics:

Understanding What It Means to Be a College Student

What to Expect of Your Professors *and* What They Expect of You

Personal Responsibilities

Getting Critical: Switching to College-Level Thinking

Finding Your Place on Campus: Diversity and New Experiences in College

Finding and Using Campus Resources

Finding a Mentor

A Major Decision: Thinking Early and Often About Majors and Careers

A Quick Overview of Which Majors Lead to Which Careers

Let's get right to the point here … you're in college for a reason. Or maybe for a lot of reasons. You always expected to get a college education. Your parents wanted you to go. Your dream job requires a college degree. Your friends were all going, so you thought you had to go. You're a good student. You had nothing better to do. The best initial investment you can make to reap the benefits of success in college is to decide why you are here. Then you can decide what you need to do to succeed. Tough questions, but answering them will yield great dividends for you over the coming years. This chapter is designed to walk you through these questions and to help you understand what college is about, what it means to be a student, what professors expect and what you can expect of them, and how you can use all the resources available to you to get the most out of your investment. It's all up to you.

First Things First

Getting into college is a lot of work. In fact, you may have been so focused on getting to college that you have spent little time actually thinking about what to do once you get there. Now that you are here, though, it's time to refocus. This can be a difficult adjustment for many students. It may be your first time away from home. You may have none of your old friends at the new school. Your first day of classes might be intimidating as you realize what your workload is going to be. At times, you may question the wisdom of your decision to attend college. Sometimes you may even feel like dropping out. It is important to realize that the first few weeks can be the hardest and that hanging in there through this period is part of the process. You must keep your goals in mind and even begin thinking ahead to where your career as a college student will lead you. But the first thing you need to do is get used to your new role as a college student.

Think About It

Answer the following questions in the space provided.

Why am I in college right now? _____

_____

What would I be doing if I were not in college? _____

_____

Understanding What It Means to Be a College Student

College, you will soon discover, is much different from high school. First of all, the workload is considerably different. On the surface, it may seem like you have less work. After all, the typical college student is in class only about 15 hours a week, half of the time a typical high school student spends in the classroom. This, however, means that you have to learn to manage your time better, because more of the responsibility of ensuring that you learn all the material falls on your own shoulders. Furthermore, many students enroll in colleges that are much bigger than their high schools.

Now that you are in college, you may not have your parents to make sure you get out of bed in the morning. You may not get an extra day to turn in an assignment. You may not be told exactly what to do on a paper. You may have to read five chapters in one night . . . and the list goes on. College, you will find, is going to demand that you be an independent learner.

That, luckily, is not as hard as it may seem. Being an independent learner, after all, doesn't mean that you have to do everything on your own. There are lots of resources on campus that will help you. What it *does* mean is that you will sometimes have to take the lead in seeking out help, looking for opportunities, and making the most of them.

The Hard Way

"I thought I knew it all when I first got to college. I went to the local state university, where my brother and sister also went a few years before. I had visited many times, and I knew where all the good parties were and the best place to live. What I didn't know, I later found out, was how to be a good student." Jake recalls with some regret the time he lost after leaving college at the end of his freshman year. He is now back, a senior ready to graduate with a degree in business, six years after he began. "It turns out I didn't really try to understand why I was in college. I went because my brother and sister went. It was just expected of me. I started out as a psychology major, with little idea of why I chose that. But what I really majored in was partying. After my freshman year, I had a 1.2 GPA. I hardly ever made it to class. I never talked to my professors or asked questions about what was expected of me. I flunked test after test but never went for help. I never asked myself what I should be majoring in or what I wanted to do when I got out of college. Then I realized, after my freshman year, that I needed to take time out. My parents said so too. So for the next two years I went to work at a small construction company. I did some pretty hard labor, since I did not have a degree, but soon the boss was letting me come with him to seek clients and close deals. I knew I had what it took to do that, to be my own boss. I knew I wouldn't get anywhere without finishing school. So I returned to the same university and majored in business. And this time, I talked to my professors, got involved in campus activities, and sought out tutors when the going got tough. I will soon graduate with a 3.0. I hope to own my own company some day."

What to Expect of Your Professors *and* What They Expect of You

You will soon discover that your professors have some pretty high expectations of you, the new college student. They expect you to attend class. They expect that you will contact them when you miss a class. They expect that you will arrange to get the information and assignments that you missed. They expect that you will ask questions and seek help during their office hours or from a tutor. They expect that you will put time into the course and take pride in your work. In short, they expect you to care.

In turn, you can expect them to provide you with a syllabus; their office hours, phone number, and e-mail address; and plenty of work. They will also provide you with assistance in completing that work. Be sure to take advantage of posted office hours; most professors are more than happy to meet with you and appreciate the extra effort on your part. This is a good way to get to know your professors and to begin the networking that is an important part of success in college. If you make an appointment during a professor's office hours, be prepared. Have a plan. You want to come across as a well-organized student. If you're visiting because you don't understand the material, you should have questions written down for your visit. Some professors, particularly those who teach large classes, have TAs (Teaching Assistants)

Time Out Tip

Always talk to your professors outside of class. Visit them during their scheduled office hours. Ask them specific questions about upcoming tests. Let them see that you are a hard-working student. Taking this kind of initiative will pay off in the long run.

who are assigned to help. These are typically graduate students who are becoming experts in the field and may even be preparing to become professors themselves.

Even though professors have high expectations of you, they will treat you a lot differently than teachers did in high school. In high school, if you skipped class, your teacher would know right away, and you would probably get detention. In college, you're certainly not going to get detention. Many of your college professors (though not all) will say little or nothing if you miss class. In a large lecture class, they probably won't even notice. But that doesn't mean that you should attend class only when you please. One of the main reasons why students fail in college is that they don't go to class. And don't be fooled by students who seem to be having a great time and not going to any classes. Unfortunately, many of those students won't be around to enjoy themselves the next semester. Don't be one of them.

Personal Responsibilities

What are all of the personal responsibilities of a college student? If you're entering college right out of high school, this is really the first time in your life that you have been totally responsible for yourself. Let's take a look at some of the major responsibilities of a first-year college student:

- ▶ Getting out of bed in the morning on your own.
- ▶ Going to class—every day, even if it starts at 8:00 a.m., and even if you have a slight headache or minor sore throat.
- ▶ Eating a healthy diet and getting enough rest.
- ▶ Managing your time.
- ▶ Managing your money.
- ▶ Balancing work and school.
- ▶ Getting exercise.
- ▶ Doing your laundry.
- ▶ Cleaning your room.
- ▶ Studying—going to class is not enough.
- ▶ Turning in projects and papers on time.
- ▶ Knowing what's on the syllabus and following it.
- ▶ Getting the notes and assignments from a fellow student when you miss class and not expecting your professor to give them to you.
- ▶ Taking responsibility for your own decisions.
- ▶ Drinking responsibly—or not drinking at all.
- ▶ Learning to deal appropriately with conflict (roommate problems, disagreements with a professor, and the like).
- ▶ Maintaining healthy relationships.
- ▶ Meeting college deadlines that govern registering for classes, paying bills, withdrawing from courses, applying for financial aid, signing up for campus housing, and so on.
- ▶ Getting help when you need it, whether it be academic, personal, or financial help. Knowing whom to ask is an important part of this.

That's a lot of stuff. Although many of the items on this list may be new to you, help is always available. Usually an advisor, counselor, faculty member, or more experienced student can at least point you in the right direction.

But you can begin on your own right now. Simple steps such as putting your alarm clock on the other side of the room instead of right next to your bed can make a big difference. If it's right next to your bed, it's all too easy just to hit the snooze or shut it off and go right back to sleep. And don't set your clock radio to your favorite station. Getting up in the morning isn't about listening to your favorite songs. If you like rock music but hate country, set your radio alarm to a country station. That makes it more likely that you will get up to shut it off.

For finances, keep an active eye on your budget. In Chapter 9, we will talk more about specific ways of managing your money. Watch out for the easy lure of credit cards. Set up a schedule of when your assignments are due—and when you are going to work on them. When you go to do your laundry, don't go empty-handed. Take some notes, or, better yet, go with a friend who is in the same class and turn it into an impromptu study session.

Get to know your college catalogue; it will list dates for such activities as registering for class, add-drop, and course withdrawals. Try to recognize potential conflicts before they get out of hand. If you are unhappy with your roommate because he listens to loud music late at night, try talking to him, and if that doesn't work, the two of you should sit down with your RA (resident assistant) or hall director and work things out. Be prepared to learn the importance of compromise. In real life, a "my way or the highway" philosophy isn't going to get you very far. It's no secret that a lot of students run into problems in college for reasons that have nothing to do with their ability to handle the academics. They get into trouble because they aren't prepared for the numerous responsibilities that have suddenly been thrust upon them.

Getting Critical: Switching to College-Level Thinking

It may be obvious, but it's nevertheless worth repeating here: College is not high school. At this level, the expectations of you as a student are much different. How? First of all, you must start becoming a critical thinker. It's not just memorization any more, although you certainly have some of that, too. You probably had some practice in critical thinking in high school, but now it's the rule rather than the exception. Your opinion matters. How well others respond to your opinion will be tied to how well you can learn to express your opinion, to frame an argument, and to convince others. What that means is that the rule will no longer be "Here's what you need to study for the test" and then you simply recite that information. Professors will question you more in class about your attitudes toward issues. Of course, we all have a right to an opinion, but getting other people to understand why we feel the way we do—and even swaying others' opinions—is what you'll be doing in college.

Along with this freedom to express your opinion comes the responsibility for taking your learning into your own hands. You will have to locate a lot of infor-

What Worked for Me

"I was the first person in my family to go to college." Ashley, a senior education major, looks back with amazement at how far she has come. "My parents never went to college, and I am the oldest child in my family. Everything was new. I also chose a college that none of my friends from high school attended — four hours away from home. I knew when I first got here that it was sink or swim. I came to college undeclared, because I had no sense of direction. My parents own a restaurant and I knew I did not want to do that for the rest of my life. I always thought I would make a good elementary school teacher, but I didn't know any teachers, and I didn't know if I had what it would take."

Ashley now credits a campus scavenger hunt project with helping find key people and resources that helped her become a successful education major. "During my first-year seminar, my professor gave us a scavenger hunt project. During this project, I located the Advising Center. In the Advising Center, I met a great professor who walked me through the process of declaring a major and reviewing the courses I would need to take. I went to see her every week. She was a former high school teacher and became the role model I never had. She helped calm my fears and show me I had what it takes. By the end of my first semester, I had a 3.0 GPA and was accepted into the Elementary Education program. I never looked back."

Ashley is currently student teaching in a first grade classroom and knows she made the right decision. Her advice for freshmen is to find an advocate, a professor or staff member who can answer the questions that may overwhelm them. "It may have been easy to quit, but instead, I found a person who believed in me. She told me what classes to take, where to get a tutor when I was failing math my first semester and what to do to declare a major. One person really can make a difference. I hope I can do the same when I am a teacher."

mation on your own. You will have to find your own way around the library, for instance, and your college library may be extremely intimidating when you first arrive. In any given course, you could be expected to take responsibility for locating materials that will supplement information presented in your textbook and in the lectures. A critical thinker does not wait for information to be provided. A critical thinker seeks out information independently. If you do not have enough information about a subject, you can't really think critically about it. The responsibility for equipping yourself with enough information lies in your own hands.

Learning to be a critical thinker doesn't end in the classroom. As you move through life, you will be held responsible for your own actions. You will need to make critical decisions every day when you are in college. This can be as simple as deciding to eat healthy foods or something as complex as trying to decide how to help a friend who has mentioned suicide. Learning how to deal with these issues is not easy, but it is part of becoming an educated person. The relatively simple issue of deciding when and whether to renew your housing contract is an example. You could end up missing important deadlines if you do not take it upon yourself to seek out information you may not have been given. You may not even realize how many housing opportunities you have unless you gather information, think critically about your options, and make an informed decision.

For most students, the biggest difference between high school and college is not the work itself but the need to navigate through the decision making necessitated by the independence that college brings.

Finding Your Place on Campus: Diversity and New Experiences in College

Your first few days or even weeks on campus can be an overwhelming experience. You may have a roommate who comes from a totally different environment. You may see people dressing differently from what you encountered at your high school. You may be surprised at the number of religious organizations represented on campus. Racial, ethnic, and socioeconomic diversity will also play a role in your college experience. From the very beginning, you may find that the students in your classes and in your residence hall are from much more diverse backgrounds than you were used to in high school. You may realize that you're no longer the best athlete in the school or that you're suddenly surrounded by students of all different ages. The faculty members may act very differently from your high school teachers, and they will probably have very different expectations of you. You may come to ask yourself, after the first few days or weeks, "Where do I fit in?" That is a good question, and sooner or later, everyone finds the answer.

Finding your place on campus and coming to enjoy and benefit from the diversity of a college campus is your responsibility, as much as becoming the critical thinker and independent learner you are expected to be. This is not to say, however, that you will not get any help. Help is all around you. Here are some things you can do early in your college experience to find your way:

- ▶ Try to get to know your roommate, if you don't know each other already. Even if you seem to have only differences, you can learn from those differences.
- ▶ Talk to your resident assistant or floor supervisor if you live on campus. In the beginning, residence halls often have socials that can help you get to know people right away so that you don't feel like an outsider.
- ▶ Try to get to know at least one person in each of your classes. Not only will this help you avoid feeling alone in the class, but it will also give you someone you can turn to if you have a question, if you need study help, or if you miss some of the notes.
- ▶ If you get to know your professors outside of class, they may not seem as intimidating or as different from the teachers you have learned from in the past.
- ▶ Try to join at least one extracurricular activity as soon as possible. Whether you like politics, chess, art, or music, there's probably a club for you. And if there isn't, consider taking the lead and forming one. These clubs give you a chance to socialize and share your interests with others.
- ▶ Go to a cultural event on campus that you would not normally see. For example, you could go to a ballet, a symphony, a drum circle, or a gallery opening. This sort of exploration could lead to a whole new area of interest.

- If you think your schedule will permit, consider working on campus, even for a few hours a week. This will make you feel more connected, and it will also help you to meet new people.
- If you're a commuter, your campus may have a commuter lounge or group where you can share lunch and meet others who have a similar experience.
- If you're a nontraditional student, remember that most campuses have a nontraditional student group that may be very supportive and helpful. It may also be especially important for nontraditional students with families to think about striking an effective balance so that they maintain a healthy family life while being a student. One suggestion is to get your family involved in your college experiences. Many campuses have family days, festivals, or cultural activities that spouses, children, and other family members can attend. Such opportunities can help them feel more familiar with what you're doing in college.
- Sports are a good way to get to know others. You don't have to be a state champion to get involved. Most colleges have intramural sport leagues. And any trip to the campus gym should give you an opportunity to play pick-up basketball, racquetball, or tennis.
- Fraternities and sororities have long been a tradition at many college campuses. They can be a great way to get to know other students. Often, members end up living together in the "house." The best of these organizations not only support strong academic performance but also actively encourage it.
- College parties are also a long-standing tradition. And, of course, they can be a good way to meet and get to know others. As with anything else, moderation is the key. Save the parties for the weekend and don't overdo it.

The best time to try to find your place on campus is from the very beginning. Remember that all the other new students are trying to do the same thing. If you wait too long, you may miss out on some opportunities. Also, a few weeks could go by, and you could start to feel very isolated from the campus community. Trying to find your place right away will prevent this isolation and help you feel more connected.

College students traditionally think of their courses as the main sources of learning. This is partly true—you do learn in your courses—but it is also true that you will learn as much, if not more, from the experiences that you have outside the classroom. In other words, if you simply go to classes and then go home and study, you're not going to have all that much to say for yourself when you graduate. Most employers and graduate schools are looking for a well-rounded person —for someone who, in addition to having made good grades, can show that he or she has been involved in activities that go beyond the classroom.

> **DIY: Do-It-Yourself Activity**
>
> Find and arrange to meet a professor in the field you are interested in pursuing. You can find a professor in a particular field by checking the campus directory or your school's website, which would identify professors and their respective departments. When you meet with the professor, ask him or her the following questions:
>
> 1. How did you get into your field?
> 2. What level of education do you recommend?
> 3. Am I in the right major?
> 4. What can I do now to prepare for this career?
>
> You may find some of the answers surprising, and you just might be laying the foundation for a mentoring relationship—and a letter of recommendation when you graduate!

Finding and Using Campus Resources

Campus resources are there for you. Only you can decide what you can get out of them by investing your time and effort. Campus resources may include

- **Career Services Office** Houses information about specific jobs, job outlooks, job qualifications, résumé writing and interviewing, and graduate schools. But don't wait until you're a senior to take advantage of Career Services. These offices also can help you find summer jobs and internships in areas related to your major. This will be an enormous help to you down the road.
- **Student Activities Office** Provides information on clubs and activities that students can participate in both on and off campus. Everything from the outdoor club, which might take canoeing trips, to the finance club for future entrepreneurs. You can start networking today.
- **Residence Life Office** If you're living on campus, you're going to need to know this office, which is the place to go for everything from changing roommates to getting a job as a resident assistant (RA).

Tutoring Center Provides tutors to students in various subjects and general study skills. This is also a good source of employment on campus. If you're good in math, for example, why not get paid to help somebody else learn it while building your résumé at the same time?

Greek Life Office If you're on a campus with fraternities and sororities, the Greek Life Office will be the focal point for coordinating activities and housing.

Financial Aid Office Don't stay in the dark about student loans, grants, and scholarships. Much more may be out there than you know about, and the Financial Aid Office is a veritable warehouse of valuable information that can help you stay in school. Also, the Financial Aid Office can often provide information about work study jobs (which are tied to financial need).

Bursar's Office Pay your bills here!

Registrar's Office This office is responsible for helping you register for classes, drop and add classes, and withdraw from classes and for maintaining academic records. Also, if you need a transcript for a job or graduate school, this is where you will go.

Advising Office Many campuses provide full-time academic advisors to help you develop an appropriate academic plan. Take advantage of this service so you can avoid staying in school longer than you need to.

Counseling Center College can be a stressful and difficult time emotionally and psychologically. If at any time you feel that you're getting overly stressed, you don't have to bear the burden alone. Trained counselors are there to help you, and that help can often very quickly get you back on track.

Volunteer Center Besides being a nice thing to do, volunteering is another great way to build your résumé. It also can give you a taste of a job that interests you, and you can help people along the way. Many colleges work with both local organizations such as soup kitchens and national organizations such as Habitat for Humanity and the Red Cross. Feel good about yourself while learning more about careers and meeting other students.

Teamwork Activity

For this assignment, work in a group. Each member of the group will find out about a specific service or office on your campus that will help you achieve academic success. You are being given no clues. It's up to you to find such resources and complete your assignment. Good luck!

Oral Portion: All group members will present their findings orally. Include helpful handouts and visuals.

Written Portion: Each group member should write down the answers.

Answer the following questions individually.
1. Who is your advisor?
2. Where is his or her office?
3. What single most important piece of advice did she or he provide to help you achieve academic success in your first year of college?

Answer the following questions in groups.
1: What is tutoring? Who is in charge of this service here on campus? How can you take advantage of it? How might it benefit you? How will you be able to use this information in the future for your academic success?

2: Where is the Career Services Office? What services does it provide for students? How can you utilize it as a first-year student?

3: What does the Counseling Center provide for students on campus? Where is it located? Who is the contact person for this office? Besides the other services that this office provides, how does the staff in this office help students achieve academic success?

4: Where can you go to become a volunteer? What do you need to do to get involved? What are some of the volunteering opportunities that are available? How can these be of value to you as a first-year student?

5: What is the Student Activities Office? Where is it located? What are some of the activities on campus? How can becoming involved in student activities enrich your first year on campus?

Finding a Mentor

Another thing to consider early in your college career is finding the people who can help you through the many twists and turns of college life. A mentor is one such person, and finding one promptly can be one of the best things you can do for yourself. In *The Odyssey,* Mentor was a close friend of Odysseus. Athena, the goddess of wisdom, disguised herself as Mentor in order to serve as a guide for Telemachus in the search for his father. From Homer's classic tale, the term *mentor* has come to mean a guide or an advisor to someone less experienced. How does this work in today's world? A rookie pitcher in baseball may be guided by a veteran. A new account executive at an advertising agency, showing some potential, may be taken under the wing of a senior executive. In college, a professor of biology may show a promising undergraduate the ropes. Or a senior may help a new student learn her way around campus and pick the best professors. Mentoring can mean many different things, and it has advantages for both parties. The mentor gets to share his or her knowledge. The person being mentored gets to learn from someone who has already done what he or she is about to do. Mentoring relationships take time to cultivate, however, and the best time to find a mentor is now, in your first year.

How do you find a mentor? You can begin by going to class. Of course, going to class is no guarantee that you will find a mentor. But it opens up the possibility that you might find a mentor in the person of one of your professors. You're even more likely to cultivate a mentoring relationship by visiting your professors outside of the classroom. Where? Professors usually have posted office hours. They might serve as advisors to different student groups, such as honor societies, volunteer groups, and the student branches of various professional organizations. Another way to get to know professors in a way that might lead to a mentoring relationship is through campus employment. Interested in psychology? See whether any jobs are available in the department office. Or perhaps you could become a tutor in the subject.

Professors are not the only potential mentors, however. People working in your future field can also be valuable mentors. How do you meet them? One of the best ways is through summer employment, starting with the summer immediately following your first year of college. Let's say you want to be an accountant with a major accounting firm. You're not going to be working as an accountant during your first year out of college (you might not even have taken an accounting class yet), but you could certainly get a job in the company in another position (such as the legendary mailroom). In these jobs, take advantage of opportunities to talk with people who have the kinds of jobs you are seeking. You might find someone who is interested in helping you get ahead in that field. The one summer you spend in the mailroom could lead to a job the next summer that is closer to your desired position.

Finally, you may not have to do all the work yourself. Many campuses have organized peer mentoring programs in place. They can be set up by majors, honor societies, residence halls, and athletics programs. Don't be afraid to give these a try. You may find after a year or two that you've gone from mentee to mentor and are sharing *your* knowledge with a new student.

A Major Decision: Thinking Early and Often About Majors and Careers

"So, what's your major?" If you haven't heard this line already, you will soon enough. To the world at large, you're identified by which college you attend: "I go to --- College." Within your college, though, along with your fraternity/sorority, sports team, residence hall, clubs, or even hometown, your major is one of the key identifiers that tells your peers about you. You might feel a little frustration if your answer to that question right now is "Undeclared" or "Biology, but I am switching to something else," but you don't need to worry just yet. Studies show that the average college student switches majors three to four times. Yet even though you may need this year to get your feet wet in college, now is still as good a time as any to start *thinking* about your major. You should do it now—and do it often. There are plenty of opportunities to get started on this important process:

▶ **Reflect on the classes you are taking.** Usually, in your first year in college, you have a number of general education classes in everything from speech and composition to psychology and mathematics. What courses do you enjoy the most? How are you doing in these courses? You might find you are fascinated by something you never even considered when you were in high school.

▶ **If there's a course you like and in which you are doing well, talk to the professor.** He or she may have some insights to share with you about how the course is related to particular majors or career choices you could pursue.

▶ **Join a special-interest club.** You might find more information about a particular major or career and also meet people with similar interests—not only students but also professors and other professionals in the field.

▶ **Talk to your advisor.** Your advisor is trained to give you advice not only on what courses to take but also on what courses fit into what degree programs. He or she can help you decide whether a change in major is appropriate. If you are undeclared, speaking with your advisor is especially important as you sharpen your focus.

▶ **Visit the career office on campus.** In addition to providing information about careers, this office gives students an opportunity to take self-assessments that will help them zero in on a major or possible career. It's a good idea to take these self-assessments early, especially if you did not do so in high school. You

Lifeline

If you think you might need a tutor for a course, sign up early in the semester. Studies show that tutoring works best with repeated visits. If you wait until the last minute, it is not likely to help much. Besides, at most campuses, tutors are assigned on a first-come, first-served basis, so if you wait too long, a tutor may not be available.

A Quick Overview of Which Majors Lead to Which Careers

Getting a bachelor's degree is like becoming a member of an exclusive club; having the degree can open many doors for you, regardless of what your major is. In other words, even if you have a degree in English, you may be able to get a job in business. If you have a degree in psychology, you may find yourself with an opportunity to break into sales. Except in very technical fields—such as nursing, accounting, and chemical engineering, where you would be required to have a specialized degree—a bachelor's degree in almost any subject will be enough to get your foot in the door. What happens after that, of course, is up to you. Even so, your choice of major will provide direction for the types of opportunities you pursue. There are plenty of majors that really do provide you with a very straight path to particular job opportunities if that's the way you choose to go:

Major	Typical Jobs*	Other Possibilities*
Education	Elementary Teacher	Corporate Trainer
	High School Teacher	Tour or Museum Guide
	Day Care Provider	Public Relations Trainee
Business	Accountant	Restaurateur
	Manager	Sports Agent
	Financial Planner	Computer Consultant
Physical Science	Chemist	Sales Representative
	Flavorist	Teacher
	Quality Control Inspector	Chef
Psychology	Counselor	Sales Representative
	Social Service Position	Web Designer
	Psychologist	Manager
Mass Media	Radio/TV Personality	Sales Representative
	Public Relations Staffer	Corporate Trainer
	Radio/TV Producer	Web Designer
English	Editor	Sales Representative
	Writer	Corporate Trainer
	Public Relations Staffer	Teacher
History	Teacher	Journalist
	Researcher	Antiques Dealer
	Museum Curator	Art or Furniture Restorer
Visual and Performing Arts	Artist	Teacher
	Dancer	Architect
	Actor	Interior or Set Designer

(continued)

Major	Typical Jobs*	Other Possibilities*
Math	Actuary	Sales Representative
	Mathematician	Claims Adjuster
	Computer Programmer	Teacher
Technology	Programmer	Technical Writer
	Network Administrator	Technology Reporter
	Web Page Designer	Computer Sales Person

*Some fields may require further education or training.
For more information on job possibilities related to different majors, go to the website at **http://studentsuccess.college.hmco.com/students**.

You will notice that some fields, such as sales, are open to people from just about any major. The point of a chart like this is to suggest the possibilities and also to illustrate the lack of limitations. There are many examples of English majors who became business executives and business majors who decided to become teachers. Don't be limited by the stereotypes, but do research the possibilities. The time to start is now.

Now that you have a good idea of what is expected of you and how you can begin to meet those expectations, it's a good time to reflect on what you have learned about what lies ahead. Ask yourself: **What do I need to do to be a successful college student?**

Get Involved!

"Plain and simple—I was lost." Pedro, now a senior communications major, looks back on his first year in college with a laugh. "My senior class in high school had 45 students in it. Then I came here, and there were four thousand freshmen on campus. I didn't know what to do. I went from knowing everybody in my whole school—teachers and students—to knowing, out of all five classes, exactly one other student."

"I had gone to a college in another state because I didn't want to go where all my friends were going. But I had no idea how big a challenge I was facing. Everything was new, I didn't know anybody, and after a little while, I started to feel like I was invisible." Pedro says he spent a couple of weeks hanging out alone in his room. "My roommate and I didn't have much in common, and he was never there anyway, so I just kind of hid out. But I realized I couldn't do that forever. If I didn't find something soon, I'd be heading home." A sign in the student union one afternoon captured his attention. "The student newspaper was looking for some people for the layout staff. I didn't think of myself as much of a writer, and I didn't know anything about newspapers, but I had a little experience with some of the computer programs they mentioned, so I thought I'd give it a try. Turns out they had all the people they needed for layout, but they took my name and number, along with those of about 20 other people." Pedro left the meeting thinking that was the end of that. "I was shocked when the sports editor called the next morning and asked me to cover the football game that day. Nobody else could do it. I asked her if she had the right number, but she said they were desperate. The regular reporter was sick, and she was tied up at the office. They would set me up in the press box. I just had to take notes, and she would help me write it up if I needed it. I actually did very well on my own and gained the confidence to write more."

Chapter 2

Learning Styles

2 Learning about Learning

YOU'RE ABOUT TO DISCOVER...

> How learning changes your brain
> How people are intelligent in different ways
> How you learn through your senses
> How your personality affects your learning style
> How to become a more efficient and effective learner

"They know enough who know how to learn."
John Adams, second President of the United States

FOCUS CHALLENGE CASE

Tammy Ko

"How depressing!" Tammy Ko whispered under her breath as she walked out of her "Introduction to Criminology" class on a dark, rainy Thursday afternoon. *What's with him, anyway?* she asked herself pointedly about the professor.

Tammy was a first-semester student at a large state campus several hours from her tiny hometown, where she'd been a popular student. If you leafed through her high school yearbook, you'd see Tammy's picture on nearly every page. There Tammy had been a big fish in a small pond, but now it was the other way around.

Even though she found college life at the large state university overwhelming, Tammy was excited about her major, forensic chemistry. The crime shows on TV were her favorites. She watched them all each week. She rationalized how much time it took by thinking of it as career development. The fun was picturing herself as an investigator solving headline cases: "Man Slain, Found in City Park" or "Modern Day 'Jack the Ripper' Terrorizes Las Vegas." She could envision herself hunched over laboratory equipment, testing intently for fibers or DNA, and actually breaking the case.

When she registered for classes, her academic advisor had told her that taking an "Introduction to Criminology" course from the sociology department would be a good idea. "It'll teach you how to think," he'd said, "and it'll give you the background you need to understand the criminal mind. At the end of this class," he said, "you'll know if you really want to pursue a career in forensics." *Maybe it would teach me how to think*, Tammy thought to herself now that the term was underway, *if only I could understand the professor. Forget understanding the criminal mind—I'd just like a glimpse into his!*

Professor Caldwell was quiet and reserved, and he seemed a bit out of touch. He dressed as if he hadn't bought a new article of clothing in as many years as he'd been at the university. In class, he was very articulate, knowledgeable, and organized with his handouts neatly piled on the desk, and he covered each day's material methodically, point by point. Tammy wished he'd venture from his notes occasionally to explore fascinating, related tangents. Tammy had always preferred teachers who created exciting things to do in class over teachers who went completely by the book.

Tammy's biggest complaint about Professor Caldwell was that he only talked about *theories* of criminology. When was he ever going to get to the hands-on part of the course? She couldn't help thinking, *When will we stop talking about theories and start working on real cases—like the ones on all those TV shows?*

To make matters worse, learning from lectures was not Tammy's strong suit. She hadn't done well on the first exam because she'd had to resort to memorizing things that didn't make much sense to her, and her D grade showed it. The exam consisted of one question: "Compare and contrast two theories of criminology discussed in class thus far." Tammy hated essay tests. She was at her best on tests with right or wrong answers, like true-false or multiple-choice questions. Making sense out of spoken words that go by very quickly during a lecture and trying to psych out professors' preferred answers on essay tests were challenges to her.

But her "Introduction to Criminology" class was far from hands-on. In fact, Tammy had noticed that many of her teachers preferred talking about things to doing things. They seemed to take more interest in theories than in the real world. *Too bad*, she thought, *the real world is where exciting things happen.* Although she hated to admit it, sometimes Tammy couldn't wait for college to be over so that she could begin her career in the real world. A few of Tammy's friends had taken Professor Caldwell's classes. "Just try and memorize the stuff; that's all you can do," they'd advised her. Regardless of what they happened to be talking about, somehow the conversation always came around to Professor Caldwell and how impossible it was to learn in his classes.

WHAT DO YOU THINK?

Now that you've read about Tammy Ko, answer the following questions. You may not know all the answers yet, but you'll find out what you know and what you stand to gain by reading this chapter.

1. Why is Tammy having difficulty learning in her "Introduction to Criminology" class?
2. Is Tammy smart? If so, in what ways? What is she particularly good at?
3. What sensory modality does Tammy prefer for taking in information?
4. What do you think Tammy's personality type is? How does her personality type relate to her learning style?
5. How would you describe Professor Caldwell's teaching style? His personality type? How does his personality type relate to his teaching style?
6. What are the differences between Professor Caldwell's teaching style and Tammy's learning style? How do these differences impact Tammy's learning?
7. What should Tammy do to become a better learner in Professor Caldwell's class?

"O! this learning, what a thing it is."

William Shakespeare

READINESS CHECK

Before beginning to read this chapter, take two minutes to answer the following questions on a scale of 1 to 10. Your answers will help you assess how ready you are to focus.

1 = not very/not much/very little/low   10 = very/a lot/very much/high

Based on reading the "You're about to discover..." list and skimming this chapter, how much do you think you probably already know about the subject matter?

1 2 3 4 5 6 7 8 9 10

How much do you think this information might affect your college success?

1 2 3 4 5 6 7 8 9 10

How much do you think this information might affect your career success after college?

1 2 3 4 5 6 7 8 9 10

In general, how motivated are you to learn the material in this chapter?

1 2 3 4 5 6 7 8 9 10

This book describes four key factors related to intrinsic, or internal, motivation: curiosity, control, career outlook, and challenge The next four questions relate to these **C-Factors:**

How *curious* are you about the content you expect to read in this chapter?

1 2 3 4 5 6 7 8 9 10

How much *control* do you expect to have over mastering the material in this chapter?

1 2 3 4 5 6 7 8 9 10

How much do you think this chapter might help you develop your *career outlook*?

1 2 3 4 5 6 7 8 9 10

How *challenging* do you expect the material in this chapter to be for you?

1 2 3 4 5 6 7 8 9 10

Before beginning any task, including studying, it's important to check in with yourself to ensure that you're physically, intellectually, and emotionally ready to focus. How ready are you, physically, to focus on this chapter? (Are you rested, feeling well, and so on?)

1 2 3 4 5 6 7 8 9 10

How ready are you, intellectually, to focus on this chapter? (Are you thinking clearly, focused on this course, interested in this subject?)

1 2 3 4 5 6 7 8 9 10

How ready are you, emotionally, to focus on this chapter? (Are you calm, confident, composed?)

1 2 3 4 5 6 7 8 9 10

If your answer to any of the last three questions is below a 5 on the scale, you may need to address the issue you're facing prior to beginning this chapter. For example, if you're hungry, get a quick bite to eat. If you're feeling scattered, take a few moments to settle down and focus.

Finally, how long do you think it will take you to complete this chapter?
_____ Hour(s) _____ Minutes

Go to the HEAD of the Class: Learning and the Brain

CHALLENGE ⇨ REACTION

Challenge: What is learning?

Reaction: The following statements represent common student views on learning. Think about each statement, and mark it **true** or **false** based on your honest opinion.

_____ 1. Learning is often hard work and really not all that enjoyable.

_____ 2. Memorization and learning are basically the same thing.

_____ 3. The learning done in school is often gone in a few weeks or months.

_____ 4. In college, most learning takes place in class.

_____ 5. Learning is usually the result of listening to an instructor lecture or reading a textbook.

_____ 6. The best way to learn is by working alone.

_____ 7. Most students know intuitively how they learn best.

_____ 8. Teachers control what students learn.

_____ 9. Learning only deals with subjects taught in school.

_____ 10. The learning pace is controlled by the slowest learner in the class.

You probably noticed that many of these statements attempt to put learning in a negative light. How many did you mark true? This chapter will help you understand more about learning as a process and about yourself as a learner. As you read, your goal should be to use the insights you gain to become a better learner.

Let's start our exploration of the learning process close to home—in our own heads. What's going on up there, anyway? While your hands are busy manipulating test tubes in chemistry lab, or your eyes are watching your psychology professor's PowerPoint presentation, or your ears are taking in a lecture on American politics, what's your brain up to? The answer? Plenty.

Use It or Lose It

The human brain consists of a complex web of connections between neurons. This web grows in complexity as it incorporates new knowledge. But if the connections are not reinforced frequently, they degenerate. As you learn new things, you work to hardwire these connections, making them less susceptible to degeneration. When your professors repeat portions of the previous week's lecture or assign follow-up homework to practice material covered in class, they're helping you to form connections between neurons through repeated use—or, in other words, to learn. Repetition is vital to learning. You must use and reuse information in order to hardwire it.

American humorist Will Rogers once said, "You know, you've got to exercise your *brain* just like your muscles." He was right. Giving your brain the exercise it needs—now and in your years after college—will help you form connections between neurons that, if you keep using them, will last a lifetime. From a biological point of view, that's what being a lifelong learner means. The age-old advice "use it or lose it" is true when it comes to learning.

Ask Questions and Hardwire Your Connections

Your professors have been studying their disciplines for years, perhaps decades. They have developed extensive hardwired connections between their brain neurons. They are *experts*. Woodrow Wilson once said, "I not only use all the brains I have, but all that I can borrow." Think of college as an ideal time to borrow some excellent brains—your professors'!

By contrast, you are a *novice* to whatever discipline you're studying. You've not yet developed the brain circuitry that your

"Learning is not so much an additive process, with new learning simply piling up on top of existing knowledge, as it is an active, dynamic process in which the connections are constantly changing and the structure reformatted."

K. Patricia Cross, Professor Emerita of Higher Education, University of California, Berkeley

> "The art and science of asking questions is the source of all knowledge."
>
> Thomas Berger, American novelist

professors have developed. This realization points to a potential problem. Sometimes professors are so familiar with what they already know from years of traveling the same neuron paths that what you're learning for the first time seems obvious to them. Without even realizing it, they can expect what is familiar to them to be obvious to you. Sometimes, it isn't obvious at all. One learning expert says this: "The best learners . . . often make the worst teachers. They are, in a very real sense, perceptually challenged. They cannot imagine what it must be like to struggle to learn something that comes so naturally to them."[1] Think of how challenging it is when you try to teach something that you understand thoroughly to another person who doesn't, like teaching someone who has never used a computer before how to upload an assignment.

Since you're a novice, you may not understand everything your professors say. Ask questions, check, clarify, probe, and persist until you do understand. Sometimes your confusion is not due to a lack of knowledge, but a lack of the *correct* knowledge. You may be getting interference from misinformation or unproductive habits of thinking and learning that have become hardwired in your brain. For example, you may study for a test by doing only one thing—reading and re-reading the textbook. Actually, it's important to be familiar with an array of study tools and choose the ones that work best for you.

Think of it this way. Some of the neural connections you brought with you to college are positive and useful, and some are counterproductive. When you learn, you not only add new connections, but you rewire some old connections. While you're in college, you're under construction![2]

Take Charge and Create the Best Conditions for Learning

Throughout this discussion, we've been talking about internal processes in your brain. *Your* brain, not anyone else's. The bottom line is this: Learning must be *internally initiated*—by you. It can only be *externally encouraged*—by someone else. You're in charge of your own learning. Learning changes your brain.

Let's look at food as an analogy: If learning is a process that is as biological as digestion, then no one can learn for you, in the same way that no one can eat for you. The food in the refrigerator doesn't do you a bit of good unless you walk over, open the door, remove the object of your desire, and devour it. It's there for the taking, but you must make that happen. To carry the analogy further, you eat on a daily basis, right? "No thanks, I ate last week" is a senseless statement. Learning does for your brain what food does for your body. Nourish yourself!

CULTIVATE Your Curiosity

CAN YOU BUILD A BETTER BRAIN?

Don't look now, but you're a very busy person! If you were watching a movie of your life at this moment, what would the scene look like? A cell phone in your hand, a website open on your computer screen, your iPod plugged in, the TV lit up, and this book propped in your lap? So much to do, so little time! There's no way to squeeze more than twenty-four hours into a day. All we can hope for is that some scientist somewhere will develop a way to get a bigger, better brain! But let's face it: brain enhancement surgery won't be available any time soon.

Even so, scientists have been busy recently learning more about this heady organ of ours. Now in new and fascinating ways, the sciences of biology and psychology are joining hands to study the human brain.[3]

A healthy adult brain weighs about two pounds—about the size and weight of a cauliflower—and the more we use this *pliable* organ, the more efficient it gets. A sample the size of a rice kernel contains a million neurons, twenty miles of axons, and ten billion synapses. It's crowded up there—sounds like a headache waiting to happen!

From birth to adolescence, we lay the brain's basic circuitry. Stimulation is critical. When children grow up in isolated, sterile environments, their brains suffer. But when they grow up in fertile, rich environments, their brains thrive. The more our Moms and Dads read to us and play learning games with us, the better. By the time we're eighteen or so, we have an individual "brain-print." Our basic circuitry is hardwired for life. Once that occurs, certain opportunities are lost—forever. It's unlikely that learning a new language now at this time in your life, for example, will ever come as naturally to you as learning your native tongue did.

What's the secret to a healthy brain? When we think of fitness, most of us think from the neck down—strong abs, bulging pecs, and tight glutes. But brain health tops them all. New evidence shows that physical exercise helps our brains shrug off damage, reinforce old neural networks, and forge new ones. Denser neural networks help us process information better, store it, and ultimately result in a smarter brain!

Current research focuses on a protein called BDNF, for brain-derived neurotrophic factor. BDNF, which helps nerve cells in our brains grow and connect, is important for development in the womb, but it's also important in adult brains. Simply put: it helps us learn. According to researchers, rats that eat a high-calorie, fast-food diet and have a couch-potato lifestyle have less BDNF in their brains. Omega-3 fatty acids found in fish normalize BDNF levels and counteract learning disabilities in rats with brain injuries. Scientists are working to see if the same thing may be true for humans.[4]

"Exercise your brain. Nourish it well. And the earlier you start the better," scientists tell us.[5] New research indicates that the goal should be to store up a cognitive reserve. And just how do we do that? Education! People who are less educated have twice the risk of getting Alzheimer's disease in later life, and people who are less educated and have ho-hum, nonchallenging jobs have three to four times the risk. According to researchers, "College seems to pay off well into retirement."[6] It *can* help you build a better brain!

Brain researchers tell us the best state for learning has ten conditions. Read each one, along with some suggestions about how to get there.

1. **You're intrinsically motivated (from within yourself) to learn material that is appropriately challenging.**

   > *Examine where your motivation to learn comes from.* Are you *internally* motivated because you're curious about the subject and want to learn about it or externally motivated to get an A or avoid an F? Can you generate your own internal motivation, rather than relying on external "carrots" and "sticks"? This book has built-in reminders to boost your intrinsic motivation. Use them to your advantage as a learner.

   > *Adjust the level of challenge yourself.* If you're too challenged in a class, you become anxious. Make sure you're keeping up with the workload and that you've completed the prerequisites. In many disciplines, you must know the fundamentals before tackling more advanced concepts. If you're not challenged enough, you can become bored and disengaged. Your professor will provide the baseline challenge for everyone in the class. But it's up to you to fine-tune that challenge for yourself. Get extra help if you aren't quite up to the task or bump up the challenge a notch or two if you're ahead of the game so that you're continually motivated to learn.

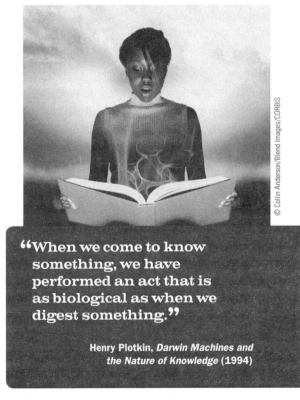

> "When we come to know something, we have performed an act that is as biological as when we digest something."
>
> Henry Plotkin, *Darwin Machines and the Nature of Knowledge* (1994)

2. You're appropriately stressed, but generally relaxed.

> *Assess your stress.* According to researchers, you learn best in a state of *relaxed alertness*, a state of high challenge and low threat.[7] While relaxed alertness may sound like an oxymoron, it can be achieved. No stress at all is what you'd find in a no-brainer course. Some stress is useful; it helps engage you in learning. How stressed are you—and why—when you get to class? Are you overstressed because you've rushed from your last class, cruised the parking lot for half an hour to find a good spot, or because you haven't done the reading and hope you won't be called on? Prepare for class so that you're ready to jump in. Or instead of too much stress, are you understressed because you don't value the course material? Consider how the information can be useful to you—perhaps in ways you've never even thought of. Here's the vital question to ask yourself: How much stress do I need in order to trigger my best effort?

> *Attend to your overall physical state.* Are you taking care of your physical needs so that you can stay alert, keep up with the lecture, and participate in the discussion?

3. You enter into a state researchers call "flow" when you're so totally absorbed in what you're doing that you lose track of everything else.[8]

> *Identify the kinds of learning situations that help you "flow."* Do you get fully engaged by hands-on activities? Do you find that certain courses naturally capture your attention such that you're surprised when it's time for class to end? Understanding your own preferences and style as a learner are key here.

> *Think about what you can do as a learner to get yourself there.* Not all classes or subjects will naturally induce a flow state in you. Nevertheless, ask yourself what *you* can do to focus on learning and exclude distractions. How can you become more engrossed in what you're learning?

4. You're curious about what you're learning, and you look forward to learning it.

> *Get ready to learn by looking back and by looking ahead.* When you're about to cross the street, you must look both ways, right? Keep that image in mind because that's what you should do before each class. What did class consist of last time? Can you predict what it will consist of next time? Considering the big picture can help you fit your learning into a larger whole.

> *Focus on substance, not style.* Part of Tammy's bias against Professor Caldwell focused on his appearance. Despite society's obsession with attractiveness, grooming, and fashion, a student's job is to ask: What can I learn from this person? Passing judgment on physical appearance just encourages you to play the blame game and derails your learning.

5. You're slightly confused, but only for a short time.[9]

> *Use confusion as a motivator.* You may not be getting the lecture's main points because you don't understand new terms used along the way. Look them up early on in the learning process. Ask yourself what background information would help things click—and find out the answers to those questions.

> *Ask questions!* To your professor, questions indicate *interest*, not *idiocy*. Don't be afraid to probe more deeply into the material. As they say, "The only stupid question is the one you don't ask."

6. You search for personal meaning and patterns.

> *Ask yourself: What's in it for me?* Why is knowing this important? How can I use this information in the future? Instead of dismissing material that appears unrelated to your life, try figuring out how it *could* relate. You may be surprised!

> *Think about how courses relate to one another.* How does this new knowledge align with other things you're learning in other courses? Does sociology have anything to do with history? Psychology with economics?

7. Your emotions are involved, not just your mind.

> *Evaluate your attitudes and feelings.* Do you like the subject matter? Do you admire the teacher? Remember your high school teacher, Mr. Brown (let's call him), whose class you just couldn't stand? Studying for Mr. Brown's tests was absolute torture. Not every class will be your favorite. That's natural. But if a class turns you off as a learner, instead of allowing your emotions to take over, ask why and whether your feelings are in your best interest.

> *Make a deliberate decision to change negative feelings.* Fortunately, feelings can be changed. Hating a course or disliking a professor can only build resentment and threaten your success. It's possible to do a one-eighty and transform your negative emotions into positive energy.

8. You realize that as a learner you use what you already know in constructing new knowledge.[10]

> *Remember that passive learning is an oxymoron.* When it comes to learning, you are the construction foreman, building on what you already know to construct new knowledge. You're not just memorizing facts someone else wants you to learn. You're a full partner in the learning process!

> *Remind yourself that constructing knowledge takes work.* No one ever built a house by simply sitting back or just hanging out. Builders work hard, but in the end, they have something to show for their efforts. In your college courses, you must identify what you already know and blend new knowledge into the framework you've built in your mind. By constructing new knowledge, you are building yourself into a more sophisticated, more polished, and most certainly, a more educated person.

"Personal participation is the universal principle of knowing."

Michael Polanyi, Hungarian-British scholar (1891–1976)

9. You understand that learning is both conscious and unconscious.

> *Watch where your mind goes when it's off duty.* Does learning take place when you're not deliberately trying to learn? Some of what you learn will be immediately obvious to you, and some will dawn on you after class is over, while you're in the shower, or eating lunch, or falling asleep at night, for example. Pay attention to your indirect learning and move it into your line of vision.

> *Remember that both kinds of learning are important.* Both conscious learning and unconscious learning count. There are no rules about when and where learning can occur. Capitalize on both.

10. You're given a degree of choice in terms of what you learn, how you do it, and feedback on how you're doing.

> *Make the most of the choices you're given.* As Yogi Berra said, "When you come to a fork in the road, take it." College isn't a free-for-all in which you can take any classes you like toward earning a degree. However, which electives you choose will be up to you. Or in a particular course, if your instructor allows you to write a paper or shoot a video, choose the option that will be more motivating for you. When you receive an assignment, select a topic that fires you up. It's easier to generate energy to put toward choices you've made yourself.

> *Use feedback to improve, and if feedback is not given, ask for it.* It's possible to get really good at doing something the wrong way. Take

"It is what we think we know already that often prevents us from learning."

Claude Bernard, French physiologist (1813–1878)

a golf swing or a swimming stroke, for example. Without someone intervening to give you feedback, it may be difficult to know how to improve. Your instructors will most likely write comments on your assignments to explain their grades. Assessing your work is their job; it's what they must do to help you improve. Take their suggestions to heart and try them out.

All of us are already good learners in some situations. Let's say you're drawn to technology, for example. You're totally engrossed in computers and eagerly learn everything you can from books, classes, and online sources—and you sometimes totally lose yourself in a flow state as you're learning. No one has to force you to practice your technology skills or pick up an issue of *Wired* or *PC World*. You do it because you want to. In this case, you're self-motivated and therefore learning is easy. This chapter provides several different tools to help you understand your own personal profile as a learner so that you can try to learn at your best in *all* situations.

C CONTROL Your Learning

YOUR TOP-TEN LIST

Reflect on yourself as a learner in each of the classes you're enrolled in this term. How optimal are the conditions for learning? How can you adjust the learning environment *yourself* to optimize it? Label the classes you're taking this term, and put checkmarks next to the conditions that are present in each class. Reflect on why you chose to mark these items (or didn't) in each class.

Ten Conditions for Optimal Learning

COURSE NAMES	Class 1: MATH	Class 2:	Class 3:	Class 4:	Class 5:
1. You're intrinsically motivated to learn material that is appropriately challenging.	☐	☐	☐	☐	☐
2. You're appropriately stressed, but generally relaxed.	✓	☐	☐	☐	☐
3. You enter into a state researchers call flow.	✓	☐	☐	☐	☐
4. You're curious about what you're learning, and you look forward to learning it.	☐	☐	☐	☐	☐
5. You're slightly confused, but only for a short time.	✓	☐	☐	☐	☐
6. You search for personal meaning and patterns.	☐	☐	☐	☐	☐
7. Your emotions are involved, not just your mind.	☐	☐	☐	☐	☐
8. You realize that as a learner you use what you already know in constructing new knowledge.	✓	☐	☐	☐	☐
9. You understand that learning is both conscious and unconscious.	✓	☐	☐	☐	☐
10. You're given a degree of choice in terms of what you learn, how you do it, and feedback on how you're doing.	☐	☐	☐	☐	☐

Which course has the most checkmarks? Is this the course that you find easiest? The most engaging? Which course has the least number of checkmarks? Is this the course that you find the most difficult? The least interesting? Considering these ten optimal conditions for learning, what specific actions can you take to enhance your learning in your most challenging class?

> "It is of the utmost importance that we recognize and nurture all of the varied human intelligences, and all of the combinations of intelligences. We are all so different largely because we all have different combinations of intelligences. If we recognize this, I think we will have at least a better chance of dealing appropriately with the many problems that we face in the world."
>
> Howard Gardner, Harvard Professor of Psychology

Multiple Intelligences: *How* Are You Smart?

CHALLENGE → REACTION

Challenge: Are people smart in different ways? How so?

Reaction: On each line, put checkmarks next to all the statements that best describe you.

Linguistic Intelligence: **The capacity to use language to express what's on your mind and understand others ("word smart")**

_____ I'm a good storyteller.

_____ I enjoy word games, puns, and tongue twisters.

_____ I'd rather listen to the radio than watch TV.

_____ I've recently written something I'm proud of.

_____ I can hear words in my head before I say or write them.

_____ When riding in the car, I sometimes pay more attention to words on billboards than I do to the scenery.

_____ In high school, I did better in English, history, or social studies than I did in math and science.

_____ I enjoy reading.

Logical-Mathematical Intelligence: **The capacity to understand cause/effect relationships and to manipulate numbers ("number/reasoning smart")**

_____ I can easily do math in my head.
_____ I enjoy brainteasers or puzzles.
_____ I like it when things can be counted or analyzed.
_____ I can easily find logical flaws in what others do or say.
_____ I think most things have rational explanations.
_____ Math and science were my favorite subjects in high school.
_____ I like to put things into categories.
_____ I'm interested in new scientific advances.

Spatial Intelligence: **The capacity to represent the world visually or graphically ("picture smart")**

_____ I like to take pictures of what I see around me.
_____ I'm sensitive to colors.
_____ My dreams at night are vivid.
_____ I like to doodle or draw.
_____ I'm good at navigating with a map.
_____ I can picture what something will look like before it's finished.
_____ In school, I preferred geometry to algebra.
_____ I often make my point by drawing a picture or diagram.

Bodily-Kinesthetic Intelligence: **The capacity to use your whole body or parts of it to solve a problem, make something, or put on a production ("body smart")**

_____ I regularly engage in sports or physical activities.
_____ I get fidgety when asked to sit for long periods of time.
_____ I get some of my best ideas while I'm engaged in a physical activity.
_____ I need to practice a skill in order to learn it, rather than just reading or watching a video about it.
_____ I enjoy being a daredevil.
_____ I'm a well-coordinated person.
_____ I like to think through things while I'm doing something else like running or walking.
_____ I like to spend my free time outdoors.

Musical Intelligence: **The capacity to think in music, hear patterns and recognize, remember, and perhaps manipulate them ("music smart")**

_____ I can tell when a musical note is flat or sharp.
_____ I play a musical instrument.
_____ I often hear music playing in my head.
_____ I can listen to a piece of music once or twice, and then sing it back accurately.
_____ I often sing or hum while working.
_____ I like music playing while I'm doing things.
_____ I'm good at keeping time to a piece of music.
_____ I consider music an important part of my life.

Interpersonal Intelligence: **The capacity to understand other people ("people smart")**

_____ I prefer group activities to solo activities.
_____ Others think of me as a leader.

(continued)

_____ I enjoy the challenge of teaching others something I like to do.
_____ I like to get involved in social activities at school, church, or work.
_____ If I have a problem, I'm more likely to get help than tough it out alone.
_____ I feel comfortable in a crowd of people.
_____ I have several close friends.
_____ I'm the sort of person others come to for advice about their problems.

Intrapersonal Intelligence: **The capacity to understand yourself, who you are, and what you can do ("self-smart")**
_____ I like to spend time alone thinking about important questions in life.
_____ I have invested time in learning more about myself.
_____ I consider myself to be independent minded.
_____ I keep a journal of my inner thoughts.
_____ I'd rather spend a weekend alone than at a place with a lot of other people around.
_____ I've thought seriously about starting a business of my own.
_____ I'm realistic about my own strengths and weaknesses.
_____ I have goals for my life that I'm working on.

Naturalistic Intelligence: **The capacity to discriminate between living things and show sensitivity toward the natural world ("nature smart")**
_____ Environmental problems bother me.
_____ In school, I always enjoyed field trips to places in nature or away from class.
_____ I enjoy studying nature, plants, or animals.
_____ I've always done well on projects involving living systems.
_____ I enjoy pets.
_____ I notice signs of wildlife when I'm on a walk or hike.
_____ I can recognize types of plants, trees, rocks, birds, and so on.
_____ I enjoy learning about environmental issues.

Which intelligences have the most checkmarks? Although this is an informal instrument, it can help you think about the concept of multiple intelligences, or MI. *How* are you smart?

Based on Armstrong, T. (1994). *Multiple intelligences in the classroom.* Alexandria, VA: Association for Supervision and Curriculum Development, pp. 18–20.

Have you ever noticed that people are smart in different ways? Consider the musical genius of Mozart, who published his first piano pieces at the age of five. Or think about Tiger Woods, who watched his father hit golf balls and mimicked his dad's swing while still in his crib. When he was two, Tiger played golf with comedian and golfer Bob Hope on national television, and he was featured in *Golf Digest* at the age of five. Not many of us are as musically gifted as Mozart or as physically gifted as Tiger Woods, but we all have strengths. We're all smart in different ways. You may earn top grades in math, and not-so-top grades in English, and your best friend's grades may be just the opposite.

According to Harvard psychologist Howard Gardner, people can be smart in at least eight different ways. Most schools focus on particular types of intelligence, linguistic and logical-mathematical intelligence, reflecting the three R's: reading, writing, and 'rithmetic. But Gardner claims intelligence is actually multifaceted. It can't be measured by traditional one-dimensional standardized IQ tests and represented by a three-digit number: 100 (average), 130+ (gifted), or 150+ (genius). Gardner defines intelligence as "the ability to find and solve problems and create products of value in one or more cultural setting."[11]

So instead of asking the traditional question "How smart are you?" a better question is "How are you smart?" The idea is to find out *how*, and then apply this understanding of yourself to your academic work in order to achieve your best results.

Translate Content into Your Own Intelligences

Do you sometimes wonder why you can't remember things for exams? Some learning experts believe that memory is intelligence-specific. You may have a good memory for people's faces but a bad memory for their names. You may be able to remember the words of a country-western hit but not the dance steps that go with it. The Theory of Multiple Intelligences may explain why.[12]

Examine your own behaviors in class. If your instructors use their linguistic intelligence to teach, as many do, and your intelligences lie elsewhere, can you observe telltale signs of your frustration? Instead of zeroing in on the lecture, do you fidget (bodily-kinesthetic), doodle (spatial), or socialize (interpersonal)? You may need to translate the information into your own personal intelligences, just as you would if your professor speaks French and you speak English. This strategy might have worked for Tammy Ko from the "FOCUS Challenge Case." Professor Caldwell's most developed intelligence is linguistic, whereas Tammy's are bodily-kinesthetic (manipulating test tubes) and interpersonal (interacting with people). Tammy's learning problems are partially due to a case of mismatched intelligences between Professor Caldwell and herself.

Let's say one of your courses this term is "Introduction to Economics," and the current course topic is the Law of Supply and Demand. Basically, "the theory of supply and demand describes how prices vary as a result of a balance between product availability at each price (supply) and the desires of those with purchasing power at each price (demand)."[13] To understand this law, you could read the textbook (linguistic); study mathematical formulas (logical-mathematical); examine charts and graphs (spatial); observe the Law of Supply and Demand in the natural world, through the fluctuating price of gasoline, for example (naturalist); look at the way the Law of Supply and Demand is expressed in your own body, using food as a metaphor (bodily-kinesthetic); reflect on how and when you might be able to afford something you desperately want, like a certain model of car (intrapersonal); or write (or find) a song that helps you understand the law (musical). How about the 1964 Beatles' hit, "[Money] Can't Buy Me Love"?[14] You needn't try all eight ways, but it's intriguing to speculate about various ways to learn that may work for you, rather than assuming you're doomed because your intelligences don't match your instructor's.

Use Intelligence-Oriented Study Techniques

What if your strongest intelligence is different from the one through which course material is presented? What can you do about it? Take a look at the following techniques for studying using different intelligences. Tweaking the *way* you study may make a world of difference.

Linguistic →	1. Rewrite your class notes. 2. Record yourself reading through your class notes and play it as you study. 3. Read the textbook chapter aloud.
Logical Mathematical →	1. Create hypothetical conceptual problems to solve. 2. Organize chapter or lecture notes into logical flow. 3. Analyze how the textbook chapter is organized and why.
Spatial →	1. Draw a map that demonstrates your thinking on course material. 2. Illustrate your notes by drawing diagrams and charts. 3. Mark up your textbook to show relationships between concepts.
Bodily-Kinesthetic →	1. Study course material while engaged in physical activity. 2. Practice skills introduced in class or in the text. 3. Act out a scene based on chapter content.
Musical →	1. Create musical memory devices by putting words into well-known melodies. 2. Listen to music while you're studying. 3. Sing or hum as you work.
Interpersonal →	1. Discuss course material with your classmates in class. 2. Organize a study group that meets regularly. 3. Meet a classmate before or after class for coffee and course conversation.
Intrapersonal →	1. Keep a journal to track your personal reactions to course material. 2. Study alone and engage in internal dialogue about course content. 3. Coach yourself on how to best study for a challenging class.
Naturalistic →	1. Search for applications of course content in the natural world. 2. Study outside (if weather permits and you can resist distractions). 3. Go to a physical location that exemplifies course material (for example, a park for your geology course).

Choose a Major and Career That Fit Your Intelligences

If linguistic intelligence isn't your most developed type, but spatial intelligence is, architecture would probably be a much better major for you than English. If you're an adult student returning to school in order to change careers, perhaps the Theory of Multiple Intelligences can help you understand why. For example, perhaps you've always enjoyed working outdoors. But you may have disliked working a construction job that required heavy physical labor (bodily-kinesthetic, a lesser intelligence for you) and returned to school to pursue a degree in geology (naturalist, your most developed intelligence). Take a look at Figure 2.1 for ideas about careers that emphasize particular intelligences and famous achievers in each category.

Intelligence Type	Careers in Intelligences	Well-Known Examples
Linguistic	journalist	Diane Sawyer
	teacher	Your instructor
	lawyer	Lin Wood
	talkshow host	Oprah Winfrey
Logical-Mathematical	accountant	Henry W. Bloch (H&R Block)
	engineer	Dean Kamen, inventor
	computer programmer	Bill Gates, entrepreneur
Spatial	architect	Norma Merrick Sklarek, first African American woman architect, designed the Los Angeles International Airport Terminal
	artist	Christo, environmental artist
	artistic director	Grant Major, Academy Award Winner, *Lord of the Rings: The Return of the King*, 2003
Bodily-Kinesthetic	professional athlete	Venus Williams, tennis player
	coach	Mike Shanahan, Denver Broncos
	actor	Brad Pitt
Musical	musician	Faith Hill, country singer
	composer	John Williams, composer/conductor
Interpersonal	salesperson	Sam Walton, Wal-Mart Founder
	teacher	Your instructor
	counselor	Carl Rogers (1902–1987)
Intrapersonal	theorist	Ilya Prigogine (1917–2003), Nobel prize winner, chemistry, 1977
	researcher	John Wheeler, physicist
	philosopher	W. V. Quine, American philosopher
Naturalistic	landscape architect	Frederick Law Olmsted
	anthropologist	Jane Goodall
	botanist	Peter Raven

Figure 2.1

Choosing an Intelligence-Based Career

Develop Your Weaker Intelligences

It's important to cultivate your weaker intelligences. Why? Because life isn't geared to one kind of intelligence. It's complex. Even in the particular career fields listed for each intelligence in the preceding chart, more than one intelligence may be required. A photo journalist for *National Geographic*, for example, might need linguistic intelligence, spatial intelligence, interpersonal intelligence, and naturalist intelligence. Being well-rounded, as the expression goes, is truly a good thing. Artist Pablo Picasso once said, "I am always doing that which I cannot do, in order that I may learn how to do it."

Use your multiple intelligences to multiply your success. Remember that no one is naturally intelligent in all eight areas. Each individual is a unique blend of intelligences. But the Theory of Multiple Intelligences claims that we all have the capacity to develop all of our eight intelligences further. That's good news! Howard Gardner puts it this way: "We can all get better at each of the intelligences, although some people will improve in an intelligence area more readily than others, either because biology gave them a better brain for that intelligence or because their culture gave them a better teacher."[15]

INSIGHT → ACTION

1. What are your most developed intelligences? Describe a situation in which you excelled as a learner and how the Theory of Multiple Intelligences helps explain your success.

2. Now do the opposite. Describe a situation in which you did not excel as a learner and how the Theory of Multiple Intelligences helps explain your difficulty.

3. Identify a career field you are interested in. Which intelligences would be important?

4. Which of your intelligences would you like to develop further? Why? What actions can you take to do so?

How Do You Perceive and Process Information?

CHALLENGE → REACTION

Challenge: You've lived with yourself for many years now, but how well do you know yourself as a learner?

Reaction: List as many descriptive phrases about your learning preferences as you can. For example, you might write, "I learn best when I listen to an instructor lecture" or "I learn best when I make color-coded binders for each class." Use this activity to discover some specifics about your learning style.

Style—we all have it, right? What's yours? Baggy jeans and a T-shirt? Sandals, even in the middle of winter? A signature hairdo that defies gravity? A stocking cap that translates into I-just-rolled-out-of-bed-before-class? When it comes to appearance, you have your own style. You know it, and so does everyone who knows you.

Think about how your mind works. For example, how do you decide what to wear in the morning? Do you turn on the radio or TV for the weather forecast? Jump on the Internet? Stick your head out the front door? Ask someone else's opinion? Try on your new jeans to see how they feel? Throw on whatever happens to be clean? We all have different styles, don't we?

So what's a learning style? A learning style is defined as your "characteristic and preferred way of gathering, interpreting, organizing, and thinking about information."[16]

Here's one way of looking at things. The way you perceive information and the way you process it—your perceiving/processing preferences—are based in part on your senses. Which sensory modalities do you prefer to use to take in information—your eyes (visual-graphic or visual-words), your ears (aural), or all your senses using your whole body (kinesthetic)? Which type of information sinks in best? Which type of information do you most trust to be accurate? Do you prefer teachers who lecture? Teachers who use visuals such as charts, web pages, and diagrams to explain things? Or teachers who plan field trips, use role-plays, and create simulations?

"Learning how to learn is life's most important skill."

Tony Buzan, memory expert

To further understand your preferred sensory channel, let's take this hypothetical example. Assume a rich relative you didn't even know you had leaves you some money, and you decide to use it to buy a new car. You must first answer many questions: What kind of car do you want to buy—an SUV, a sedan, a sports car, a van, or a truck? What are the differences between various makes and models? How do prices, comfort, and safety compare? Who provides the best warranty? Which car do consumers rate highest? How would you go about learning the answers to all these questions?

- **Visual.** Some of us would **look**. We'd study charts and graphs comparing cars, mileage, fuel tank capacity, maintenance costs, and customer satisfaction. We learn through symbolic representations that explain what could have been said in normal text format.

- **Aural.** Some of us would **listen**. We'd ask all our friends what kind of cars they drive and what they've heard about cars from other people. We'd pay attention as showroom salespeople describe the features of various cars. We learn through sounds by listening.

- **Read/Write.** Some of us would **read** or **write**. We'd buy a copy of *Consumer Reports* annual edition on automobiles, or copies of magazines such as *Car and Driver* or *Road and Track*, and write lists of each car's pros and cons. We learn through words by reading and writing.

- **Kinesthetic.** Some of us would want to **do it**. We'd go to the showroom and test drive a few cars to physically try them out. We learn through experience when all our sensory modalities are activated.

What would you do? Eventually, as you're deciding which vehicle to buy, you might do all these things, and do them more than once. But learning style theory says we all have preferences in terms of how we perceive and process information.

After reading the car-buying description, you probably have a gut feeling about your own style. However, take a few minutes to answer the questions about yourself in Exercise 2.1—for confirmation or revelation—to verify your hunches or to learn something new about yourself.

You can take the VARK online at http://www.vark-learn.com/english/page.asp?p=questionnaire and your results will be tabulated for you.

EXERCISE 2.1 VARK Learning Styles Assessment

Choose the answer which best explains your preference and circle the letter. Please select more than one response if a single answer does not match your perception. Leave blank any question that does not apply.

1. You are helping someone who wants to go downtown, find your airport or locate the bus station. You would:
   a) draw or give her a map.
   b) tell her the directions.
   c) write down the directions (without a map).
   d) go with her.

2. You are not sure whether a word should be spelled "dependent" or "dependant." You would:
   a) see the word in your mind and choose by the way different versions look.
   b) think about how each word sounds and choose one.
   c) find it in a dictionary.
   d) write both words on paper and choose one.

3. You are planning a group vacation. You want some feedback from your friends about your plans. You would:
   a) use a map or website to show them the places.
   b) phone, text or email them.
   c) give them a copy of the printed itinerary.
   d) describe some of the highlights.

4. You are going to cook something as a special treat for your family. You would:
   a) look through the cookbook for ideas from the pictures.
   b) ask friends for suggestions.
   c) use a cookbook where you know there is a good recipe.
   d) cook something you know without the need for instructions.

5. A group of tourists want to learn about the parks or wildlife reserves in your area. You would:
   a) show them internet pictures, photographs or picture books.
   b) talk about, or arrange a talk for them, about parks or wildlife reserves.
   c) give them a book or pamphlets about the parks or wildlife reserves.
   d) take them to a park or wildlife reserve and walk with them.

6. You are about to purchase a digital camera or cell phone. Other than price, what would most influence your decision?
   a) Its attractive design that looks good.
   b) The salesperson telling me about its features.

c) Reading the details about its features.
d) Trying or testing it.

7. Remember a time when you learned how to do something new. Try to avoid choosing a physical skill, like riding a bike. You learned best by:
    a) diagrams and charts—visual clues.
    b) listening to somebody explaining it and asking questions.
    c) written instructions—e.g. a manual or textbook.
    d) watching a demonstration.

8. You have a problem with your knee. You would prefer that the doctor:
    a) showed you a diagram of what was wrong.
    b) described what was wrong.
    c) gave you a pamphlet to read about it.
    d) used a plastic model of a knee to show what was wrong.

9. You want to learn a new software program, skill or game on a computer. You would:
    a) follow the diagrams in the book that came with it.
    b) talk with people who know about the program.
    c) read the written instructions that came with the program.
    d) use the controls or keyboard and try things out.

10. I like websites that have:
    a) interesting design and visual features.
    b) audio channels where I can hear music, radio programs or interviews.
    c) interesting written descriptions, lists and explanations.
    d) things I can click on or try out.

11. Other than price, what would most influence your decision to buy a new non-fiction book?
    a) The cover looks appealing.
    b) A friend talks about it and recommends it.
    c) You'd quickly read parts of it.
    d) It contains real-life stories, experiences and examples.

12. You are using a book, CD or website to learn how to take photos with your new digital camera. You would like to have:
    a) diagrams showing the camera and what each part does.
    b) a chance to ask questions and talk about the camera and its features.
    c) clear written instructions with lists and bullet points about what to do.
    d) many examples of good and poor photos and how to improve them.

13. Do you prefer a teacher or a presenter who uses:
    a) diagrams, charts or graphs?
    b) question and answer, talk, group discussion or guest speakers?
    c) handouts, books or readings?
    d) demonstrations, models, fieldtrips, role plays or practical exercises?

14. You have finished a competition or test and would like some feedback. You would like to have feedback:
    a) using graphs showing what you had achieved.
    b) from somebody who talks it through with you.

(continued)

c) in a written format, describing your results.

d) using examples from what you have done.

15. You are going to choose food at a restaurant or cafe. You would:
    a) look at what others are eating or look at pictures of each dish.
    b) ask the server or friends to recommend choices.
    c) choose from the written descriptions in the menu.
    d) choose something that you have had there before.

16. You have to give an important speech at a conference or special occasion. You would:
    a) make diagrams or create graphs to help explain things.
    b) write a few key words and practice your speech over and over.
    c) write out your speech and learn from reading it over several times.
    d) gather many examples and stories to make the talk real and practical.

Source: N. Fleming. (2001-2007). *VARK, a Guide to Learning Styles.* Version 7.0. Available at http://www.vark-learn.com/english/page.asp?p=questionnaire. Adapted and used with permission from Neil Fleming.

Scoring the VARK

The VARK learning style assessment was created by two professors, Neil Fleming and Colleen Mills, working with students at Lincoln University in Canterbury, New Zealand. They began with three traditional sensory modalities: visual, aural, and kinesthetic. Later, based on student input, they divided the visual mode (in which we use our eyes) into two categories: Visual (pictures, graphs, colors, symbols, and so on) and Read/Write (printed information). Let's tabulate your results.

Count your choices in each of the four VARK categories.	(a)	(b)	(c)	(d)
	Visual	**Aural**	**Read/Write**	**Kinesthetic**

Now that you've calculated your scores, do they match your perceptions of yourself as a learner? Could you have predicted them? The VARK's creators believe that *you* are best qualified to verify and interpret your own results.[17]

Using Your Sensory Preferences

Knowing your preferences can help you in your academic coursework. If your highest score (by 4 or 5 points) is in one of the four VARK modalities, that particular learning modality is your preferred one.[18] If your scores are more or less even between several or all four modalities, these scores mean that you don't have a strong preference for any single modality. It's estimated that 55 to 65 percent of the population is multimodal, which gives most of us flexibility in the way we learn.[19] A lower score in a preference simply means that you are more comfortable using other styles. If your VARK results contain a zero in a particular learning modality, you may realize that you do indeed dislike this mode or find it unhelpful. "Why would anyone want to use *that* mode?" you may have asked yourself in the past. It may be helpful to reflect on why you omit this learning modality. To learn more about your results and suggestions for applying them, see Figure 2.2 for your preferred modality.

Figure 2.2
Visual, Aural, Read/Write, and Kinesthetic Learning Strategies

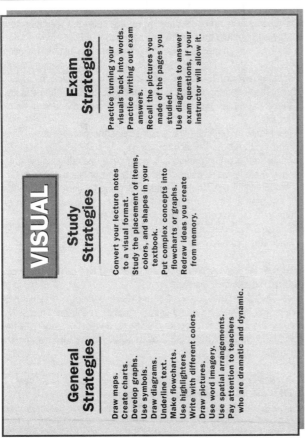

Your highest score represents your preferred learning style; your lowest score, your least preferred. Most college classes emphasize reading and writing; however, if your lowest score is in the Read/Write modality, don't assume you're academically doomed. VARK can help you discover alternative, more productive ways to learn the same course material.

Learning style descriptions aren't meant to put you into a cubbyhole or stereotype you. And they certainly aren't meant to give you an excuse when you don't like a particular assignment. It might work in a restaurant to send back your entrée if it's not cooked to your liking, but most of the time in life, we don't get to choose how information is served. (Imagine saying to your professor: "I'm afraid this won't do. Can you bring me information I can digest in my own learning style?") You may learn to adapt naturally to a particular instructor or discipline's preferences, using a visual modality in your economics class to interpret graphs and a kinesthetic modality in your chemistry lab to conduct experiments.

However, you may also find that you need to deliberately and strategically re-route your learning methods in some of your classes, and knowing your VARK preferences can help you do that. Learning to capitalize on your preferences and translate challenging course material into your preferred modality

FOCUS ON CAREERS: NEIL FLEMING, University Professor, Creator of the VARK

Q1: What's it like to be a college teacher? What are the pros and cons of the profession?

Although I write and speak widely, teaching is my favorite job because you get to talk with so many interesting people (students) and you sometimes make a difference in their lives. There are those great moments when you see that a student has "gotten it." Those "Aha!" moments are priceless. They may exist in other careers, but I wouldn't know about that. You also get to learn new things with your students so you stay a learner for life and never "mature"! The bad days are those when you realize that you have "missed" some students or that they have somehow lost interest in you and what you teach.

Q2: What sensitivities to student learning have you developed over time? How do you use your knowledge in the classroom?

Over time I have moved through several stages. When I first began my teaching career, I was simply trying to survive for fifty minutes by filling the room with my voice. Later I realized that teaching was about learning, and that there were students in the room, too! I became so engrossed in my subject that I wanted to teach it to everyone! I eventually learned that students learn in different ways. And I finally realized that I was not at all necessary for my students to learn. They could, with some guidance from me, learn very well without me.

Q3: Do most students understand how they learn? Do most teachers understand learning? What is your understanding of how learning happens?

Unfortunately, some students have to experience failure before they learn about their own learning, and that is a tragic waste. Many students know in some detail how they learn, but they are seldom asked by teachers. Many teachers know a great deal about how to teach about their disciplines—history or math or psychology, for example—but they may never have had anyone help them learn how to teach it.

I think learning happens when students accept, adjust, and alter the "scripts" they carry in their heads. That may sound like a contradiction of terms, but it really isn't. "Scripts" are the outcome of neural pathways in our brain. Those pathways can be clear and unobstructed, open and inviting, sheathed and insulated against change, or overgrown and in danger of being lost.

We all learn in particular ways. Sometimes those ways serve us well. We need to understand what those ways are and cultivate them. But other times our learning preferences don't serve us well because of the particular material we're trying to learn. It's sort of like trying to build a house without the right tools. It's just not going to work, or at the very least, it's going to be a struggle. In those cases, we need to adjust our learning to fit the content and the situation.

In general, I know students have learned something well when they can teach it to someone else.

Q4: What do the best teachers know about learning? How do they incorporate what they know into their teaching?

The best teachers are aware of some basic principles that enhance learning, and they keep doing those things that assist that process. For example, they know that students like variety and options and that they learn in different ways. They also know that students want to learn in an atmosphere without fear or bias.

Q5: Do you believe in multiple intelligences? Are people smart in different ways? How does this manifest itself in the classroom?

Yes, I believe that people are smart in different ways. Students prove may serve you well. Remember these suggestions about the VARK, and try them out to see if they improve your academic results.

1. VARK preferences are not necessarily strengths. However VARK is an excellent vehicle to help you reflect on how you learn and begin to reinforce the productive strategies you're already using or select ones that might work better.

2. If you have a strong preference for a particular modality, practice multiple suggestions listed in Figure 2.2 for that particular modality. Reinforce your learning through redundancy.

3. Remember that an estimated 55 to 65 percent of people are multimodal. In a typical classroom of 30 students (based on VARK data):
   - 17 students would be multimodal,
   - 1 student would be Visual,
   - 1 student would be Aural,
   - 5 students would be Read/Write,
   - 6 students would be Kinesthetic,

   and the teacher would most likely have a strong Read/Write preference![20]

C CREATE a Career Outlook

COLLEGE PROFESSOR

Have you ever considered a career as a college professor? Here are some facts about this career to consider and some questions about yourself to ponder.

Facts to Consider

Academic preparation required: A master's degree, or more often, a doctoral degree is required, although in some fields highly cultivated expertise or practical experience is sufficient. (A former politician without a Ph.D. may be hired to teach a course in political science, for example.)

Future workforce demand: Prospects for new jobs will be good in the future, although many openings will be for part-time teachers.

Work environment: College professors have flexible schedules, teach a wide variety of subjects (usually related within one field) to sixteen million full- and part-time college students nationwide, and conduct research.

Most common psychological type preferences: introverted, sensing, (and to a lesser extent, intuitive), thinking, judging[21]

Essential skills: reading, writing, communicating with individual students, to a classroom of students, or in work-related committees, collecting and analyzing data, using technology (to teach distance-learning courses, communicate with students, and present information)

Questions to Ponder

1. Do you have (or could you acquire) the skills this career requires?
2. What would you find most satisfying about this type of career?
3. What would you find most challenging about this type of career?
4. Are you interested in a career like this? Why or why not?

For more information, see U.S. Department of Labor, Bureau of Labor Statistics, *Occupational Outlook Handbook, 2006–2007 Edition.*[22]

For more career activities online, go to http://www.academic.cengage.com/collegesuccess/staley to do the Team Career exercises.

---

that every year in my classrooms, and I try not to forget it. But I think we must use the word *intelligence* cautiously, because it sounds like a "thing" that some have and others don't.

Q6: How do students sabotage their own learning?
Students often fail themselves by using methods of learning that are not suited to them. In the past, the students that saddened me were those who were trying to copy the learning methods of their sister or friend or the student who got high grades in their class. Learning requires a lot of hard work, and if there is less than a major effort, in the end, little will be learned.

Q7: In your opinion, are most students today visual, aural, read/write, or kinesthetic learners? Have learning styles shifted over the course of your teaching career? Why do you think this is? How do you teach to different learning styles in the classroom?
The VARK data I've collected indicate that the most common preference for students is kinesthetic, that is, they want to experience the learning or have the teacher relate the learning to things that they know, have seen, or can do. The plain truth is that the teacher who can provide links to the reality of students is going to reach more students. Despite popular conceptions, this is not a very "visual" world as defined by VARK, and unfortunately the "Read/Write" world is made for teachers rather than students. The power of VARK is in the practical strategies that students can use to learn efficiently, effectively, and personally.

Q8: How can students who want to go into the teaching profession best prepare themselves?
If students want to become teachers at any level, they must understand how people learn, and they must devote themselves to helping people do it. In my view, it's the best profession in the world. If students want a fulfilling career, a career in which they have the potential to bring forth lasting, and sometimes life-altering, change, they should consider teaching.

4. If you are multimodal, as most of us are, it may be necessary to use all your modalities to boost your confidence in your learning. Practice the suggestions for all of your preferred modalities.

5. While in an ideal world, it would be good to try to strengthen lesser preferences, you may wish to save that goal for later in life. Fleming's students eventually convinced him that college isn't the place to experiment. Academic results are important, and often scholarships and graduate school acceptance hang in the balance. You, too, may decide it's better to try to strengthen existing preferences now and work on expanding your repertoire later. This book will give you an opportunity to practice your VARK learning preferences—whatever they are—in each chapter.

INSIGHT ➔ ACTION

Go back to the earliest days of your schooling and identify three peak learning experiences—times when you were most engaged as a learner. Perhaps during these learning peaks you were operating in "flow" mode. You were so engrossed in what you were learning that you lost track of everything around you and how long you had been working. After you've identified these experiences, list the primary VARK modality or modalities that you were using at the time. Does your list match your results on the VARK instrument? Were you using your most preferred modality? List some specific ways you can translate tasks in your most challenging classes into your VARK preferences.

What Role Does Your Personality Play?

CHALLENGE ➔ REACTION

Challenge: How does your personality affect your learning style?

Reaction: _____

One of the best things about college, no matter which one you've chosen to attend, is meeting so many different kinds of people. At times you may find these differences intriguing. At other times, they may baffle you. Look around and listen to other students, and you'll start to notice. Have you heard students voicing totally opposite opinions about college life by saying things like this?

"There's no way I can study in the dorm. It's way too noisy."

"There's no way I can study in the library. It's way too quiet."

"My roommate is terrific! We're getting along great."

"My roommate is unbearable! I can hardly stand being around him."

> "Each person is an exception to the rule."
>
> Carl Jung, Swiss psychiatrist (1875–1961)

"I'm so glad I've already decided on a major. Now I can go full steam ahead."

"My sociology prof is great. She talks about all kinds of things in class, and her essay tests are actually fun!"

"I have no idea what to major in. I can think of six different majors I'd like to choose."

"My sociology prof is so confusing. She talks about so many different things in class. How am I supposed to know what to study for her tests?"[23]

You're likely to run into all kinds of viewpoints and all kinds of people, but as you're bound to discover in college, differences make life much more interesting! We're each unique. You've seen it on sappy greeting cards, "There's only one you." But it's true. Perhaps your friends comment on your personality by saying, "She's really quiet," or "He's the class clown," or "He's incredibly logical," or "She trusts her gut feelings." What you may not know is how big a role your personality plays in how you prefer to learn.

The Myers-Briggs Type Indicator® (MBTI) is the most well known personality assessment instrument in the world. Each year, approximately four million people worldwide obtain significant insights about their personalities, their career choices, their interaction with others, and their learning styles by completing it.

This chapter will introduce you to a shorter instrument based on the MBTI, the SuccessTypes Learning Style Type Indicator. Created by Dr. John Pelley at Texas Tech University, this instrument focuses specifically on how you prefer to learn. If you are able to complete the full Myers-Briggs Type Indicator in the class for which you're using this textbook, or through your college counseling center or learning center, do so. You'll learn even more about yourself.

Here's an important point: Both the SuccessTypes Learning Style Type Indicator and the Myers-Briggs Type Indicator show you your preferences. These instruments are not about what you *can* do. They're about what you *prefer* to do. That's an important distinction. Here's an illustration. Try writing your name on the line below.

_____

Now put the pen in your other hand, and try writing your name again.

_____

What was different the second time around? For most people, the second try takes longer, is less legible, probably feels odd, and requires more concentration. But could you do it? Yes. It's just that you prefer doing it the first way. The first way is easier and more natural; the second way makes a simple task seem like hard work! It's possible that you might have to try "writing with your other hand" in college—doing things that don't come naturally. Practice, rehearsal, and focus might be extra important, but you can do it!

Throughout this book, you will find "Your Type Is Showing" features. These articles will summarize MBTI research that investigates the chapter's topic. They are intended to pique your interest and invite you to go beyond what you see in the chapter. Chances are you'll be fascinated by what you can learn about yourself through the MBTI. But in the meantime, let's zero in on how your personality affects your learning style, specifically.

EXERCISE 2.2 The SuccessTypes Learning Style Type Indicator

Each of the following statements represents opposites in your thinking when you are learning. Choose the one that describes the way you really are. It is common to want to choose the one that represents what you want to be or what others think you ought to be. Try to imagine that you are learning for yourself and not for a teacher and that there is no grade involved. For example, you are learning about something that interests you like a new hobby or outside interest. Just choose the description that best fits you, and write the letter associated with that sentence in the box to the left, and you will total them when you are done.

1. ☐   E   I study best with other people.
          I   I study best by myself.

2. ☐   E   When I study with other people, I get the most out of expressing my thoughts.
          I   When I study with other people, I get the most out of listening to what others have to say.

3. ☐   E   When I study with other people, I get the most out of quick, trial-and-error thinking.
          I   When I study with other people, I get the most out of thinking things through before I say them.

4. ☐   E   I prefer to start my learning by doing something active and then considering the results later.
          I   I prefer to start my learning by considering something thoroughly and then doing something active with it later.

5. ☐   E   I need frequent breaks when I study and interruptions don't bother me.
          I   I can study for very long stretches and interruptions are *not* welcome.

6. ☐ E I prefer to demonstrate what I know.
   I I prefer to describe what I know.
7. ☐ E I like to know what other people expect of me.
   I I like to set my own standards for my learning.
8. ☐ S I am more patient with routine or details in my study.
   N I am more patient with abstract or complex material.
9. ☐ S I am very uncomfortable with errors of fact.
   N I consider errors of fact to be another useful way to learn.
10. ☐ S I am very uncomfortable when part of my learning is left to my imagination.
    N I am bored when everything I am supposed to learn is presented explicitly.
11. ☐ S I prefer to learn fewer skills and get really good at them.
    N I prefer to keep learning new skills and I'll get good at them when I have to.
12. ☐ S I learn much better in a hands-on situation to see what-is.
    N I learn much better when I'm thinking about the possibilities to imagine what might be.
13. ☐ S I prefer to learn things that are useful and based on established principles.
    N I prefer to learn things that are original and stimulate my imagination.
14. ☐ S I always re-examine my answers on test questions just to be sure.
    N I usually trust my first hunches about test questions.
15. ☐ S I emphasize observation over imagination.
    N I emphasize imagination over observation.
16. ☐ S I'm more comfortable when the professor sticks closely to the handout.
    N I'm likely to get bored if the professor sticks closely to the handout.
17. ☐ T I prefer to have a logical reason for what I learn.
    F I prefer to see the human consequences of what I learn.
18. ☐ T I prefer a logically organized teacher to a personable teacher.
    F I prefer a personable teacher to a logically organized teacher.
19. ☐ T I prefer group study as a way to give and receive critical analysis.
    F I prefer group study to be harmonious.
20. ☐ T I prefer to study first what should be learned first.
    F I prefer to study first what appeals to me the most.
21. ☐ T The best way to correct a study partner is to be blunt and direct.
    F The best way to correct a study partner is to be tactful and understanding.
22. ☐ J I prefer to study in a steady, orderly fashion.
    P I prefer to study in a flexible, even impulsive, way.

(continued)

23.	☐	J	I stay on schedule when I study regardless of how interesting the assignment is.
		P	I tend to postpone uninteresting or unpleasant assignments.
24.	☐	J	I tend to be an overachiever in my learning.
		P	I tend to be an underachiever in my learning.
25.	☐	J	I prefer to structure my study now to avoid emergencies later.
		P	I prefer to stay flexible in my study and deal with emergencies when they arise.
26.	☐	J	I prefer to give answers based on the information I already have.
		P	I prefer to seek more information before deciding on an answer.
27.	☐	J	I prefer to finish one assignment before starting another one.
		P	I prefer to have several assignments going at once.
28.	☐	J	I like well defined learning assignments.
		P	I like learning from open-ended problem solving.

Let's boil it down to four letters:

E or I	☐	Record the letter which occurred the most for questions 1–7.
S or N	☐	Record the letter which occurred the most for questions 8–16.
T or F	☐	Record the letter which occurred the most for questions 17–21.
J or P	☐	Record the letter which occurred the most for questions 22–28.

Adapted from Table 5.1 in SuccessTypes for Medical Students, J. W. Pelley and B. K. Dalley (Texas Tech Univ. Extended Learning, 1997). Used by permission of John W. Pelley.

You can take the SuccessTypes Learning Style Type Indicator online at http://www.ttuhsc.edu/SOM/Success/LSTI.htm.

Interpreting Your SuccessTypes Learning Style Type Profile

Look at your four-letter profile. Are you an ESFP? An ESTP? An INTJ? What do those four letters say about you? There are many sources of information about the sixteen possible combinations of letters, or type, in books and online resources.[24] However, here are some things you need to know about measuring psychological type.

First, most abbreviated type indicators—even this one—are not scientifically reliable. They are designed to illustrate type, not prove it. As the instrument's creator asserts, "Your type is the starting line, not the finish line.... Type is more than the sum of its parts."[25]

Second, the SuccessTypes Learning Style Type Indicator forces you to make a choice between two opposites. That's because, theoretically, you can't simultaneously prefer two opposite things at once. That doesn't mean you'd never under any circumstances choose the other one. It just means that most of the time the one you chose would be your preference.

Third, any Myers-Briggs type instrument answers four questions about you (see Figure 2.3 for further explanations of typical characteristics of the preferences):

Figure 2.3
Learning Style Preferences

Extravert (E)	Introvert (I)	Thinking (T)	Feeling (F)
"How do you recharge your batteries"? Students who prefer extraversion pay attention to people and things around them. That's also where they get their energy. As learners, they:	Students who prefer introversion focus on the world inside their heads. They pay attention to their own thoughts, feelings, and ideas, and draw energy from their inner experience. As learners, they:	Students who are thinkers like to make decisions objectively using logic, principles, and analysis. They weigh evidence in a detached manner. As learners, they:	Students who are feelers value harmony and focus on what is important to them or to others when they make decisions. As learners, they:
· Learn best when actively involved · Like to study with others · Like background noise while studying · Don't particularly enjoy writing papers · Want teachers to encourage discussion in class	· Learn best by pausing to think · Like to study alone · Say they aren't good public speakers · Need to study in quiet · Want teachers to give clear lectures	· Use their logic to guide their learning · Like to critique ideas · Learn through challenge and debate · Can find flaws in an argument · Want teachers to present logically	· Want information to apply to them personally · Like to please their teachers · Find value or good in things · Learn when they are supported or appreciated · Want teachers to establish rapport with students

Sensing (S)	Intuition (N)	Judging (J)	Perceiving (P)
What kind of information do you rely on? Students who are sensors become aware of things that are real through their senses: sound, touch, taste, feel, and smell. They focus on what is happening in the here and now. As learners, they:	Students who trust their intuition, or sixth sense, look for patterns, possibilities, and the big picture. As learners, they:	Students who are judgers like to make quick decisions, settle things, and structure and organize their worlds. As learners, they:	Students who are perceivers want to adapt to the world around them. They don't like to close off options; instead they'd rather experience whatever comes up. As learners, they:
· Look for specific information · Memorize facts · Follow instructions · Like hands-on experiences · Want teachers to give clear assignments	· Look for quick insights · Like theories and abstract thinking · Read between the lines · Create their own directions · Want teachers to encourage independent thinking	· Like more formal class structures · Plan their work in advance · Work steadily toward their goals · Like to be in charge · Want teachers to be organized	· Like informal learning situations · Enjoy spontaneity · Stay open to new information · Work in energy bursts · Want teachers to entertain and inspire

Source: Based on J. K. DiTiberio & A. L. Hammer. (1993). *Introduction to Type in College.* Palo Alto, CA: Consulting Psychologists Press.

1. What energizes you and where do you direct energy? E or I
2. How do you gather information and what kind of information do you trust? S or N
3. How do you make decisions, arrive at conclusions, and make judgments? T or F
4. How do you relate to the outer world? J or P

Using Your SuccessTypes Learning Style Type Profile

What does it all mean? Now that you know some important things about yourself as a learner, there are several other points about learning styles you should know.

First, look at your first and second letters (ES, IS, EN, or IN). Statistically, twice as many instructors as students are Introverted Intuitives (IN). By and large, students are Extraverted Sensors (ES), preferring concrete, practical learning, while instructors often prefer theories and learning for its own sake.[26]

In the "FOCUS Challenge Case," Tammy's extraverted sensing (ES) learning style clashed with Professor Caldwell's introverted intuitive (IN) learning style. It's unlikely that Professor Caldwell will change his teaching style, and even if he did, students in his class have a variety of learning styles. Whose style would he try to match? Both Tammy's personality and Professor Caldwell's are representative of the most common types found in college classrooms.

Now look at your second and last letters (SP, SJ, NP, or NJ). Three times as many college students prefer sensing and perceiving (SP) as their professors, who are likely to be intuitive and judging (NJ). Generally, students want a more concrete, flexible approach to learning while instructors like to teach abstract, structured theories.[27]

While simply knowing about these mismatches is good, it's important to go further and act on that knowledge. As a single learner in a larger class, you will need to adjust to the teaching style of your instructor in ways such as the following:

> **Translate for maximum comfort.** The way to maximize your comfort as a learner is to find ways to translate from your instructor's preferences to yours. If you know that you prefer feeling over thinking, and your instructor's style is based on thinking, make the course material come alive by personalizing it. How does the topic relate to you, your lifestyle, your family, and your future choices?

> **Make strategic choices.** While learning preferences can help explain your academic successes, it's also important not to use them to rationalize your nonsuccesses. An introvert could say, "I could have aced that assignment if the professor had let me work on an individual project instead of a group one! I really dislike group projects." Become the best learner you can be at what you're naturally good at. But also realize that you'll need to become more versatile over time. In the

workforce, you won't always be able to choose what you do and how you do it. Actively choose your learning strategies, rather than simply hoping for the best. Remember: no one can learn for you, just as no one can eat for you.

> **Take full advantage.** College will present you with an extensive menu of learning opportunities. You will also build on your learning as you move beyond your general, introductory classes into courses in your chosen major—and across and between disciplines. Don't fall victim to the temptation to rationalize and victimize as some students do ("I could have been more successful in college if . . . I hadn't had to work so many hours . . . I hadn't had a family to support . . . my friends had been more studious . . . my roommate had been easier to live with . . . my professors had been more supportive. . . ." If, if, if. College may well be the most concentrated and potentially powerful learning opportunity you'll ever have.

Ultimately, learning at your best is up to you. Each chapter of this book will remind you of your VARK preferences with special activities to reinforce your sensory modalities. And you'll have a chance to re-explore your SuccessType Learning Style preferences in short sections called "Your Type Is Showing," in which you'll get a short flash of current research findings on the Myers-Briggs Type Indicator and the chapter's particular focus.

Gaining the insights provided in this chapter and acting on them have the potential to greatly affect your college success. Understand yourself, capitalize on your preferences, build on them, focus, and learn!

EXERCISE 2.3 VARK Activity

Complete the recommended activity for your preferred VARK learning modality. If you are multimodal, select more than one activity. Your instructor may ask you to (a) give an oral report on your results in class, (b) send your results to him or her via e-mail, (c) post them online, or (d) contribute to a class chat.

Visual: Think about a particular course or exam you studied for in the past. Create a personal chart that compares the learning strategies for each of the four VARK modalities you used and the degree of success you had using each one.

Aural: Interview another student who is a member of a campus honor society. Which VARK strategies does this student use and why? Determine whether these strategies would work for you.

Read/Write: Write a one-page summary of what you have learned about yourself as a result of reading this chapter.

Kinesthetic: If your campus has a Learning Center, visit it to gather additional information about your learning style. Apply what you have learned to create a plan to prepare for your next exam.

For more practice online, go to http://www.academic.cengage.com/collegesuccess/staley to take the Challenge Yourself online quizzes.

NOW WHAT DO YOU THINK?

FOCUS CHALLENGE CASE At the beginning of this chapter, Tammy Ko, a frustrated and disgruntled student, faced a challenge. Now after reading this chapter, would you respond differently to any of the questions you answered about the "FOCUS Challenge Case"?

REALITY CHECK

On a scale of 1 to 10, answer the following questions now that you've completed this chapter.

1 = not very/not much/very little/low   10 = very/a lot/very much/high

In hindsight, how much did you *really* know about this subject matter before reading the chapter?

1 2 3 4 5 6 7 8 9 10

How much do you think this information might affect your college success?

1 2 3 4 5 6 7 8 9 10

How much do you think this information might affect your career success after college?

1 2 3 4 5 6 7 8 9 10

How long did it actually take you to complete this chapter (both the reading and writing tasks)? _____ Hour(s) _____ Minutes

Take a minute to compare these answers to your answers from the "Readiness Check" at the beginning of this chapter. What gaps exist between the similar questions? How might these gaps between what you thought before starting the chapter and what you now think after completing the chapter affect how you approach the next chapter in this book?

To download mp3 format audio summaries of this chapter, go to http://www.academic.cengage.com/collegesuccess/staley.

Chapter 3

Project Management

2 Time

MASTER STUDENT MAP

why this chapter matters...

Procrastination and lack of planning can quickly undermine your success in school.

how you can use this chapter...

Discover the details about how you currently use time.
Set goals that make a difference in the quality of your life.
Know exactly what to do today, this week, and this month in order to achieve your goals.
Eliminate procrastination.

as you read, ask yourself
what if...

I could meet my goals with time to spare?

what is included...

You've got the time   61
Setting and achieving goals   67
The ABC daily to-do list   70
More strategies for planning   73
Stop procrastination now   75
25 ways to get the most out of now   78
Beyond time management: Stay focused on what matters   83
Gearing up: Using a long-term planner   89
Power Process: "Be here now"   92
Master Student Profile: Malcolm X   97

STUDENT VOICES

Making lists has been one of my favorite tools to stay on track and prioritize. Not much gives me more pleasure than to cross off duties one by one and to see the number of items left to do shrink to nothing, or what can be put off until another time.

—LAURIE MURRAY

Goal setting is a very real pursuit in a master student's life. Not only are goals set and strived for, they are also re-evaluated on a periodic basis. This re-evaluation process is more than an "Am I still on course?" A master student also asks, "Is this still the best course?"

—KEITH BELLOWS

You've got the time

The words *time management* can call forth images of restriction and control. You might visualize a prune-faced Scrooge hunched over your shoulder, stopwatch in hand, telling you what to do every minute. Bad news.

Good news: You do have enough time for the things you want to do. All it takes is thinking about the possibilities and making conscious choices.

Time is an equal opportunity resource. All of us, regardless of gender, race, creed, or national origin, have exactly the same number of hours in a week. No matter how famous we are, no matter how rich or poor, we get 168 hours to spend each week—no more, no less.

Time is also an unusual commodity. It cannot be saved. You can't stockpile time like wood for the stove or food for the winter. It can't be seen, felt, touched, tasted, or smelled. You can't sense time directly. Even scientists and philosophers find it hard to describe. Because time is so elusive, it is easy to ignore. That doesn't bother time at all. Time is perfectly content to remain hidden until you are nearly out of it. And when you are out of it, you are out of it.

Time is a nonrenewable resource. If you're out of wood, you can chop some more. If you're out of money, you can earn a little extra. If you're out of love, there is still hope. If you're out of health, it can often be restored. But when you're out of time, that's it. When this minute is gone, it's gone.

Time seems to pass at varying speeds. Sometimes it crawls and sometimes it's faster than a speeding bullet. On Friday afternoons, classroom clocks can creep. After you've worked a 10-hour day, reading the last few pages of an economics assignment can turn minutes into hours. A year in school can stretch out to an eternity.

At the other end of the spectrum, time flies. There are moments when you are so absorbed in what you're doing that hours disappear like magic.

Approach time as if you are in control. Sometimes it seems that your friends control your time, that your boss controls your time, that your teachers or your parents or your kids or somebody else controls your time. Maybe that is not true. When you say you don't have enough time, you might really be saying that you are not spending the time you *do* have in the way that you want.

Everything written about time management boils down to two topics. One is knowing exactly *what* you want. The other is knowing *how* to get what you want. State your wants as written goals. Then choose activities that will help you meet those goals.

Spend your most valuable resource in the way you choose. Start by observing how you use time. The next exercise gives you this opportunity.

journal entry 6

Discovery/Intention Statement

Think back to a time during the past year when you rushed to finish a project or when you did not find time for an activity that was important to you. List one thing you might have done to create this outcome.

I discovered that I . . .

_____
_____
_____

Take a few minutes to skim this chapter. Find three to five articles that might help you avoid such outcomes in the future and list them below.

Title	Page number

If you don't have time to read these articles in depth right now, schedule a time to do so.

I intend to . . .

_____
_____
_____
_____

exercise 6

THE TIME MONITOR/TIME PLAN PROCESS

The purpose of this exercise is to transform time into a knowable and predictable resource. You can do this by repeating a two-phase cycle of monitoring and planning. This exercise takes place over two weeks. During the first week, you can monitor your activities to get a detailed picture of how you spend your time. Then you can plan the second week thoughtfully. Monitor your time during the second week, compare it to your plan, and discover what changes you want to make in the following week's plan.

Monitor your time in 15-minute intervals, 24 hours a day, for seven days. Record how much time you spend sleeping, eating, studying, attending lectures, traveling to and from class, working, watching television, listening to music, taking care of the kids, running errands—everything.

If this sounds crazy, hang on for a minute. This exercise is not about keeping track of the rest of your life in 15-minute intervals. It is an opportunity to become conscious of how you spend your time, your life. Use the Time Monitor/Time Plan process only for as long as it is helpful to do so.

When you know how your time is spent, you can find ways to adjust and manage it so that you spend your life doing the things that are most important to you. Monitoring your time is a critical first step toward putting you in control of your life.

Some students choose to keep track of their time on 3x5 cards, calendars, campus planners, or software designed for this purpose. You might even develop your own form for monitoring your time.

1. Get to know the Time Monitor/Time Plan. Look at the Time Monitor/Time Plan on page 63. Note that each day has two columns, one labeled "monitor" and the other labeled "plan." During the first week, use only the "monitor" column. After that, use both columns simultaneously to continue the monitor-plan process.

To become familiar with the form, look at the example on page 63. When you begin an activity, write it down next to the time you begin and put a line just above that spot. Round off to the nearest 15 minutes. If, for example, you begin eating at 8:06, enter your starting time as 8:00. Over time, it will probably even out. In any case, you will be close enough to realize the benefits of this exercise. (Note that you can use the blank spaces in the "monitor" and "plan" columns to cover most of the day.)

On Monday, the student in this example got up at 6:45 a.m., showered, and got dressed. He finished this activity and began breakfast at 7:15. He put this new activity in at the time he began and drew a line just above it. He ate from 7:15 to 7:45. It took him 15 minutes to walk to class (7:45 to 8:00), and he attended classes from 8:00 to 11:00.

Keep your Time Monitor/Time Plan with you every minute you are awake for one week. Take a few moments every two or three hours to record what you've done. Or enter a note each time you change activities.

Here's an eye opener for many students. If you think you already have a good idea of how you manage time, predict how many hours you will spend in a week on each category of activity listed in the form on page 64. (Four categories are already provided; you can add more at any time.) Do this before your first week of monitoring. Write your predictions in the margin to the left of each category. After monitoring your time for one week, see how accurate your predictions were.

2. Remember to use your Time Monitor/Time Plan. It might be easy to forget to fill out your Time Monitor/Time Plan. One way to remember is to create a visual reminder for yourself. You can use this technique for any activity you want to remember.

Relax for a moment, close your eyes, and imagine that you see your Time Monitor/Time Plan. Imagine that it has arms and legs and is as big as a person. Picture the form sitting at your desk at home, in your car, in one of your classrooms, or in your favorite chair. Visualize it sitting wherever you're likely to sit. When you sit down, the Time Monitor/Time Plan will get squashed.

You can make this image more effective by adding sound effects. The Time Monitor/Time Plan might scream, "Get off me!" Or since time can be related to money, you might associate the Time Monitor/Time Plan with the sound of an old-fashioned cash register. Imagine that every time you sit down, a cash register rings.

Complete this exercise online.

62   Chapter Two   TIME

MONDAY 9/12	
Monitor	Plan
Get up	
Shower	
7:00	7:00
7:15 Breakfast	
7:30	
7:45 Walk to	
8:00 class	8:00
8:15	
8:30 Econ 1	
8:45	
9:00	9:00
9:15	
9:30	
9:45	
10:00 Bio 1	10:00
10:15	
10:30	
10:45	
11:00	11:00
11:15 Study	
11:30	
11:45	
12:00	12:00
12:15 Lunch	
12:30	
12:45	
1:00	1:00
1:15 Eng. Lit	
1:30	
1:45	
2:00	2:00
2:15 Coffeehouse	
2:30	
2:45	
3:00	3:00
3:15	
3:30	
3:45	
4:00	4:00
4:15 Study	
4:30	
4:45	
5:00	5:00
5:15 Dinner	
5:30	
5:45	
6:00	6:00
6:15	
6:30 Babysit	
6:45	
7:00	7:00

TUESDAY 9/13	
Monitor	Plan
Sleep	
7:00	7:00
7:15	
7:30	
7:45 Shower	
8:00 Dress	8:00
8:15 Eat	
8:30	
8:45	
9:00 Art	9:00
9:15 Apprec.	
9:30 Project	
9:45	
10:00	10:00
10:15	
10:30	
10:45	
11:00 Data	11:00
11:15 process	
11:30	
11:45	
12:00	12:00
12:15	
12:30	
12:45	
1:00	1:00
1:15 Lunch	
1:30	
1:45	
2:00 Work	2:00
2:15 on book	
2:30 report	
2:45	
3:00 Art	3:00
3:15 Apprec.	
3:30	
3:45	
4:00	4:00
4:15	
4:30	
4:45	
5:00 Dinner	5:00
5:15	
5:30	
5:45	
6:00 Letter to	6:00
6:15 Uncle Jim	
6:30	
6:45	
7:00	7:00

3. Evaluate the Time Monitor/Time Plan. After you've monitored your time for one week, group your activities together by categories. The form on page 64 lists the categories "sleep," "class," "study," and "meals." Think of other categories you could add. "Grooming" might include showering, putting on makeup, brushing teeth, and getting dressed. "Travel" can include walking, driving, taking the bus, and riding your bike. Other categories might be "exercise," "entertainment," "work," "television," "domestic," and "children."

Write in the categories that work for you, and then add up how much time you spent in each of your categories.

exercise 6 continued

Put the totals in the "monitored" column. Make sure that the grand total of all categories is 168 hours.

Now take a minute and let these numbers sink in. Compare your totals to your predictions and notice your reactions. You might be surprised. You might feel disappointed or even angry about where your time goes. Use those feelings as motivation to plan your time differently. Go to the "planned" column and decide how much time you want to spend on various daily activities. As you do so, allow yourself to have fun. Approach planning in the spirit of adventure. Think of yourself as an artist who's creating a new life.

In several months you might want to take another detailed look at how you spend your life. You can expand the two-phase cycle of monitoring and planning to include a third phase: evaluating. Combine this with planning your time, following the suggestions in this chapter. You can use a continuous cycle: monitor, evaluate, plan; monitor, evaluate, plan. When you make it a habit, this cycle can help you get the full benefits of time management for the rest of your life. Then time management becomes more than a technique. It's transformed into a habit, a constant awareness of how you spend your lifetime.

WEEK OF ___ / ___ / ___ /

Category	Monitored	Planned
Sleep		
Class		
Study		
Meals		

MONDAY __/__/__/		TUESDAY __/__/__/		WEDNESDAY __/__/__/	
Monitor	Plan	Monitor	Plan	Monitor	Plan
7:00	7:00	7:00	7:00	7:00	7:00
7:15		7:15		7:15	
7:30		7:30		7:30	
7:45		7:45		7:45	
8:00	8:00	8:00	8:00	8:00	8:00
8:15		8:15		8:15	
8:30		8:30		8:30	
8:45		8:45		8:45	
9:00	9:00	9:00	9:00	9:00	9:00
9:15		9:15		9:15	
9:30		9:30		9:30	
9:45		9:45		9:45	
10:00	10:00	10:00	10:00	10:00	10:00
10:15		10:15		10:15	
10:30		10:30		10:30	
10:45		10:45		10:45	
11:00	11:00	11:00	11:00	11:00	11:00
11:15		11:15		11:15	
11:30		11:30		11:30	
11:45		11:45		11:45	
12:00	12:00	12:00	12:00	12:00	12:00
12:15		12:15		12:15	
12:30		12:30		12:30	
12:45		12:45		12:45	
1:00	1:00	1:00	1:00	1:00	1:00
1:15		1:15		1:15	
1:30		1:30		1:30	
1:45		1:45		1:45	
2:00	2:00	2:00	2:00	2:00	2:00
2:15		2:15		2:15	
2:30		2:30		2:30	
2:45		2:45		2:45	
3:00	3:00	3:00	3:00	3:00	3:00
3:15		3:15		3:15	
3:30		3:30		3:30	
3:45		3:45		3:45	
4:00	4:00	4:00	4:00	4:00	4:00
4:15		4:15		4:15	
4:30		4:30		4:30	
4:45		4:45		4:45	
5:00	5:00	5:00	5:00	5:00	5:00
5:15		5:15		5:15	
5:30		5:30		5:30	
5:45		5:45		5:45	
6:00	6:00	6:00	6:00	6:00	6:00
6:15		6:15		6:15	
6:30		6:30		6:30	
6:45		6:45		6:45	
7:00	7:00	7:00	7:00	7:00	7:00
7:15		7:15		7:15	
7:30		7:30		7:30	
7:45		7:45		7:45	
8:00	8:00	8:00	8:00	8:00	8:00
8:15		8:15		8:15	
8:30		8:30		8:30	
8:45		8:45		8:45	
9:00	9:00	9:00	9:00	9:00	9:00
9:15		9:15		9:15	
9:30		9:30		9:30	
9:45		9:45		9:45	
10:00	10:00	10:00	10:00	10:00	10:00
10:15		10:15		10:15	
10:30		10:30		10:30	
10:45		10:45		10:45	
11:00	11:00	11:00	11:00	11:00	11:00
11:15		11:15		11:15	
11:30		11:30		11:30	
11:45		11:45		11:45	
12:00	12:00	12:00	12:00	12:00	12:00

Student Website — college.hmco.com/pic/bams12e

exercise 6 continued

THURSDAY __ / __ / __ /		FRIDAY __ / __ / __ /		SATURDAY __ / __ / __ /	
Monitor	**Plan**	**Monitor**	**Plan**	**Monitor**	**Plan**
7:00	7:00	7:00	7:00		
7:15		7:15			
7:30		7:30			
7:45		7:45			
8:00	8:00	8:00	8:00		
8:15		8:15			
8:30		8:30			
8:45		8:45			
9:00	9:00	9:00	9:00		
9:15		9:15			
9:30		9:30			
9:45		9:45			
10:00	10:00	10:00	10:00		
10:15		10:15			
10:30		10:30			
10:45		10:45			
11:00	11:00	11:00	11:00		
11:15		11:15			
11:30		11:30			
11:45		11:45			
12:00	12:00	12:00	12:00		
12:15		12:15			
12:30		12:30			
12:45		12:45			
1:00	1:00	1:00	1:00		
1:15		1:15			
1:30		1:30			
1:45		1:45			
2:00	2:00	2:00	2:00		
2:15		2:15			
2:30		2:30			
2:45		2:45			
3:00	3:00	3:00	3:00		
3:15		3:15			
3:30		3:30			
3:45		3:45			

THURSDAY (cont.)		FRIDAY (cont.)		SUNDAY __ / __ / __ /	
				Monitor	**Plan**
4:00	4:00	4:00	4:00		
4:15		4:15			
4:30		4:30			
4:45		4:45			
5:00	5:00	5:00	5:00		
5:15		5:15			
5:30		5:30			
5:45		5:45			
6:00	6:00	6:00	6:00		
6:15		6:15			
6:30		6:30			
6:45		6:45			
7:00	7:00	7:00	7:00		
7:15		7:15			
7:30		7:30			
7:45		7:45			
8:00	8:00	8:00	8:00		
8:15		8:15			
8:30		8:30			
8:45		8:45			
9:00	9:00	9:00	9:00		
9:15		9:15			
9:30		9:30			
9:45		9:45			
10:00	10:00	10:00	10:00		
10:15		10:15			
10:30		10:30			
10:45		10:45			
11:00	11:00	11:00	11:00		
11:15		11:15			
11:30		11:30			
11:45		11:45			
12:00	12:00	12:00	12:00		

Setting and achieving goals

Many of us have vague, idealized notions of what we want out of life. These notions float among the clouds in our heads. They are wonderful, fuzzy, safe thoughts such as "I want to be a good person," "I want to be financially secure," or "I want to be happy."

Such outcomes are great possible goals. Left in a generalized form, however, these goals can leave us confused about ways to actually achieve them. If you really want to meet a goal, translate it into specific, concrete behaviors. Find out what that goal looks like. Listen to what it sounds like. Pick it up and feel how heavy that goal is. Inspect the switches, valves, joints, cogs, and fastenings of the goal. Make your goal as real as a chain saw.

There is nothing vague or fuzzy about chain saws. You can see them, feel them, and hear them. They have a clear function. Goals can be every bit as real and useful.

Writing down your goals exponentially increases your chances of meeting them. Writing exposes undefined terms, unrealistic time frames, and other symptoms of fuzzy thinking. If you've been completing Intention Statements as explained in the Introduction to this book, then you've already had experience writing goals. Both goals and Intention Statements address changes you want to make in your behavior, your values, your circumstances—or all of these. To keep track of your goals, write each one on a separate 3x5 card or key them all into a word processing file on your computer.

There are many useful methods for setting goals. Following is one of them. This method is based on writing specific goals in several time frames and areas of your life. Experiment with it and modify it as you see fit. You're also encouraged to reflect regularly on your goals. The key words to remember are *specific*, *time*, *areas*, and *reflect*. Combine the first letter of each word and you get the acronym *STAR*. Use this acronym to remember the suggestions that follow.

journal entry 7

Discovery Statement

After one week of monitoring my time, I discovered that . . .

I want to spend more time on . . .

I want to spend less time on . . .

I was surprised that I spent so much time on . . .

I was surprised that I spent so little time on . . .

I had strong feelings about my use of time when (describe the feeling and the situation) . . .

Write specific goals. In writing, state your goals as observable actions or measurable results. Think in detail about how things will be different once your goals are attained. List the changes in what you'd see, feel, touch, taste, hear, be, do, or have.

Suppose that one of your goals is to become a better student by studying harder. You're headed in a powerful direction; now translate that goal into a concrete action, such as "I will study two hours for every hour I'm in class." Specific goals make clear what actions are needed or what results are expected. Consider these examples:

Vague goal	Specific goal
Get a good education.	Graduate with B.S. degree in engineering, with honors, by 2009.
Enhance my spiritual life.	Meditate for 15 minutes daily.
Improve my appearance.	Lose six pounds during the next six months.

When stated specifically, a goal might look different to you. If you examine it closely, a goal you once thought you wanted might not be something you want after all. Or you might discover that you want to choose a new path to achieve a goal that you are sure you want.

Write goals in several time frames. To get a comprehensive vision of your future, write down:

- *Long-term goals.* Long-term goals represent major targets in your life. These goals can take five to 20 years to achieve. In some cases, they will take a lifetime. They can include goals in education, careers, personal relationships, travel, financial security—whatever is important to you. Consider the answers to the following questions as you create your long-term goals: What do you want to accomplish in your life? Do you want your life to make a statement? If so, what is that statement?

- *Mid-term goals.* Mid-term goals are objectives you can accomplish in one to five years. They include goals such as completing a course of education, paying off a car loan, or achieving a specific career level. These goals usually support your long-term goals.

- *Short-term goals.* Short-term goals are the ones you can accomplish in a year or less. These goals are specific achievements, such as completing a particular course or group of courses, hiking down the Appalachian Trail, or organizing a family reunion. A financial goal would probably include an exact dollar amount. Whatever your short-term goals are, they will require action now or in the near future.

Write goals in several areas of life. People who set goals in only one area of life—such as their career—can find that their personal growth becomes one-sided. They could experience success at work while neglecting their health or relationships with family members and friends.

To avoid this outcome, set goals in a variety of categories. Consider what you want to experience in your:

- education
- career
- financial life
- family life
- social life
- spiritual life
- level of health

Add goals in other areas as they occur to you.

Reflect on your goals. Each week, take a few minutes to think about your goals. You can perform the following "spot checks":

- *Check in with your feelings.* Think about how the process of setting your goals felt. Consider the satisfaction you'll gain in attaining your objectives. If you don't feel a significant emotional connection with a written goal, consider letting it go or filing it away to review later.

- *Check for alignment.* Look for connections between your goals. Do your short-term goals align with your mid-term goals? Will your mid-term goals help you achieve your long-term goals? Look for a "fit" between all of your goals and your purpose for taking part in higher education, as well as your overall purpose in life.

- *Check for obstacles.* All kinds of things can come between you and your goals, such as constraints on time and money. Anticipate obstacles and start looking now for workable solutions.

- *Check for immediate steps.* Here's a way to link goal setting to time management. Decide on a list of small, achievable steps you can take right away to accomplish each of your short-term goals. Write these small steps down on a daily to-do list. If you want to accomplish some of them by a certain date, enter them in a calendar that you consult daily. Then, over the coming weeks, review your to-do list and calendar. Take note of your progress and celebrate your successes.

exercise 7

GET REAL WITH YOUR GOALS

One way to make goals effective is to examine them up close. That's what this exercise is about. Using a process of brainstorming and evaluation, you can break a long-term goal into smaller segments until you have taken it completely apart. When you analyze a goal to this level of detail, you're well on the way to meeting it.

For this exercise, you will use a pen, extra paper, and a watch with a second hand. (A digital watch with a built-in stopwatch is even better.) Timing is an important part of the brainstorming process, so follow the stated time limits. This entire exercise takes about an hour.

Part one: Long-term goals

Brainstorm. Begin with an eight-minute brainstorm. For eight minutes write down everything you think you want in your life. Write as fast as you can and write whatever comes into your head. Leave no thought out. Don't worry about accuracy. The object of a brainstorm is to generate as many ideas as possible. Use a separate sheet of paper for this part of the exercise.

Evaluate. After you have finished brainstorming, spend the next six minutes looking over your list. Analyze what you wrote. Read the list out loud. If something is missing, add it. Look for common themes or relationships between goals. Then select three long-term goals that are important to you—goals that will take many years to achieve. Write these goals below in the space provided.

_____

_____

_____

Before you continue, take a minute to reflect on the process you've used so far. What criteria did you use to select your top three goals?

Part two: Mid-term goals

Brainstorm. Read out loud the three long-term goals you selected in Part One. Choose one of them. Then brainstorm a list of goals you might achieve in the next one to five years that would lead to the accomplishment of that one long-term goal. These are mid-term goals. Spend eight minutes on this brainstorm. Go for quantity.

Complete this exercise online.

Student Website

Evaluate. Analyze your brainstorm of mid-term goals. Then select three that you determine to be important in meeting the long-term goal you picked. Allow yourself six minutes for this part of the exercise. Write your selections below in the space provided.

_____

_____

_____

Again, pause for reflection before going on to the next part of this exercise. Why do you see these three goals as more important than the other mid-term goals you generated? On a separate sheet of paper, write about your reasons for selecting these three goals.

Part three: Short-term goals

Brainstorm. Review your list of mid-term goals and select one. In another eight-minute brainstorm, generate a list of short-term goals—those you can accomplish in a year or less that will lead to the attainment of that mid-term goal. Write down everything that comes to mind. Do not evaluate or judge these ideas yet. For now, the more ideas you write down, the better.

Evaluate. Analyze your list of short-term goals. The most effective brainstorms are conducted by suspending judgment, so you might find some bizarre ideas on your list. That's fine. Now is the time to cross them out. Next evaluate your remaining short-term goals and select three that you are willing and able to accomplish. Allow yourself six minutes for this part of the exercise, then write your selections below in the space provided.

_____

_____

_____

The more you practice, the more effective you can be at choosing goals that have meaning for you. You can repeat this exercise, employing the other long-term goals you generated or creating new ones.

The ABC daily to-do list

One of the most effective ways to stay on track and actually get things done is to use a daily to-do list. While the Time Monitor/Time Plan gives you a general picture of the week, your daily to-do list itemizes specific tasks you want to complete within the next 24 hours.

One advantage of keeping a daily to-do list is that you don't have to remember what to do next. It's on the list. A typical day in the life of a student is full of separate, often unrelated tasks—reading, attending lectures, reviewing notes, working at a job, writing papers, researching special projects, running errands. It's easy to forget an important task on a busy day. When that task is written down, you don't have to rely on your memory.

The following steps present one method for to-do lists. Experiment with these steps, modify them as you see fit, and invent new techniques that work for you.

Step 1 — Brainstorm tasks.
To get started, list all of the tasks you want to get done tomorrow. Each task will become an item on a to-do list. Don't worry about putting the entries in order or scheduling them yet. Just list everything you want to accomplish on a sheet of paper or a planning calendar, or in a special notebook. You can also use 3x5 cards, writing one task on each card. Cards work well because you can slip them into your pocket or rearrange them, and you never have to copy to-do items from one list to another.

Step 2 — Estimate time.
For each task you wrote down in step 1, estimate how long it will take you to complete it. This can be tricky. If you allow too little time, you end up feeling rushed. If you allow too much time, you become less productive. For now, give it your best guess. Your estimates will improve with practice. Now pull out your calendar or Time Monitor/Time Plan. You've probably scheduled some hours for activities such as classes or work. This leaves the unscheduled hours for tackling your to-do lists.

Add up the time needed to complete all your to-do items. Also add up the number of unscheduled hours in your day. Then compare the two totals. The power of this step is that you can spot overload in advance. If you have eight hours' worth of to-do items but only four unscheduled hours, that's a potential problem. To solve it, proceed to step 3.

Step 3 — Rate each task by priority.

To prevent overscheduling, decide which to-do items are the most important given the time you have available. One suggestion for doing this comes from the book *Take Control of Your Time and Life* by Alan Lakein: Simply label each task A, B, or C.[1]

The A's on your list are those things that are the most critical. These are assignments that are coming due or jobs that need to be done immediately. Also included are activities that lead directly to your short-term goals.

The B's on your list are important, but less so than the A's. B's might someday become A's. For the present, these tasks are not as urgent as A's. They can be postponed, if necessary, for another day.

The C's do not require immediate attention. C priorities include activities such as "shop for a new blender" and "research genealogy on the Internet." C's are often small, easy jobs with no set timeline. These, too, can be postponed.

Once you've labeled the items on your to-do list, schedule time for all of the A's. The B's and C's can be done randomly during the day when you are in between tasks and are not yet ready to start the next A.

Step 4 — Cross off tasks.

Keep your to-do list with you at all times, crossing off activities when you finish them and adding new ones when you think of them. If you're using 3x5 cards, you can toss away or recycle the cards with completed items. Crossing off tasks and releasing cards can be fun—a visible reward for your diligence. This step fosters a sense of accomplishment.

When using the ABC priority method, you might experience an ailment common to students: C fever. This is the uncontrollable urge to drop that A task and begin crossing C's off your to-do list. If your history paper is due tomorrow, you might feel compelled to vacuum the rug, call your third cousin in Tulsa, and make a trip to the store for shoelaces. The reason C fever is so common is that A tasks are usually more difficult or time-consuming to achieve, with a higher risk of failure.

If you notice symptoms of C fever, ask yourself: "Does this job really need to be done now?" "Do I really need to alphabetize my CD collection, or might I better use this time to study for tomorrow's data processing exam?" Use your to-do list to keep yourself on task, working on your A's. Don't panic or berate yourself when you realize that in the last six hours, you have completed 11 C's and not a single A. Calmly return to the A's.

Step 5 — Evaluate.

At the end of the day, evaluate your performance. Look for A priorities you didn't complete. Look for items that repeatedly turn up as B's or C's on your list and never seem to get done. Consider changing these to A's or dropping them altogether. Similarly, you might consider changing an A that didn't get done to a B or C priority. When you're done evaluating, start on tomorrow's to-do list. Be willing to admit mistakes. You might at first rank some items as A's only to realize later that they are actually C's. Some of the C's that lurk at the bottom of your list day after day might really be A's. When you keep a daily to-do list, you can adjust these priorities *before* they become problems.

The ABC system is not the only way to rank items on your to-do list. Some people prefer the "80-20" system. This is based on the idea that 80 percent of the value of any to-do list comes from only 20 percent of the tasks on that list. So on a to-do list of 10 items, find the two that will contribute most to your life, and complete those tasks without fail.

Another option is to rank items as "yes," "no," or "maybe." Do all of the tasks marked "yes." Ignore those marked "no." And put all of the "maybe's" on the shelf for later. You can come back to the "maybe's" at a future point and rank them as "yes" or "no."

Or you can develop your own style for to-do lists. You might find that grouping items by categories such as "errands" or "reading assignments" works best. Be creative.

Keep in mind the power of planning a whole week or even two weeks in advance. Planning in this way can make it easier to put activities in context and see how your daily goals relate to your long-term goals. Weekly planning can also free you from feeling that you have to polish off your whole to-do list in one day. Instead, you can spread tasks out over the whole week.

In any case, make starting your own to-do list an A priority.

exercise 8

CREATE A LIFELINE

On a large sheet of paper, draw a horizontal line. This line will represent your lifetime. Now add key events in your life to this line in chronological order. Examples are birth, first day at school, graduation from high school, and enrollment in higher education.

Now extend the lifeline into the future. Write down key events you would like to see occur in one year, five years, and 10 or more years from now. Choose events that align with your core values. Work quickly in the spirit of a brainstorm, bearing in mind that this is not a final plan.

Afterward, take a few minutes to review your lifeline. Select one key event for the future and list any actions you could take in the next month to bring yourself closer to that goal. Do the same with the other key events on your lifeline. You now have the rudiments of a comprehensive plan for your life.

Finally, extend your lifeline another 50 years beyond the year when you would reach age 100. Describe in detail what changes in the world you'd like to see as a result of the goals you attained in your lifetime.

Do this exercise online.  Student Website

mastering technology

HIGH-TECH WAYS TO MANAGE TIME

It's a paradox: Computers have given us ways to increase productivity *and* to waste time. Surfing Websites, sending e-mail, and instant messaging can be fun. They can also make hours disappear. With a few simple techniques, you can actually use a computer to accomplish more rather than less.

Lengthen your online attention span. When researching the online behavior of office workers, psychologist Gloria Mark discovered that they focused on a single project for only 11 minutes at a time. And that 11 minutes broke down into a series of three-minute tasks, such as creating a spreadsheet, sending an e-mail, or accessing Websites.[2] It might come as shock to discover that your online attention span amounts to three minutes or less. Write Intention Statements about gradually increasing the time.

Clear your desktop. Limit the number of windows that you have open at one time. Or see if you can minimize windows that you aren't using at the moment. Clearing your screen could clear your mind as well. Research indicates that working with a cleaner desktop can significantly boost productivity.[3]

Surf with purpose. Set aside some random hours to just aimlessly surf Websites. When using the Web at other times, however, know your purpose. Express that purpose as a specific question you want to answer. Scan pages quickly for a direct answer. After you find it, get offline.

Use keyboard shortcuts. Executing commands with keystrokes rather than a mouse can save effort and time. Check the help screens and manuals for your favorite software to find lists of keyboard shortcuts.

Check e-mail at specific times. Checking your e-mail every few minutes produces a steady stream of interruptions. Set aside specific times of the day—between periods of productive activity—to check your e-mail. Also change the settings on your e-mail software so that it does *not* notify you when a new message arrives.

Filter your e-mail. Use separate e-mail accounts for work-related and personal messages. When you're at work, avoid opening personal messages. In addition, consider a special account for e-mail newsletters and other messages that don't demand immediate attention. Check this account just once each week.

Use instant-messaging only when it creates real value. A one-minute break for "IM-ing" can easily add up to twenty minutes or more—the time it takes to shift mental gears away from the interruption and back into the flow of concentrated work. Instant-messaging in class is a particularly potent way to waste your time and tuition money. It also distracts the instructor and other students.

Stop procrastination NOW

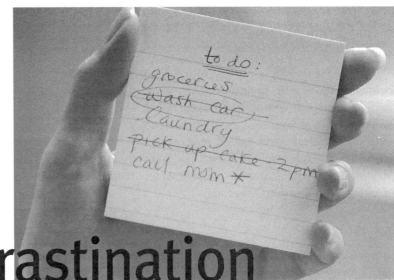

Consider a bold idea: The way to begin to stop procrastinating is to choose to stop procrastinating. Giving up procrastination is actually a simple choice, and people just try to make it complicated.

Test this idea for yourself. Think of something that you've been putting off. Choose a small, specific task—one that you can complete in five minutes or less. Then do it today.

Tomorrow, choose another task and do it. Repeat this strategy each day for one week. Notice what happens to your habit of procrastination.

If the above suggestion just doesn't work for you, then experiment with any strategy from the list on page 76. (Just don't put it off.)

Discover the costs. Find out if procrastination keeps you from getting what you want. Clearly seeing the costs of procrastination can help you kick the habit.

Discover your procrastination style. Psychologist Linda Sapadin identifies different styles of procrastination.[4] For example, *dreamers* have big goals that they seldom translate into specific plans. *Worriers* focus on the "worst case" scenario and are likely to talk more about problems than about solutions. *Defiers* resist new tasks or promise to do them and then don't follow through. *Overdoers* create extra work for themselves by refusing to delegate tasks and neglecting to set priorities. And *perfectionists* put off tasks for fear of making a mistake.

Awareness of procrastination styles is a key to changing your behavior. If you exhibit the characteristics of an overdoer, for example, then say no to new projects. Also ask for help in completing your current projects.

To discover your procrastination style, observe your behavior. Avoid judgments. Just be a scientist and record the facts. Write Discovery Statements about specific ways you procrastinate. Follow up with Intention Statements about what to do differently.

Trick yourself into getting started. If you have a 50-page chapter to read, then grab the book and say to yourself, "I'm not really going to read this chapter right now. I'm just going to flip through the pages and scan the headings for ten minutes." Tricks like these can get you started on a task you've been dreading.

Let feelings follow action. If you put off exercising until you feel energetic, you might wait for months. Instead, get moving now. Then watch your feelings change. After five minutes of brisk walking, you might be in the mood for a 20-minute run. This principle—action generates motivation—can apply to any task that's been put on the back burner.

Choose to work under pressure. Sometimes people thrive under pressure. As one writer put it, "I don't do my *best* work under deadline. I do my *only* work under deadline." Used selectively, this strategy might also work for you.

Put yourself in control. If you choose to work with a due date staring you right in the face, then schedule a big block of time during the preceding week. Until then, enjoy!

Think ahead. Use the monthly calendar on page 87 or the long-term planner on page 91 to list due dates for assignments in all your courses. Using these tools, you can anticipate heavy demands on your time and take action to prevent last-minute crunches. Make *Becoming a Master Student* your "home base," the first place to turn in taking control of your schedule.

Give up "some day." Procrastination rests on this vague notion: *I'll do it some day*. Other people reinforce this notion by telling you that your life will *really* start when you.... (Fill in the blank with phrases like *graduate from college, get married, have kids, get promoted,* or *retire*.) Using this logic, you could wait your whole life to start living. Avoid this fate. Take action today.

Create goals that draw you forward. A goal that grabs you by the heart strings is an inspiration to act now. If you're procrastinating, then set some goals that excite you. Then you might wake up one day and discover that procrastination is part of your past.

The seven-day antiprocrastination plan

Listed here are seven strategies you can use to reduce or eliminate many sources of procrastination. The suggestions are tied to the days of the week to help you remember them. Use this list to remind yourself that each day of your life presents an opportunity to stop the cycle of procrastination.

MONDAY Make it meaningful. What is important about the task you've been putting off? List all the benefits of completing it. Look at it in relation to your short-, mid-, or long-term goals. Be specific about the rewards for getting it done, including how you will feel when the task is completed. To remember this strategy, keep in mind that it starts with the letter *M*, like the word *Monday*.

TUESDAY Take it apart. Break big jobs into a series of small ones you can do in 15 minutes or less. If a long reading assignment intimidates you, divide it into two-page or three-page sections. Make a list of the sections and cross them off as you complete them so you can see your progress. Even the biggest projects can be broken down into a series of small tasks. This strategy starts with the letter *T*, so mentally tie it to *Tuesday*.

WEDNESDAY Write an intention statement. For example, if you can't get started on a term paper, you might write, "I intend to write a list of at least 10 possible topics by 9 p.m. I will reward myself with an hour of guilt-free recreational reading." Write your intention on a 3 × 5 card and carry it with you, or post it in your study area where you can see it often. In your memory, file the first word in this strategy—*write*—with **Wednesday**.

THURSDAY Tell everyone. Publicly announce your intention to get a task done. Tell a friend that you intend to learn 10 irregular French verbs by Saturday. Tell your spouse, roommate, parents, and children. Include anyone who will ask whether you've completed the assignment or who will suggest ways to get it done. Make the world your support group. Associate *tell* with **Thursday**.

FRIDAY Find a reward. Construct rewards to yourself carefully. Be willing to withhold them if you do not complete the task. Don't pick a movie as a reward for studying biology if you plan to go to the movie anyway. And when you legitimately reap your reward, notice how it feels. Remember that *Friday* is a fine day to *find* a reward. (Of course, you can find a reward on any day of the week. Rhyming *Friday* with *fine* day is just a memory trick.)

SATURDAY Settle it now. Do it now. The minute you notice yourself procrastinating, plunge into the task. Imagine yourself at a cold mountain lake, poised to dive. Gradual immersion would be slow torture. It's often less painful to leap. Then be sure to savor the feeling of having the task behind you. Link *settle* with **Saturday**.

SUNDAY Say no. When you keep pushing a task into a low-priority category, re-examine your purpose for doing it at all. If you realize that you really don't intend to do something, quit telling yourself that you will. That's procrastinating. Just say no. Then you're not procrastinating. You don't have to carry around the baggage of an undone task. *Sunday*—the last day of this seven-day plan—is a great day to finally let go and just *say* no.

Power Process | Put It to Work | **Quiz** | Learning Styles Application | Master Student Profile

Name _____ Date _____/_____/_____

1. Describe a strategy for managing interruptions when you study.

2. Rewrite the statement "I want to study harder" so that it becomes a specific goal.

3. The text suggests that you set long-term goals. Write one example of a long-term goal.

4. Write a mid-term and short-term goal that can help you achieve the long-term goal that you listed for question 3.

5. What are at least five of the 25 ways to get the most out of now?

6. In time-management terms, what is meant by "This ain't no piano"?

7. Define "C fever" as it applies to the ABC priority method.

8. Scheduling marathon study sessions once in a while is generally an effective strategy. True or False? Explain your answer.

9. According to the text, overcoming procrastination is a complex process that can take months or even years. True or False? Explain your answer.

10. The Power Process: "Be here now" suggests ways to return your attention to the present moment. Describe two of them.

Chapter 4

Business Writing

Three phases of effective writing

Writing is a way to learn. Professional writers report that one of the joys of their craft is the opportunity to explore new fields. They constantly learn new subjects by researching and writing about them. They know that you can literally write your way into a subject.

Through writing, you can get a much clearer picture of what you know, what you don't know, and where to look for the missing pieces. Through writing, you can turn raw data into useful insight.

This chapter outlines a three-phase process for writing any paper or speech:

1. Getting ready to write
2. Writing a first draft
3. Revising your draft

Even though the following articles lay out a step-by-step process, remember that writing is highly personal. You might go through the steps in a different order or find yourself working on several at once.

PHASE 1 Getting ready to write

Schedule and list writing tasks

You can divide the ultimate goal—a finished paper—into smaller steps that you can tackle right away. Estimate how long it will take to complete each step. Start with the date your paper is due and work backward to the present. Say that the due date is December 1 and you have about three months to write the paper. Schedule November 20 as your targeted completion date, plan what you want to get done by November 1, then list what you want to get done by October 1.

Generate ideas for a topic

Brainstorm with a group. There's no need to create in isolation. Forget the myth of the lonely, frustrated artist hashing out his ideas alone in a dimly lit Paris café. You can harness the energy and the natural creative power of a group to assist you. For ideas about ways to brainstorm, see Chapter Seven: Thinking.

Speak it. To get ideas flowing, start talking. Admit your confusion or lack of a clear idea. Then just speak. By putting your thoughts into words, you'll start thinking more clearly. Novelist E. M. Forster said, "'Speak before you think' is creation's motto."[6]

Use free writing. Free writing, a technique championed by writing teacher Peter Elbow, sends a depth probe into your creative mind.[7] This is one way to bypass your internal censors, those little voices in your head that constantly say, "That sentence wasn't very good. Why don't you stop this before you get hurt?"

There's only one rule in free writing: Write without stopping. Set a time limit—say, 10 minutes—and keep your pencil in motion or your fingers dancing across the keyboard the whole time.

Give yourself permission to keep writing. Ignore the urge to stop and rewrite, even if you think what you've written isn't very good. There's no need to worry about spelling, punctuation, or grammar. It's OK if you stray from the initial subject. Just keep writing and let the ideas flow. Experiment with free writing as soon as your instructor assigns a paper.

Refine initial ideas

Select a topic and working title. It's easy to put off writing if you have a hard time choosing a topic. However, it is almost impossible to make a wrong choice at this stage. Just choose any subject. You can choose again later.

Using your instructor's guidelines for the paper or speech, write down a list of topics that interest you. Write as many of these as you can think of in two minutes. Then choose one. If you can't decide, use scissors to cut your list into single items, put them in a box, and pull one out. To avoid getting stuck on this step, set a precise timeline: "I will choose a topic by 4 p.m. on Wednesday."

The most common pitfall is selecting a topic that's too broad. "Harriet Tubman" is not a useful topic for your American history paper. Instead, consider "Harriet Tubman's activities as a Union spy during the Civil War." Your topic statement can function as a working title.

Write a thesis statement. Clarify what you want to say by summarizing it in one concise sentence. This sentence, called a thesis statement, refines your working title. It also helps in making a preliminary outline.

You might write a thesis statement such as "Harriet Tubman's activities with the Underground Railroad led to a relationship with the Union army during the Civil War." A statement that's clear and to the point can make your paper easier to write. Remember, you can always rewrite your thesis statement as you learn more about your topic.

A thesis statement is different from a topic statement. Like newspaper headlines, a thesis statement makes an assertion or describes an action. It is expressed in a complete sentence, including a verb. "Diversity" is a topic. "Cultural diversity is valuable" is a thesis statement.

Consider your purpose

Effective writing flows from a purpose. Discuss the purpose of your assignment with your instructor. Also think about how you'd like your reader or listener to respond after considering your ideas. Do you want him to think

---

journal entry 25

Discovery Statement

This Journal Entry is for people who avoid writing. As with any anxiety, you can approach writing anxiety by accepting it fully. Realize that it's OK to feel anxious about writing. Others have shared this feeling, and many people have worked with it successfully.

Begin by telling the truth. Describe exactly what happens when you start to write. What thoughts or images run through your mind? Do you feel any tension or discomfort in your body? Where? Let the thoughts and images come to the surface without resistance. Complete the following statement.

When I begin to write, I discover that I . . .

_____
_____
_____
_____
_____
_____
_____
_____
_____
_____
_____
_____

differently, to feel differently, or to take a certain action?

Your writing strategy is greatly affected by how you answer these questions. If you want someone to think differently, make your writing clear and logical. Support your assertions with evidence. If you want someone to feel differently, consider crafting a story. Write about a character your audience can empathize with, and tell how he resolves a problem that they can relate to. And if your purpose is to move the reader into action, explain exactly what steps to take and offer solid benefits for doing so.

To clarify your purpose, state it in one sentence. For example, "The purpose of this paper is to define the term *success* in such a clear and convincing way that I win a scholarship from Houghton Mifflin."

Do initial research

At this stage, the objective of your research is not to uncover specific facts about your topic. That comes later. First, you want to gain an overview of the subject. Discover the structure of your topic—its major divisions and branches. Say that you want to persuade the reader to vote for a certain candidate. You must first learn enough about this person to summarize his background and state his stands on key issues.

Outline

An outline is a kind of map. When you follow a map, you avoid getting lost. Likewise, an outline keeps you from wandering off the topic.

To start an outline, gather a stack of 3 × 5 cards and brainstorm ideas you want to include in your paper. Write one phrase or sentence per card.

Then experiment with the cards. Group them into separate stacks, each stack representing one major category. After that, arrange the stacks in order. Finally, arrange the cards within each stack in a logical order. Rearrange them until you discover an organization that you like.

If you write on a computer, consider using outlining software. These programs allow you to record and rearrange ideas on the screen, much like the way you'd create and shuffle 3 × 5 cards.

After you write the first draft of your outline, test it. Make sure that each word relates directly to your statement of purpose.

Do in-depth research

You can find information about research skills in Chapter Four: Reading and in Chapter Five: Notes. Following are added suggestions.

Use 3 × 5 cards. If 3 × 5 cards haven't found their way into your life by now, joy awaits you. These cards work wonders when conducting research. Just write down one idea per card. This makes it easy to organize—and reorganize—your ideas.

Organizing research cards as you create them saves time. Use rubber bands to keep source cards separate from information cards and to maintain general categories.

You can also save time in two other ways. First, copy all of the information correctly. Always include the source code and page number on information cards. Second, write legibly, using the same format for all of your cards.

In addition to source cards and information cards, generate idea cards. If you have a thought while you are researching, write it down on a card. Label these cards clearly as your own ideas.

An alternative to 3 × 5 cards is a computer outlining or database program. Some word processing packages also include features that can be used for note taking.

Sense the time to begin writing. A common mistake that beginning writers make is to hold their noses, close their eyes, and jump into the writing process with both feet first—and few facts. Avoid this temptation by gathering more information than you think you can use.

You can begin writing even before your research is complete. The act of writing creates ideas and reveals areas where more research is needed.

Finding a natural place to begin is one signal to start writing. This is not to say that the skies will suddenly open up and your completed paper, flanked by trumpeting angels, will appear before your eyes. You might instead get a strong sense of how to write just one small section of your paper or speech. When this happens, write.

PHASE 2: Writing a first draft

If you've planned your writing project and completed your research, you've already done much of the hard work. Now you can relax into writing your first draft.

To create your draft, gather your notes and arrange them to follow your outline. Then write about the ideas in your notes. Write in paragraphs, one idea per paragraph. If you have organized your notes logically, related facts will appear close to each other. As you

> Avoid ~~at all costs and at all times~~ the ~~really, really terrible mistake of~~ using ~~way too many~~ unnecessary words. ~~a mistake that some student writers often make when they sit down to write papers for the various courses in which they participate at the fine institutions of higher learning which they are fortunate to attend.~~

complete this task, keep the following suggestions in mind.

Remember that the first draft is not for keeps. You can save quality for later, when you revise. Your goal at this point is simply to generate lots of material.

Don't worry about grammar, punctuation, or spelling as you write your first draft. Write as if you were explaining the subject to a friend. Let the words flow. The very act of writing will release creative energy. It's perfectly all right to crank out a draft that you heavily rewrite or even throw away. The purpose of a first draft is merely to have something to work with—period. For most of us, that's a heck of a lot better than facing a blank page. You will revise this rough draft several times, so don't be concerned if it seems rough or choppy.

Write freely. Many writers prefer to get their first draft down quickly. Their advice is just to keep writing, much as in free writing. You can pause occasionally to glance at your notes and outline. The idea is to avoid stopping to edit your work. You can save that for the next step.

Another option is to write a first draft without referring to your notes and outline. If you've immersed yourself in the topic, chances are that much of the information is already bubbling up near the surface of your mind anyway. Later, when you edit, you can go back to your notes and correct any errors.

Keep in mind that you don't have to follow your outline from beginning to end. Some professional writers prefer to write the last chapter of a novel or the last scene of a play first. With the ending firmly in mind, they can then guide the reader through all of the incidents that lead up to it. You might feel more comfortable with certain aspects of your topic than with others. Dive in where you feel most comfortable.

Be yourself. Let go of the urge to sound "official" or "scholarly," and write in a natural voice instead. Address your thoughts not to the teacher but to an intelligent student or someone you care about. Visualize this person and choose the three or four most important things you'd say to him about the topic. This helps you avoid the temptation to write merely to impress.

The flip side of this point is that we can't really write the way we speak. The spoken word is accompanied by facial expressions and gestures, as well as changes in voice tone, pitch, and volume. Slang expressions used in everyday speech are not appropriate in academic writing. Compensate for elements peculiar to the spoken language by being clear and concise in your writing and by providing smooth, logical transitions from subject to subject.

Let your inner writer take over. There might be times when ideas come to you spontaneously—when thoughts flow from your head to your hand without conscious effort. This is a "natural high," similar to states that accomplished athletes, musicians, and artists have described. Writer Natalie Goldberg says that during such moments you are in touch with your "inner writer."[8] Such "peak experiences" can yield moments of pure joy. Often, those moments come just after a period of feeling stuck. Welcome getting stuck. A breakthrough is not far behind.

Ease into it. Some people find that it works well to forget the word *writing*. Instead, they ease into the task with activities that help generate ideas. You can free-associate, cluster, meditate, daydream, doodle, draw diagrams, visualize the event you want to describe, talk into a voice recorder—anything that gets you started.

Make writing a habit. The word *inspiration* is not in the working vocabulary for many professional writers. Instead of waiting for inspiration to strike, they simply make a habit of writing at a certain time each day. You can use the same strategy. Schedule a block of time to write your first draft. The very act of writing can breed inspiration.

Respect your deep mind. Part of the process of writing takes place outside our awareness. There's nothing mysterious about this. Many people report that ideas come to them while they're doing something totally unrelated to writing. Often this happens after they've been grappling with a question and have reached a point where they feel stuck. It's like the composer who said, "There I was, sitting and eating a sandwich, and all of a sudden this darn tune pops into my head." You can trust your deep mind. It's writing while you eat, sleep, and brush your teeth.

Get physical. Writing is physical, like jogging or playing tennis. You can move your body in ways that are in tune with the flow of your ideas. While working on the first draft, take breaks. Go for a walk. Speak or sing your ideas out loud. From time to time, practice relaxation techniques and breathe deeply.

Use affirmations and visualizations. Write with the idea that the finished paper or speech is inside you, waiting to be released. Affirmations and visualizations can help you with this. Imagine what your finished paper will look like. Construct a detailed mental picture of the title page and major sections of the paper. See a clean, typed copy, and speculate how it will feel to hold the paper and flip through the pages. Visualize the reaction of audience members after you've given your speech.

Then support your writing by sprinkling your self-talk with statements that affirm your abilities. For example: "I express myself clearly and persuasively." "I am using an effective process to write my paper." "I will be pleased with the results."

Hide it in your drawer for a while. Schedule time for rewrites before you begin, and schedule at least one day between revisions so that you can let the material sit. On Tuesday night, you might think your writing sings the song of beautiful language. On Wednesday, you will see that those same words, such as the phrase "sings the song of beautiful language," belong in the trash basket.

Ideally, a student will revise a paper two or three times, make a clean copy of those revisions, then let the last revised draft sit for at least three or four days. The brain needs that much time to disengage itself from the project. Obvious grammatical mistakes, awkward constructions, and lapses in logic are hidden from us when we are in the middle of the creative process. Give yourself time to step back, and then go over the paper one last time before starting the third phase of the writing process.

PHASE 3: Revising your draft

One definition of a writer is simply anyone who rewrites. Some people who write for a living will rewrite a piece seven, eight, or even more times. Ernest Hemingway rewrote the last page of *A Farewell to Arms* 39 times before he was satisfied with it. When asked what the most difficult part of this process was, he simply said, "Getting the words right."[9]

People who rewrite care. They care about the reader. They care about precise language and careful thinking. And they care about themselves. They know that the act of rewriting teaches them more about the topic than almost any other step in the process.

There's a difference in pace between writing a first draft and revising it. Keep in mind the saying "Write in haste, revise at leisure." When you edit and revise, slow down and take a microscope to your work. One guideline is to allow 50 percent of writing time for planning, research, and writing the first draft. Then give the remaining 50 percent to revising.

An effective way to revise your paper is to read it out loud. The eyes tend to fill in the blanks in our own writing. The combination of voice and ears forces us to pay attention to the details.

Another technique is to have a friend look over your paper. This is never a substitute for your own review, but a friend can often see mistakes you miss. Remember, when other people criticize or review your work, they're not attacking you. They're just commenting on your paper. With a little practice, you can actually learn to welcome feedback.

Reading aloud and having a friend comment on your paper are techniques that can help you in each step of rewriting explained below.

Cut

Writer Theodore Cheney suggests that an efficient way to begin revising is to cut the passages that don't contribute to your purpose.[10] It might not pay to polish individual words, phrases, and sentences right now—especially if you end up deleting them later. To save time, focus instead on deciding which words you want to keep and which ones you want to let go.

Look for excess baggage. Avoid at all costs and at all times the really, really terrible mistake of using way too many unnecessary words, a mistake that some student writers often make when they sit down to write papers for the various courses in which they participate at the fine institutions of higher learning that they are fortunate enough to attend. (Example: The previous sentence could be edited to "Avoid unnecessary words.")

Approach your rough draft as if it were a chunk of granite from which you will chisel the final product. In the end, much of your first draft will be lying on the floor. What is left will be the clean, clear, polished product. Sometimes the revisions are painful. Sooner or later, every writer invents a phrase that is truly clever but makes no contribution to the purpose of the paper. Grit your teeth and let it go.

Note: For maximum efficiency, make the larger cuts first—sections, chapters, pages. Then go for the smaller cuts—paragraphs, sentences, phrases, words.

Keep in mind that cutting a passage means just for now, for this paper, for this assignment. You might want to keep a file of deleted writings to save for future use.

Paste

In deleting passages, you've probably removed some of the original transitions and connecting ideas from your draft. The next task is to rearrange what's left of your paper or speech so that it flows logically. Look for consistency within paragraphs and for transitions from paragraph to paragraph and section to section.

If your draft doesn't hang together, reorder your ideas. Imagine yourself with scissors and glue, cutting the paper into scraps—one scrap for each point. Then paste these points down in a new, more logical order.

Fix

Now it's time to look at individual words and phrases.

In general, rely on nouns and verbs. Using too many adjectives and adverbs weakens your message and adds unnecessary bulk to your writing. Write about the details and be specific. Also, use the active rather than the passive voice.

Instead of writing in the passive voice:
A project was initiated.

You can use the active voice:
The research team began a project.

Instead of writing verbosely:
After making a timely arrival and perspicaciously observing the unfolding events, I emerged totally and gloriously victorious.

You can write to the point, as Julius Caesar did:
I came, I saw, I conquered.

Instead of writing vaguely:
The speaker made effective use of the television medium, asking in no uncertain terms that we change our belief systems.

You can write specifically:
The reformed criminal stared straight into the television camera and shouted, "Take a good look at what you're doing! Will it get you what you really want?"

Also, define any terms that the reader might not know, putting them in plain English whenever you can.

Prepare

In a sense, any paper is a sales effort. If you hand in a paper with wrinkled jeans, its hair tangled and unwashed and its shoes untied, your instructor is less likely to buy it. To avoid this situation, format your paper following accepted standards for margin widths, endnotes, title pages, and other details.

Ask your instructor for specific instructions on how to cite the sources used in writing your paper. You can find useful guidelines in the *MLA Handbook for Writers of Research Papers,* a book from the Modern Language Association. Also visit the MLA Website at **http://www.mla.org/style_faq.**

If you "cut and paste" material from a Web page directly into your paper, be sure to place that material in quotation marks and cite the source. And before referencing an e-mail message, verify the sender's identity. Remember that anyone sending e-mail can pretend to be someone else.

Use quality paper for your final version. For an even more professional appearance, bind your paper with a paper or plastic cover.

Proof

As you ease down the homestretch, read your revised paper one more time. This time, go for the big picture and look for:

- A clear thesis statement.
- Sentences that introduce your topic, guide the reader through the major sections of your paper, and summarize your conclusions.
- Details—such as quotations, examples, and statistics—that support your conclusions.
- Lean sentences that have been purged of needless words.
- Plenty of action verbs and concrete, specific nouns.

Finally, look over your paper with an eye for spelling and grammar mistakes.

When you're through proofreading, take a minute to savor the result. You've just witnessed something of a miracle—the mind attaining clarity and resolution. That's the aha! in writing.

mastering technology

WRITE E-MAIL THAT GETS RESULTS

Target content to readers. Be conscious of the amount of e-mail that busy people receive. Send e-mail messages only to the people who need them, and only when necessary.

Write an informative subject line. Rather than writing a generic description, include a capsule summary of your message. "Biology 100 Report due next Tuesday" packs more information than "Report." If your message is urgent, include that word in the subject line as well.

Think short. Keep your subject line short, your paragraphs short, and your message as a whole short.

Put the point first. To make sure your point gets across, put it at the top of the first paragraph. If your message will take up more than one screen's worth of text, break it up into short sections and add a heading for each section. Then pack those headings with the main points.

Review your message. Every message you send says something about your attention to detail. Put your best electronic foot forward. If you plan to send a long message, draft it in a word processing program first so that you can take advantage of spelling checkers and other editing devices. Remember the techniques for effective letter writing and apply them to your e-mails. Follow the rules for proper spelling, capitalization, punctuation, and word choice. The tone of e-mails to instructors or coworkers should be more professional than the instant messaging you may do with friends.

Reply promptly and consciously. Provide context. If you're responding to a question from a previous e-mail, include that question in your response.

Use "reply-all" carefully. Use this feature only when everyone who received a message truly needs to know your response. People will appreciate your help in keeping their incoming messages to a minimum.

Protect your privacy. Treat all online communication as public communication. Include only content that you're willing to circulate widely, and share personal data with caution.

Chapter 5

Reading and Studying

Muscle Reading

Picture yourself sitting at a desk, a book in your hands. Your eyes are open, and it looks as if you're reading. Suddenly your head jerks up. You blink. You realize your eyes have been scanning the page for 10 minutes, and you can't remember a single thing you have read.

Or picture this: You've had a hard day. You were up at 6 a.m. to get the kids ready for school. A coworker called in sick, and you missed your lunch trying to do his job as well as your own. You picked up the kids, then had to shop for dinner. Dinner was late, of course, and the kids were grumpy.

Finally, you get to your books at 8 p.m. You begin a reading assignment on something called "the equity method of accounting for common stock investments." "I am preparing for the future," you tell yourself, as you plod through two paragraphs and begin the third. Suddenly, everything in the room looks different. Your head is resting on your elbow, which is resting on the equity method of accounting. The clock reads 11:00 p.m. Say good-bye to three hours.

Sometimes the only difference between a sleeping pill and a textbook is that the textbook doesn't have a warning on the label about operating heavy machinery.

Contrast this scenario with the image of an active reader. This is a person who:

- Stays alert, poses questions about what she reads, and searches for the answers.

- Recognizes levels of information within the text, separating the main points and general principles from supporting details.

- Quizzes herself about the material, makes written notes, and lists unanswered questions.

- Instantly spots key terms and takes the time to find the definitions of unfamiliar words.

- Thinks critically about the ideas in the text and looks for ways to apply them.

That sounds like a lot to do. Yet skilled readers routinely accomplish all this and more—while enjoying reading.[1]

One way to experience this kind of success is to approach reading with a system in mind. An example is Muscle Reading. You can use it to avoid mental minivacations and reduce the number of unscheduled naps during study time, even after a hard day.

Muscle Reading is a way to decrease difficulty and struggle by increasing energy and skill. Once you learn this system, you might actually spend less time on your reading and get more out of it.

This is not to say that Muscle Reading will make your education a breeze. Muscle Reading might even look like more work at first. Effective textbook reading is an active, energy-consuming, sit-on-the-edge-of-your-seat business. That's why this strategy is called Muscle Reading.

journal entry 10

Discovery/Intention Statement

Recall a time when you encountered problems with reading, such as words you didn't understand or paragraphs you paused to reread more than once. Sum up the experience and how you felt about it by completing the following statement.

I discovered that I . . .

_____
_____
_____
_____

Now list three to five specific reading skills you want to gain from this chapter.

I intend to . . .

_____
_____
_____
_____
_____
_____
_____
_____
_____

How Muscle Reading works

Muscle Reading is a three-phase technique you can use to extract the ideas and information you want.

Phase one includes steps to take *before* you read.
Phase two includes steps to take *while* you read.
Phase three includes steps to take *after* you read.

Each phase has three steps.

> **PHASE ONE:**
> **Before you read**
> **Step 1:** Preview
> **Step 2:** Outline
> **Step 3:** Question
>
> **PHASE TWO:**
> **While you read**
> **Step 4:** Read
> **Step 5:** Underline
> **Step 6:** Answer
>
> **PHASE THREE:**
> **After you read**
> **Step 7:** Recite
> **Step 8:** Review
> **Step 9:** Review again

A nine-step reading strategy might seem cumbersome and unnecessary for a two-page reading assignment. It is. Use the steps appropriately. Choose which ones to apply as you read.

To assist your recall of Muscle Reading strategies, memorize three short sentences:

Pry Out Questions.
Root Up Answers.
Recite, Review, and Review again.

These three sentences correspond to the three phases of the Muscle Reading technique. Each sentence is an acrostic. The first letter of each word stands for one of the nine steps listed above.

Take a moment to invent images for each of those sentences.

For *phase one*, visualize or feel yourself prying out questions from a text. These are questions you want answered based on a brief survey of the assignment. Make a mental picture of yourself scanning the material, spotting a question, and reaching into the text to pry it out. Hear yourself saying, "I've got it. Here's my question." Then for *phase two*, get your muscles involved. Feel the tips of your fingers digging into the text as you root up the answers to your questions.

Finally, you enter *phase three*. Hear your voice reciting what you have learned. Listen to yourself making a speech or singing a song about the material as you review it.

To jog your memory, write the first letters of the Muscle Reading acrostic in a margin or at the top of your notes. Then check off the steps you intend to follow. Or write the Muscle Reading steps on 3x5 cards and then use them for bookmarks.

Muscle Reading could take a little time to learn. At first you might feel it's slowing you down. That's natural when you're gaining a new skill. Mastery comes with time and practice.

PHASE 1

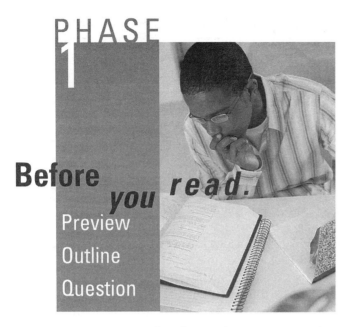

Before you read.
Preview
Outline
Question

Step 1 **Preview** Before you start reading, preview the entire assignment. You don't have to memorize what you preview to get value from this step. Previewing sets the stage for incoming information by warming up a space in your mental storage area.

If you are starting a new book, look over the table of contents and flip through the text page by page. If you're going to read one chapter, flip through the pages of that chapter. Even if your assignment is merely a few pages in a book, you can benefit from a brief preview of the table of contents.

Keep the preview short. If the entire reading assignment will take less than an hour, your preview might take five minutes. Previewing is also a way to get yourself started when an assignment looks too big to handle. It is an easy way to step into the material.

Keep an eye out for summary statements. If the assignment is long or complex, read the summary first. Many textbooks have summaries in the introduction or at the end of each chapter.

Read all chapter headings and subheadings. Like the headlines in a newspaper, these are usually printed in large, bold type. Often headings are brief summaries in themselves.

When previewing, seek out familiar concepts, facts, or ideas. These items can help increase comprehension by linking new information to previously learned material. Look for ideas that spark your imagination or curiosity. Inspect drawings, diagrams, charts, tables, graphs, and photographs. Imagine what kinds of questions will show up on a test. Previewing helps to clarify your purpose for reading. Ask yourself what you will do with this material and how it can relate to your long-term goals. Are you reading just to get the main points? Key supporting details? Additional details? All of the above? Your answers will guide what you do with each step that follows.

Step 2 **Outline** With complex material, take time to understand the structure of what you are about to read. Outlining actively organizes your thoughts about the assignment and can help make complex information easier to understand.

If your textbook provides chapter outlines, spend some time studying them. When an outline is not provided, sketch a brief one in the margin of your book or at the beginning of your notes on a separate sheet of paper. Later, as you read and take notes, you can add to your outline.

Headings in the text can serve as major and minor entries in your outline. For example, the heading for this article is "Phase one: Before you read," and the subheadings list the three steps in this phase. When you outline, feel free to rewrite headings so that they are more meaningful to you.

The amount of time you spend on this step will vary. For some assignments, a 10-second mental outline is all you might need. For other assignments (fiction and poetry, for example), you can skip this step altogether.

Step 3 **Question** Before you begin a careful reading, determine what you want from an assignment. Then write down a list of questions, including any that resulted from your preview of the materials.

Another useful technique is to turn chapter headings and subheadings into questions. For example, if a heading is "Transference and suggestion," you can ask yourself, "What are *transference* and *suggestion*? How does *transference* relate to *suggestion*?" Make up a quiz as if you were teaching this subject to your classmates.

If there are no headings, look for key sentences and turn these into questions. These sentences usually show up at the beginnings or ends of paragraphs and sections.

Have fun with this technique. Make the questions playful or creative. You don't need to answer every question that you ask. The purpose of making up questions is to get your brain involved in the assignment. Take your unanswered questions to class, where they can be springboards for class discussion.

Demand your money's worth from your textbook. If you do not understand a concept, write specific questions about it. The more detailed your questions, the more powerful this technique becomes.

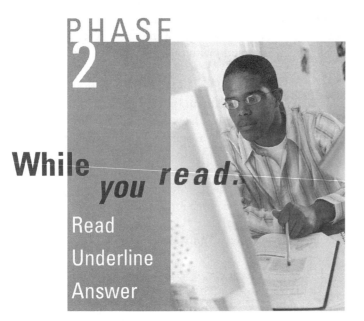

PHASE 2

While you read...
Read
Underline
Answer

Step 4
Read At last! You have previewed the assignment, organized it in your mind, and formulated questions. Now you are ready to begin reading.

Before you dive into the first paragraph, take a few moments to reflect on what you already know about this subject. Do this even if you think you know nothing. This technique prepares your brain to accept the information that follows.

As you read, be conscious of where you are and what you are doing. Use the Power Process: "Be here now" in Chapter Two. When you notice your attention wandering, gently bring it back to the present moment.

One way to stay focused is to avoid marathon reading sessions. Schedule breaks and set a reasonable goal for the entire session. Then reward yourself with an enjoyable activity for five or 10 minutes every hour or two.

For difficult reading, set more limited goals. Read for a

▶ Five smart ways to highlight a text

Underlining a text with a pen can make underlined sections—the important parts—harder to read. As an alternative, many students use colored highlighters to flag key words and sentences.

Highlighting can be a powerful tool. It also presents a danger—the ever-present temptation to highlight too much text. Excessive highlighting leads to wasted time during reviews and can also spoil the appearance of your books. Get the most out of all that money you pay for books. Highlight in an efficient way that leaves texts readable for years to come.

Read carefully first. Read an entire chapter or section at least once before you begin highlighting. Don't be in a hurry to mark up your book. Get to know the text first. Make two or three passes through difficult sections before you highlight.

Make choices up front about what to highlight. Perhaps you can accomplish your purposes by highlighting only certain chapters or sections of a text. When you highlight, remember to look for passages that directly answer the questions you posed during step 3 of Muscle Reading. Within these passages, highlight individual words, phrases, or sentences rather than whole paragraphs. The important thing is to choose an overall strategy before you put highlighter to paper.

Recite first. You might want to apply step 7 of Muscle Reading before you highlight. Talking about what you read—to yourself or with other people—can help you grasp the essence of a text. Recite first, then go back and highlight. You'll probably highlight more selectively.

Underline, then highlight. Underline key passages lightly in pencil. Then close your text and come back to it later. Assess your underlining. Perhaps you can highlight less than you underlined and still capture the key points.

Use highlighting to monitor your comprehension. Critical thinking plays a role in underlining and highlighting. When highlighting, you're making moment-by-moment decisions about what you want to remember from a text. You're also making inferences about what material might be included on a test.

Take your critical thinking a step further by using highlighting to check your comprehension. Stop reading periodically and look back over the sentences you've highlighted. See if you are making accurate distinctions between main points and supporting material. Highlighting too much—more than 10 percent of the text—can be a sign that you're not making this distinction and that you don't fully understand what you're reading. See the article "When reading is tough" later in this chapter for suggestions that can help.

half-hour and then take a break. Most students find that shorter periods of reading distributed throughout the day and week can be more effective than long sessions. You can use the following four techniques to stay focused as you read.

First, visualize the material. Form mental pictures of the concepts as they are presented. If you read that a voucher system can help control cash disbursements, picture a voucher handing out dollar bills. Using visual imagery in this way can help deepen your understanding of the text while allowing information to be transferred into your long-term memory.

Second, read the material out loud, especially if it is complicated. Some of us remember better and understand more quickly when we hear an idea.

Third, get a "feel" for the subject. For example, let's say you are reading about a microorganism, a paramecium, in your biology text. Imagine what it would feel like to run your finger around the long, cigar-shaped body of the organism. Imagine feeling the large fold of its gullet on one side and the tickle of the hairy little cilia as they wiggle in your hand.

Fourth, remember that a goal of your reading is to answer the questions you listed during phase one. After you've identified the key questions, predict how the author will answer them. Then read to find out if your predictions were accurate.

A final note: It's easy to fool yourself about reading. Just having an open book in your hand and moving your eyes across a page doesn't mean you are reading effectively. Reading textbooks takes energy, even if you do it sitting down.

If you do an informal study of chief executive officers, you'll find some who wear out the front of their chairs first. Approach your reading assignment like a company president. Sit up. Keep your spine straight. Use the edge of your chair. And avoid reading in bed—except for fun.

Step 5 Underline
Deface your books. Use them up. Have fun writing in them. Indulge yourself as you never could with your grade-school books.

The purpose of making marks in a text is to call out important concepts or information that you will need to review later. Underlining can save lots of time when you are studying for tests.

Underlining offers a secondary benefit. When you read with a pen or pencil in your hand, you involve your kinesthetic senses of touch and motion. Being physical with your books can help build strong neural pathways in your memory.

Avoid underlining too soon. Wait until you complete a chapter or section to make sure you know the key points. Then mark up the text. Sometimes, underlining after you read each paragraph works best.

Underline sparingly, usually less than 10 percent of the text. If you mark up too much on a page, you defeat the purpose—to flag the most important material for review.

In addition to underlining, you can mark up a text in the following ways:

- Place an asterisk (*) or an exclamation point (!) in the margin next to an especially important sentence or term.

- Circle key terms and words to look up later in a dictionary.

- Write short definitions of key terms in the margin.

- Write a "Q" in the margin to highlight possible test questions, passages you don't understand, and questions to ask in class.

- Write personal comments in the margin—points of agreement or disagreement with the author.

- Write mini-indexes in the margin, that is, the numbers of other pages in the book where the same topic is discussed.

- Write summaries by listing the main points or key events covered in a chapter.

- Rewrite chapter titles, headings, and subheadings so that they're more meaningful to you.

- Draw diagrams, pictures, tables, or maps that translate text into visual terms.

- Number each step in a list or series of related points.

Step 6 Answer
As you read, seek out the answers to your questions and write them down. Fill in your outline. Jot down new questions and note when you don't find the answers you are looking for. Use these notes to ask questions in class, or see your instructor personally.

When you read, create an image of yourself as a person in search of the answers. You are a detective, watching for every clue, sitting erect in your straight-back chair, demanding that your textbook give you what you want—the answers.

PHASE 3

After you read.

Recite
Review
Review again

Step 7 — Recite

Talk to yourself about what you've read. Or talk to someone else. When you're finished with a reading assignment, make a speech about it. A classic study suggests that you can profitably devote up to 80 percent of your study time to active reciting.[2] When you recite, you practice an important aspect of metacognition—synthesis, or combining individual ideas and facts into a meaningful whole.

One way to get yourself to recite is to look at each underlined point. Note what you marked, then put the book down and start talking out loud. Explain as much as you can about that particular point.

To make this technique more effective, do it in front of a mirror. It might seem silly, but the benefits can be enormous. Reap them at exam time.

Classmates are even better than mirrors. Form a group and practice teaching each other what you have read. One of the best ways to learn anything is to teach it to someone else.

In addition, talk about your reading whenever you can. Tell friends and family members what you're learning from your textbooks.

Talking about your reading reinforces a valuable skill—the ability to summarize. To practice this skill, pick one chapter (or one section of one chapter) from any of your textbooks. State the main topic covered in this chapter. Then state the main points that the author makes about this topic.

For example, the main topic up to this point in this chapter is Muscle Reading. The main point about this topic is that Muscle Reading includes three phases—steps to take before you read, while you read, and after you read. For a more detailed summary, you could name each of the nine steps.

Note: This "topic-point" method does not work so well when you want to summarize short stories, novels, plays, and other works of fiction. Instead, focus on action. In most stories, the main character confronts a major problem and takes a series of actions to solve it. Describe that problem and talk about the character's key actions—the turning points in the story.

Step 8 — Review

Plan to do your first complete review within 24 hours of reading the material. Sound the trumpets! This point is critical: A review within 24 hours moves information from your short-term memory to your long-term memory.

Review within one day. If you read it on Wednesday, review it on Thursday. During this review, look over your notes and clear up anything you don't understand. Recite some of the main points again.

This review can be short. You might spend as little as 15 minutes reviewing a difficult two-hour reading assignment. Investing that time now can save you hours later when studying for exams.

▶ Muscle Reading—a leaner approach

Keep in mind that Muscle Reading is an overall approach, not a rigid, step-by-step procedure. Here's a shorter variation that students have found helpful. Practice it with any chapter in this book:

- **Preview and question.** Flip through the pages, looking at anything that catches your eye—headings, subheadings, illustrations, photographs. Turn the title of each article into a question. For example, "How Muscle Reading works" can become "How does Muscle Reading work?" List your questions on a separate sheet of paper, or write each question on a 3x5 card.

- **Read to answer your questions.** Read each article, then go back over the text and underline or highlight answers to the appropriate questions on your list.

- **Recite and review.** When you're done with the chapter, close the book. Recite by reading each question—and answering it—out loud. Review the chapter by looking up the answers to your questions. (It's easy—they're already highlighted.) Review again by quizzing yourself one more time with your list of questions.

Step 9 Review again

The final step in Muscle Reading is the weekly or monthly review. This step can be very short—perhaps only four or five minutes per assignment. Simply go over your notes. Read the highlighted parts of your text. Recite one or two of the more complicated points.

The purpose of these reviews is to keep the neural pathways to the information open and to make them more distinct. That way, the information can be easier to recall. You can accomplish these short reviews anytime, anywhere, if you are prepared.

Conduct a five-minute review while you are waiting for a bus, for your socks to dry, or for the water to boil. Three-by-five cards are a handy review tool. Write ideas, formulas, concepts, and facts on cards and carry them with you. These short review periods can be effortless and fun.

Sometimes longer review periods are appropriate. For example, if you found an assignment difficult, consider rereading it. Start over, as if you had never seen the material before. Sometimes a second reading will provide you with surprising insights.

Decades ago, psychologists identified the primacy-recency effect, which suggests that we most easily remember the first and last items in any presentation.[3] Previewing and reviewing your reading can put this theory to work for you.

journal entry 11

Discovery Statement

Now that you've read about Muscle Reading, review your assessment of your reading skills in the Discovery Wheel on page 28. Do you still think your evaluation was accurate? What new insights do you have about the way you read? Are you a more effective reader than you thought you were? Less effective? Record your observations below.

_____
_____
_____
_____
_____
_____
_____
_____
_____
_____

When reading is tough

Sometimes ordinary reading methods are not enough. Many students get bogged down in a murky reading assignment. The solution starts with a First Step: When you are confused, tell the truth about it. Successful readers monitor their understanding of reading material. They do not see confusion as a mistake or a personal shortcoming. Instead, they take it as a cue to change reading strategies and process ideas at a deeper level. If you are ever up to your neck in textbook alligators, you can use the following techniques to drain the swamp.

Read it again. Somehow, students get the idea that reading means opening a book and dutifully slogging the text—line by line, page by page—moving in a straight line from the first word until the last. Actually, this can be an ineffective way to read much of the published material you'll encounter in college.

Feel free to shake up your routine. Make several "passes" through any reading material. During a preview, for example, just scan the text to look for key words and highlighted material. Next, skim the entire chapter or article again, spending a little more time and taking in more than you did during your preview. Finally, read in more depth, proceeding word by word through some or all of the text.

Difficult material—such as the technical writing in science texts—is often easier the second time around. Isolate difficult passages and read them again, slowly.

If you read an assignment and are completely lost, do not despair. Sleep on it. When you return to the assignment the next day, see it with fresh eyes.[4]

Look for essential words. If you are stuck on a paragraph, mentally cross out all of the adjectives and adverbs and read the sentence without them. Find the important words. These will usually be verbs and nouns.

Hold a minireview. Pause briefly to summarize—either verbally or in writing—what you've read so far. Stop at the end of a paragraph and recite, in your own words, what you have just read. Jot down some notes or create a short outline or summary.

Read it out loud. Make noise. Read a passage out loud several times, each time using a different inflection and emphasizing a different part of the sentence. Be creative. Imagine that you are the author talking.

Talk to your instructor. Admit when you are stuck and make an appointment with your instructor. Most teachers welcome the opportunity to work individually with students. Be specific about your confusion. Point out the paragraph that you found toughest to understand.

Stand up. Changing positions periodically can combat fatigue. Experiment with standing as you read, especially if you get stuck on a tough passage and decide to read it out loud.

Skip around. Jump to the next section or end of a tough article or chapter. You might have lost the big picture. Simply seeing the next step, the next main point, or summary might be all you need to put the details in context. Retrace the steps in a chain of ideas and look for examples. Absorb facts and ideas in whatever order works for you—which may be different than the author's presentation.

Find a tutor. Many schools provide free tutoring services. If tutoring services are not provided by your school, other students who have completed the course can assist you.

Use another text. Find a similar text in the library. Sometimes a concept is easier to understand if it is expressed another way. Children's books, especially children's encyclopedias, can provide useful overviews of baffling subjects.

Pretend you understand, then explain it. We often understand more than we think we do. Pretend that the material is clear as a bell and explain it to another person, or even to yourself. Write down your explanation. You might be amazed by what you know.

Ask: "What's going on here?" When you feel stuck, stop reading for a moment and diagnose what's happening. At these stop points, mark your place in the margin of the page with a penciled "S" for "Stuck." A pattern to your marks over several pages might indicate a question you want to answer before going further. Or you might discover a reading habit you'd like to change.

Stop reading. When none of the above suggestions work, do not despair. Admit your confusion and then take a break. Catch a movie, go for a walk, study another subject, or sleep on it. The concepts you've already absorbed might come together at a subconscious level as you move on to other activities. Allow some time for that process. When you return to the reading material, see it with fresh eyes.

mastering technology

FIND WHAT YOU WANT ON THE INTERNET

Joe Barker, a librarian at the University of California at Berkeley, suggests that you analyze your topic *before* you look for information about it on the Internet. Then you can determine a useful way to find what you want. His suggestions are summarized in the following chart.[5]

If...	Then...
Your topic includes distinctive words or phrases (for example, *affirmative action*)	Enclose the words or phrases in quotation marks and use a **search engine** such as Google (www.google.com) or Yahoo! (search.yahoo.com).
Your topic does *not* include distinctive words or phrases (for example, *Iraq war*)	Enclose several words or phrases related to the topic in quotation marks and use a **search engine**.
	See if you can find distinctive words or phrases related to your topic. Use a **subject directory** such as Librarians' Index (www.lii.org), Infomine (infomine.ucr.edu), About.com (www.about.com), Google Directory (directory.google.com), or Yahoo! (dir.yahoo.com).
Your topic could be summarized in a broad overview (for example, *alternative energy sources*)	Look for a specialized subject directory related to your topic. Start by searching one of the **subject directories** listed above. Look for results labeled as *directories*, *virtual libraries*, *guides*, or *gateway pages*.
	Also add the words *web directories* to your search term (for example, *alternative energy sources web directories*).
Your topic includes various words or phrases that identify the same subject (for example, *MP3 players* or *portable music players*)	Use a search engine such as Google (www.google.com) or Yahoo! (search.yahoo.com) that allows you to search with words such as *AND* and *OR* (for example, *MP3 players AND portable music players*).
You are confused about the topic or totally new to it.	Look up the topic in an encyclopedia and ask a reference librarian for help.

Power Process | Put It to Work | **Quiz** | Learning Styles Application | Master Student Profile

Name _____ Date ____/____/____

quiz

1. Name the acrostic that can help you remember the steps of Muscle Reading.

2. You must complete all nine steps of Muscle Reading to get the most out of any reading assignment. True or False? Explain your answer.

3. Give three examples of what to look for when previewing a reading assignment.

4. Briefly explain how to use headings in a text to create an outline.

5. In addition to underlining, there are other ways to mark up a text. List three possibilities.

6. To get the most benefit from marking a book, underline at least 10 percent of the text. True or False? Explain your answer.

7. Explain at least three techniques you can use when reading is tough.

8. The Power Process in this chapter includes this sentence: "The next time you discover you are angry, disappointed, or frustrated, look to see which of your pictures aren't being fulfilled." Give an example of this from your own experience.

9. Define the "topic-point" method of summarizing and give a brief example based on an article in this book.

10. List at least three techniques for increasing your reading speed.

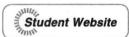

Chapter 6

Note-Taking

5 Notes

MASTER STUDENT MAP

why this chapter matters...

Note taking helps you remember information and influences how well you do on tests

how you can use this chapter...

Experiment with several formats for note taking.

Create a note-taking format that works especially well for you.

Take effective notes in special situations—such as while reading and when instructors talk fast.

As you read, ask yourself what if...

I could take notes that remain informative and useful for weeks, months, or even years to come?

what is included...

The note-taking process flows 149
Observe 150
Record 153
Review 158
Improving your handwriting 160
Enroll your instructor in your education 162
When your instructor talks *fast* 164
Taking notes while reading 165
Becoming an online learner 168
Power Process: "I create it all" 170
Master Student Profile: Craig Kielburger 175

STUDENT VOICES

Joining a study group has helped me to improve my note-taking skills. My group members rely on me to take neat notes in class, especially to help the other group members to fill in places that they've missed. Now when my psychology professor talks fast, I don't panic. Sharing the notes after class helps my whole group get the important information.

—MARCO JUAREZ

The note-taking process flows

One way to understand note taking is to realize that taking notes is just one part of the process. Effective note taking consists of three parts: observing, recording, and reviewing. First, you observe an "event"—a statement by an instructor, a lab experiment, a slide show of an artist's works, or a chapter of required reading. Then you record your observations of that event, that is, you "take notes." Finally, you review what you have recorded.

Each part of the process is essential, and each depends on the others. Your observations determine what you record. What you record determines what you review. And the quality of your review can determine how effective your next observations will be. For example, if you review your notes on the Sino-Japanese War of 1894, the next day's lecture on the Boxer Rebellion of 1900 will make more sense.

Legible and speedy handwriting is also useful in taking notes. Knowledge about outlining is handy, too. A nifty pen, a new notebook, and a laptop computer are all great note-taking devices. And they're all worthless—unless you participate as an energetic observer *in* class and regularly review your notes *after* class. If you take those two steps, you can turn even the most disorganized chicken scratches into a powerful tool.

Sometimes note taking looks like a passive affair, especially in large lecture classes. One person at the front of the room does most of the talking. Everyone else is seated and silent, taking notes. The lecturer seems to be doing all of the work.

Don't be deceived. Observe more closely, and you'll see some students taking notes in a way that radiates energy. They're awake and alert, poised on the edge of their seats. They're writing, a physical activity that expresses mental engagement. These students listen for levels of ideas and information, make choices about what to record, and compile materials to review.

In higher education, you might spend hundreds of hours taking notes. Making them more effective is a direct investment in your success. Think of your notes as a textbook that *you* create—one that's more current and more in tune with your learning preferences than any textbook you could buy.

journal entry 12

Discovery/Intention Statement

Think about the possible benefits of improving your skills at note taking. Recall a recent incident in which you had difficulty taking notes. Perhaps you were listening to an instructor who talked fast, or you got confused and stopped taking notes altogether. Describe the incident in the space below.

Now preview this chapter to find at least five strategies that you can use right away to help you take better notes. Sum up each of those strategies in a few words and note page numbers where you can find out more about each suggestion.

Strategy   *Page number*

Reflect on your intention to experiment actively with this chapter. Describe a specific situation in which you might apply the strategies you listed above. If possible, choose a situation that will occur within the next 24 hours.

I intend to . .

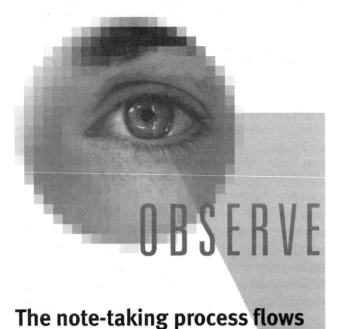

The note-taking process flows

Sherlock Holmes, a fictional master detective and student of the obvious, could track down a villain by observing the fold of his scarf and the mud on his shoes. In real life, a doctor can save a life by observing a mole—one a patient has always had—that undergoes a rapid change.

An accountant can save a client thousands of dollars by observing the details of a spreadsheet. A student can save hours of study time by observing that she gets twice as much done at a particular time of day.

Keen observers see facts and relationships. They know ways to focus their attention on the details, then tap their creative energy to discover patterns. To sharpen your classroom observation skills, experiment with the following techniques and continue to use those that you find most valuable.

Set the stage

Complete outside assignments. Nothing is more discouraging (or boring) than sitting through a lecture about the relationship of Le Chatelier's principle to the principle of kinetics if you've never heard of Henri Louis Le Chatelier or kinetics. Instructors usually assume that students complete assignments, and they construct their lectures accordingly. The more familiar you are with a subject, the more easily you can absorb important information during class lectures.

Bring the right materials. A good pen does not make you a good observer, but the lack of a pen or a notebook can be distracting enough to take the fine edge off your concentration. Make sure you have a pen, pencil, notebook, and any other materials you will need. Bring your textbook to class, especially if the lectures relate closely to the text.

If you are consistently unprepared for a class, that might be a message about your intentions concerning the course. Find out if it is. The next time you're in a frantic scramble to borrow pen and paper 37 seconds before the class begins, notice the cost. Use the borrowed pen and paper to write a Discovery Statement about your lack of preparation. Consider whether you intend to be successful in the course.

Sit front and center. Students who get as close as possible to the front and center of the classroom often do better on tests for several reasons. The closer you sit to the lecturer, the harder it is to fall asleep. The closer you sit to the front, the fewer interesting, or distracting, classmates are situated between you and the instructor. Material on the board is easier to read from up front. Also, the instructor can see you more easily when you have a question.

Instructors are usually not trained to perform. While some can project their energy to a large audience, some cannot. A professor who sounds boring from the back of the room might sound more interesting up close.

Sitting up front enables you to become a constructive force in the classroom. By returning the positive energy that an engaged teacher gives out, you can reinforce the teacher's enthusiasm and enhance your experience of the class.

In addition, sound waves from the human voice begin to degrade at a distance of eight to 12 feet. If you sit more than 15 feet from the speaker, your ability to hear and take effective notes might be compromised. Get close to the source of the sound. Get close to the energy.

Sitting close to the front is a way to commit yourself to getting what you want out of school. One reason students gravitate to the back of the classroom is that they think the instructor is less likely to call on them. Sitting in back can signal a lack of commitment. When you sit up front, you are declaring your willingness to take a risk and participate.

Conduct a short preclass review. Arrive early, then put your brain in gear by reviewing your notes from the previous class. Scan your reading assignment. Look at the sections you have underlined. Review assigned problems and exercises. Note questions you intend to ask.

Clarify your intentions. Take a 3 × 5 card to class with you. On that card, write a short Intention Statement about what you plan to get from the class. Describe your intended level of participation or the quality of attention you will bring to the subject. Be specific. If you found your previous class notes to be inadequate, write down what you intend to do to make your notes from this class session more useful.

"Be here now" in class

Accept your wandering mind. The techniques in the Power Process: "Be here now" can be especially useful when your head soars into the clouds. Don't fight daydreaming. When you notice your mind wandering during class, look at this as an opportunity to refocus your attention. If thermodynamics is losing out to beach parties, let go of the beach.

Notice your writing. When you discover yourself slipping into a fantasyland, feel the weight of your pen in your hand. Notice how your notes look. Paying attention to the act of writing can bring you back to the here and now.

You also can use writing in a more direct way to clear your mind of distracting thoughts. Pause for a few seconds and write those thoughts down. If you're distracted by thoughts of errands you need to run after class, list them on a 3x5 card and stick it in your pocket. Or simply put a symbol, such as an arrow or asterisk, in your notes to mark the places where your mind started to wander. Once your distractions are out of your mind and safely stored on paper, you can gently return your attention to taking notes.

Be with the instructor. In your mind, put yourself right up front with the instructor. Imagine that you and the instructor are the only ones in the room and that the lecture is a personal conversation between the two of you. Pay attention to the instructor's body language and facial expressions. Look the instructor in the eye.

Notice your environment. When you become aware of yourself daydreaming, bring yourself back to class by paying attention to the temperature in the room, the feel of your chair, or the quality of light coming through the window. Run your hand along the surface of your desk. Listen to the chalk on the blackboard or the sound of the teacher's voice. Be in that environment. Once your attention is back in the room, you can focus on what's happening in class.

Postpone debate. When you hear something you disagree with, note your disagreement and let it go. Don't allow your internal dialogue to drown out subsequent material. If your disagreement is persistent and strong, make note of this and then move on. Internal debate can prevent you from absorbing new information. It is OK to absorb information you don't agree with. Just absorb it with the mental tag "My instructor says . . ., and I don't agree with this."

Let go of judgments about lecture styles. Human beings are judgment machines. We evaluate everything, especially other people. If another person's eyebrows are too close together (or too far apart), if she walks a certain way or speaks with an unusual accent, we instantly make up a story about her. We do this so quickly that the process is usually not a conscious one.

Don't let your attitude about an instructor's lecture style, habits, or appearance get in the way of your education. You can decrease the power of your judgments if you pay attention to them and let them go.

You can even let go of judgments about rambling, unorganized lectures. Turn them to your advantage. Take the initiative and organize the material yourself. While taking notes, separate the key points from the examples and supporting evidence. Note the places where you got confused and make a list of questions to ask.

Participate in class activities. Ask questions. Volunteer for demonstrations. Join in class discussions. Be willing to take a risk or look foolish, if that's what it takes for you to learn. Chances are, the question you think is "dumb" is also on the minds of several of your classmates.

Relate the class to your goals. If you have trouble staying awake in a particular class, write at the top of your notes how that class relates to a specific goal. Identify the reward or payoff for reaching that goal.

Think critically about what you hear. This might seem contrary to the previously mentioned technique "Postpone debate." It's not. You might choose not to think critically about the instructor's ideas during the lecture. That's fine. Do it later, as you review and edit your notes. This is a time to list questions or write down your agreements and disagreements.

Watch for clues

Be alert to repetition. When an instructor repeats a phrase or an idea, make a note of it. Repetition is a signal that the instructor thinks the information is important.

Listen for introductory, concluding, and transition words and phrases. These include phrases such as "the following three factors," "in conclusion," "the most important consideration," "in addition to," and "on the other hand." These phrases and others signal relationships, definitions, new subjects, conclusions, cause and effect, and examples. They reveal the structure of the lecture. You can use these phrases to organize your notes.

Watch the board or overhead projector. If an instructor takes the time to write something down, consider the material to be important. Copy all diagrams and drawings, equations, names, places, dates, statistics, and definitions.

Watch the instructor's eyes. If an instructor glances at her notes and then makes a point, it is probably a signal that the information is especially important. Anything she reads from her notes is a potential test question.

Highlight the obvious clues. Instructors will often tell students point-blank that certain information is likely to appear on an exam. Make stars or other special marks in your notes next to this information. Instructors are not trying to hide what's important.

Notice the instructor's interest level. If the instructor is excited about a topic, it is more likely to appear on an exam. Pay attention when she seems more animated than usual.

journal entry 13

Discovery/Intention Statement

Think back on the last few lectures you have attended. How do you currently observe (listen to) lectures? What specific behaviors do you have as you sit and listen? Briefly describe your responses in the space below.

I discovered that I . . .
_____
_____
_____
_____

Now write an Intention Statement about any changes you want to make in the way you respond to lectures.

I intend to . .
_____
_____
_____
_____

What to do when you miss a class

For most courses, you'll benefit by attending every class session. If you miss a class, catch up as quickly as possible.

Clarify policies on missed classes. On the first day of classes, find out about your instructors' policies on absences. See if you can make up assignments, quizzes, and tests. Also inquire about doing extra-credit assignments.

Contact a classmate. Early in the semester, identify a student in each class who seems responsible and dependable. Exchange e-mail addresses and phone numbers. If you know you won't be in class, contact this student ahead of time. When you notice that your classmate is absent, pick up extra copies of handouts, make assignments lists, and offer copies of your notes.

Contact your instructor. If you miss a class, e-mail, phone, or fax your instructor, or put a note in her mailbox. Ask if she has another section of the same course that you can attend so you won't miss the lecture information. Also ask about getting handouts you might need before the next class meeting.

Consider technology. Free online services such as NoteMesh and stu.dicio.us allow students to share notes with each other. These services use wiki software, which allows you to create and edit Web pages using any browser. Before using such tools, however, check with instructors for their policies on note sharing.

The note-taking process flows

The format and structure of your notes are more important than how fast you write or how elegant your handwriting is. The following techniques can improve the effectiveness of your notes.

General techniques for note taking

Use key words. An easy way to sort the extraneous material from the important points is to take notes using key words. Key words or phrases contain the essence of communication. They include

- Concepts, technical terms, names, and numbers.
- Linking words, including words that describe action, relationship, and degree (*most, least, faster,* etc.).

Key words evoke images and associations with other words and ideas. They trigger your memory. That makes them powerful review tools. One key word can initiate the recall of a whole cluster of ideas. A few key words can form a chain from which you can reconstruct an entire lecture.

To see how key words work, take yourself to an imaginary classroom. You are now in the middle of an anatomy lecture. Picture what the room looks like, what it feels like, how it smells. You hear the instructor say:

OK, what happens when we look directly over our heads and see a piano falling out of the sky? How do we take that signal and translate it into the action of getting out of the way? The first thing that happens is that a stimulus is generated in the neurons—receptor neurons—of the eye. Light reflected from the piano reaches our eyes. In other words, we see the piano.

The receptor neurons in the eye transmit that sensory signal, the sight of the piano, to the body's nervous system. That's all they can do, pass on information. So we've got a sensory signal coming into the nervous system. But the neurons that initiate movement in our legs are effector neurons. The information from the sensory neurons must be transmitted to effector neurons or we will get squashed by the piano. There must be some kind of interconnection between receptor and effector neurons. What happens between the two? What is the connection?

Key words you might note in this example include *stimulus, generated, receptor neurons, transmit, sensory signals, nervous system, effector neurons,* and *connection.* You can reduce the instructor's 163 words to these 12 key words. With a few transitional words, your notes might look like this:

> Stimulus (piano) generated
> in receptor neurons (eye)
>
> Sensory signals transmitted
> by nervous system to
> effector neurons (legs)
>
> What connects receptor to
> effector?

Note the last key word of the lecture above *connection.* This word is part of the instructor's question and leads to the next point in the lecture. Be on the lookout for questions like this. They can help you organize your notes and are often clues for test questions.

Use pictures and diagrams. Make relationships visual. Copy all diagrams from the board and invent your own.

A drawing of a piano falling on someone who is looking up, for example, might be used to demonstrate the relationship of receptor neurons to effector neurons. Label the eyes "receptor" and the feet "effector." This picture implies that the sight of the piano must be translated into a motor response. By connecting the explanation of the process with the unusual picture of the piano falling, you can link the elements of the process together.

Write notes in paragraphs. When it is difficult to follow the organization of a lecture or to put information into outline form, create a series of informal paragraphs. These paragraphs will contain few complete sentences. Reserve complete sentences for precise definitions, direct quotations, and important points that the instructor emphasizes by repetition or other signals—such as the phrase "This is an important point."

Copy material from the board. Record all formulas, diagrams, and problems that the teacher writes down. Copy dates, numbers, names, places, and other facts. If it's on the board, put it in your notes. You can even use your own signal or code to flag that material.

Use a three-ring binder. Three-ring binders have several advantages over other kinds of notebooks. First, pages can be removed and spread out when you review. This way, you can get the whole picture of a lecture. Second, the three-ring-binder format allows you to insert handouts right into your notes. Third, you can insert your own out-of-class notes in the correct order.

Use only one side of a piece of paper. When you use one side of a page, you can review and organize all your notes by spreading them out side by side. Most students find the benefit well worth the cost of the paper. Perhaps you're concerned about the environmental impact of consuming more paper. If so, you can use the blank side of old notes and use recycled paper.

Use 3 × 5 cards. As an alternative to using notebook paper, use 3 × 5 cards to take lecture notes. Copy each new concept onto a separate 3 × 5 card.

Keep your own thoughts separate. For the most part, avoid making editorial comments in your lecture notes. The danger is that when you return to your notes, you might mistake your own idea for that of the instructor. If you want to make a comment, clearly label it as your own.

Use an "I'm lost" signal. No matter how attentive and alert you are, you might get lost and confused in a lecture. If it is inappropriate to ask a question, record in your notes that you were lost. Invent your own signal—for example, a circled question mark. When you write down your code for "I'm lost," leave space for the explanation or clarification that you will get later. The space will also be a signal that you missed something. Later, you can speak to your instructor or ask to see a fellow student's notes.

Label, number, and date all notes. Develop the habit of labeling and dating your notes at the beginning of each class. Number the page, too. Sometimes the sequence of material in a lecture is important. Write your name and phone number in each notebook in case you lose it.

Use standard abbreviations. Be consistent with your abbreviations. If you make up your own abbreviations or symbols, write a key explaining them in your notes. Avoid vague abbreviations. When you use an abbreviation such as *comm.* for *committee*, you run the risk of not being able to remember whether you meant *committee, commission, common,* or *commit.* One way to abbreviate is to leave out vowels. For example, *talk* becomes *tlk, said* becomes *sd, American* becomes *Amrcn.*

Leave blank space. Notes tightly crammed into every corner of the page are hard to read and difficult to use for review. Give your eyes a break by leaving plenty of space.

Later, when you review, you can use the blank spaces in your notes to clarify points, write questions, or add other material.

Take notes in different colors. You can use colors as highly visible organizers. For example, you can signal important points with red. Or use one color of ink for notes about the text and another color for lecture notes.

Use graphic signals. The following ideas can be used with any note-taking format:

- Use brackets, parentheses, circles, and squares to group information that belongs together.
- Use stars, arrows, and underlining to indicate important points. Flag the most important points with double stars, double arrows, or double underlines.
- Use arrows and connecting lines to link related groups.
- Use equal signs and greater-than and less-than signs to indicate compared quantities.

To avoid creating confusion with graphic symbols, use them carefully and consistently. Write a "dictionary" of your symbols in the front of your notebooks, such as the one shown here.

Use recorders effectively. There are persuasive arguments for not using a audio recorder or digital recorder. When you record a lecture, there is a strong temptation to daydream. After all, you can always listen to the lecture again later on. Unfortunately, if you let the recorder do all of the work, you are skipping a valuable part of the learning process.

I I, ( ), ○, □ = info that belongs together

*, ↘, = = important

**, ↘↘, ≡, !!! = extra important

\> = greater than < = less than
= = equal to

⟶ = leads to, becomes
Ex: school → job → money

? = huh?, lost

?? = big trouble, clear up immediately

There are more potential problems. Listening to recorded lectures can take a lot of time—more time than reviewing written notes. Recorders can't answer the questions you didn't ask in class. Also, recording devices malfunction. In fact, the unscientific Hypothesis of Recording Glitches states that the tendency of recorders to malfunction is directly proportional to the importance of the material. With those warnings in mind, some students use a recorder effectively. For example, you can use recordings as backups to written notes. (Check with your instructor first. Some prefer not to be recorded.) Turn the recorder on, then take notes as if it weren't there. Recordings can be especially useful if an instructor speaks fast.

The Cornell method

A note-taking system that has worked for students around the world is the *Cornell method*.[1] Originally developed by Walter Pauk at Cornell University during the 1950s, this approach continues to be taught across the United States and in other countries as well.

The cornerstone of this method is what Pauk calls the *cue column*—a wide margin on the left-hand side of the paper. The cue column is the key to the Cornell method's many benefits. Here's how to use it.

Format your paper. On each sheet of your note paper, draw a vertical line, top to bottom, about two inches from the left edge of the paper. This line creates the cue column—the space to the left of the line. You can also find Websites that allow you to print out pages in this format. Just do an Internet search using the keywords *cornell method pdf*.

Take notes, leaving the cue column blank. As you read an assignment or listen to a lecture, take notes on the right-hand side of the paper. Fill up this column with sentences, paragraphs, outlines, charts, or drawings. Do not write in the cue column. You'll use this space later, as you do the next steps.

Condense your notes in the cue column. Think of the notes you took on the right-hand side of the paper as a set of answers. In the cue column, list potential test questions that correspond to your notes. Write one question for each major term or point.

As an alternative to questions, you can list key words from your notes. Yet another option is to pretend that your notes are a series of articles on different topics. In the cue column, write a newspaper-style headline for each "article." In any case, be brief. If you cram the cue column full of words, you defeat its purpose—to reduce the number and length of your notes.

Write a summary. Pauk recommends that you reduce your notes even more by writing a brief summary at the bottom of each page. This step offers you another way to engage actively with the material.

Cue column	Notes
What are the 3 phases of Muscle Reading?	Phase 1: Before you read Phase 2: While you read Phase 3: After you read
What are the steps in phase 1?	1. Preview 2. Outline 3. Question
What are the steps in phase 2?	4. Read 5. Underline 6. Answer
What are the steps in phase 3?	7. Recite 8. Review 9. Review again
What is an acronym for Muscle Reading?	Pry = preview Out = outline Questions = question Root = read Up = underline Answers = answer Recite Review Review again
Summary	
Muscle Reading includes 3 phases: before, during, and after reading. Each phase includes 3 steps. Use the acronym to recall all the steps.	

Use the cue column to recite. Cover the right-hand side of your notes with a blank sheet of paper. Leave only the cue column showing. Then look at each item you wrote in the cue column and talk about it. If you wrote questions, answer each question. If you wrote key words, define each word and talk about why it's important. If you wrote headlines in the cue column, explain what each one means and offer supporting details. After reciting, uncover your notes and look for any important points you missed.

Mind mapping

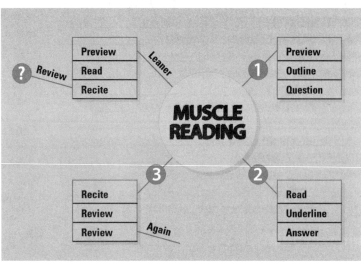

This system, developed by Tony Buzan,[2] can be used in conjunction with the Cornell format. In some circumstances, you might want to use mind maps exclusively.

To understand mind maps, first review the features of traditional note taking. Outlines (explained in the next section) divide major topics into minor topics, which, in turn, are subdivided further. They organize information in a sequential, linear way.

This kind of organization doesn't reflect certain aspects of brain function, a point that has been made in discussions about "left-brain" and "right-brain" activities. People often use the term *right brain* when referring to creative, pattern-making, visual, intuitive brain activity. They use the term *left brain* when talking about orderly, logical, step-by-step characteristics of thought. Writing teacher Gabrielle Rico uses another metaphor. She refers to the left-brain mode as our "sign mind" (concerned with words) and the right-brain mode as our "design mind" (concerned with visuals).[3] A mind map uses both kinds of brain functions. Mind maps can contain lists and sequences and show relationships. They can also provide a picture of a subject. They work on both verbal and nonverbal levels.

One benefit of mind maps is that they quickly, vividly, and accurately show the relationships between ideas. Also, mind mapping helps you think from general to specific. By choosing a main topic, you focus first on the big picture, then zero in on subordinate details. And by using only key words, you can condense a large subject into a small area on a mind map. You can review more quickly by looking at the key words on a mind map than by reading notes word for word.

Give yourself plenty of room. Use blank paper that measures at least 11 by 17 inches. If that's not available, turn regular notebook paper on its side so that you can take notes in a horizontal (instead of vertical) format. Another option is to find software that allows you to draw flow charts or diagrams.

Determine the main concept of the lecture. Write that concept in the center of the paper and circle it, underline it, or highlight it with color. You can also write the concept in large letters. Record concepts related to the main concept on lines that radiate outward from the center. An alternative is to circle these concepts.

Use key words only. Whenever possible, reduce each concept to a single word per line or circle in your mind map. Though this might seem awkward at first, it prompts you to summarize and to condense ideas to their essence. That means fewer words for you to write now and fewer to review when it's time to prepare for tests. (Using shorthand symbols and abbreviations can help.) Key words are usually nouns and verbs that communicate the bulk of the speaker's ideas. Choose words that are rich in associations and that can help you re-create the lecture.

Create links. One mind map doesn't have to include all of the ideas in a book or an article. Instead, you can link mind maps. For example, draw a mind map that sums up the five key points in a chapter, and then make a separate, more detailed mind map for each of those key points. Within each mind map, include references to the other mind maps. This helps explain and reinforce the relationships among many ideas. Some students pin several mind maps next to each other on a bulletin board or tape them to a wall. This allows for a dramatic—and effective—look at the big picture.

Outlining

An outline shows the relationship between major points and supporting ideas. One benefit of taking notes in the outline format is that doing so can totally occupy your attention. You are recording ideas and also organizing them. This can be an advantage if the material has been presented in a disorganized way. By playing with variations, you can discover the power of outlining to reveal relationships between ideas. Technically, each word, phrase, or sentence that appears in an outline is called a *heading*. These are arranged in different levels:

- In the first or "top" level of headings, note the major topics that are presented in a lecture or reading assignment.

- In the second level of headings, record the key points that relate to each topic in the first-level headings.

- In the third level of headings, record specific facts and details that support or explain each of your second-level headings. Each additional level of subordinate heading supports the ideas in the previous level of heading.

Roman numerals offer one way to illustrate the difference between levels of headings. See the following example.

You can also use other heading styles, as illustrated at right.

Distinguish levels with indentations only:

Muscle Reading includes 3 phases
   Phase 1: Before you read
      Preview

Distinguish levels with bullets and dashes:

MUSCLE READING INCLUDES 3 PHASES
   • Phase 1: Before you read
      – Preview

Distinguish headings by size:

MUSCLE READING INCLUDES 3 PHASES
Phase 1: Before you read
Preview

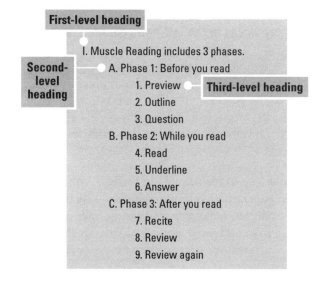

Combining formats

Feel free to use different note-taking systems for different subjects and to combine formats. Do what works for you.

For example, combine mind maps along with the Cornell format. You can modify the Cornell format by dividing your note paper in half, reserving one half for mind maps and the other for linear information, such as lists, graphs, and outlines, as well as equations, long explanations, and word-for-word definitions. You can incorporate a mind map into your paragraph-style notes whenever you feel one is appropriate. Minds maps are also useful for summarizing notes taken in the Cornell format.

John Sperry, a teacher at Utah Valley State College, developed a note-taking system that can include all of the formats discussed in this article:

- Fill up a three-ring binder with fresh paper. Open your notebook so that you see two blank pages—one on the left and one on the right. Plan to take notes across this entire two-page spread.

- During class or while reading, write your notes only on the left-hand page. Place a large dash next to each main topic or point. If your instructor skips a step or switches topics unexpectedly, just keep writing.

- Later, use the right-hand page to review and elaborate on the notes that you took earlier. This page is for anything you want. For example, add visuals such as mind maps. Write review questions, headlines, possible test questions, summaries, outlines, mnemonics, or analogies that link new concepts to your current knowledge.

- To keep ideas in sequence, place appropriate numbers on top of the dashes in your notes on the left-hand page. Even if concepts are presented out of order during class, they'll still be numbered correctly in your notes.

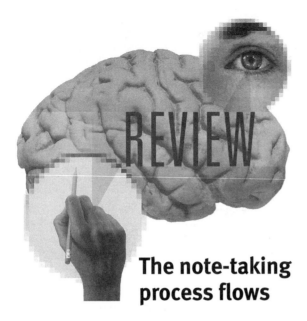

The note-taking process flows

Think of reviewing as an integral part of note taking rather than as an added task. To make new information useful, encode it in a way that connects to your long-term memory. The key is reviewing.

Review within 24 hours. In the last chapter, when you read the suggestion to review what you've read within 24 hours, you were asked to sound the trumpet. Well, if you have one, get it out and sound it again. This might be the most powerful note-taking technique you can use. It might save you hours of review time later in the term.

Many students are surprised that they can remember the content of a lecture in the minutes and hours after class. They are even more surprised by how well they can read the sloppiest of notes. Unfortunately, short-term memory deteriorates quickly. The good news is that if you review your notes soon enough, you can move that information from short-term to long-term memory. And you can do it in just a few minutes—often 10 minutes or less.

The sooner you review your notes, the better, especially if the class was difficult. In fact, you can start reviewing during class. When your instructor pauses to set up the overhead projector or erase the board, scan your notes. Dot the i's, cross the t's, and write out unclear abbreviations. Another way to use this technique is to get to your next class as quickly as you can. Then use the four or five minutes before the lecture begins to review the notes you just took in the previous class. If you do not get to your notes immediately after class, you can still benefit by reviewing later in the day. A review right before you go to sleep can also be valuable.

Think of the day's unreviewed notes as leaky faucets, constantly dripping, losing precious information until you shut them off with a quick review. Remember, it's possible to forget most of the material within 24 hours—unless you review.

Edit notes. During your first review, fix words that are illegible. Write out abbreviated words that might be unclear to you later. Make sure you can read everything. If you can't read something or don't understand something you *can* read, mark it, and make a note to ask your instructor or another student. Check to see that your notes are labeled with the date and class and that the pages are numbered.

Fill in key words in the left-hand column. This task is important if you are to get the full benefit of using the Cornell method. Using the key word principles described earlier in this chapter, go through your notes and write key words or phrases in the left-hand column.

These key words will speed up the review process later. As you read your notes, focus on extracting important concepts.

Use your key words as cues to recite. With a blank sheet of paper, cover your notes, leaving only the key words in the left-hand margin showing. Take each key word in order and recite as much as you can about the point. Then uncover your notes and look for any important points you missed.

Conduct short weekly review periods. Once a week, review all of your notes again. The review sessions don't need to take a lot of time. Even a 20-minute weekly review period is valuable. Some students find that a weekend review, say, on Sunday afternoon, helps them stay in continuous touch with the material. Scheduling regular

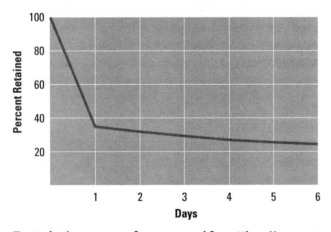

To study the process of memory and forgetting, Hermann Ebbinghaus devised a method for testing memory. The results, shown here in what has come to be known as the Ebbinghaus forgetting curve, demonstrate that forgetting occurs most rapidly shortly after learning and then gradually declines over time.

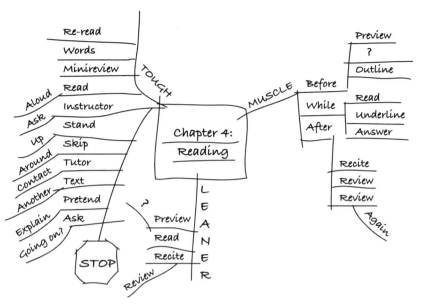

review sessions on your calendar helps develop the habit.

As you review, step back to see the larger picture. In addition to reciting or repeating the material to yourself, ask questions about it: "Does this relate to my goals? How does this compare to information I already know, in this field or another? Will I be tested on this material? What will I do with this material? How can I associate it with something that deeply interests me?"

Consider typing your notes. Some students type their handwritten notes using a computer. The argument for doing so is threefold. First, typed notes are easier to read. Second, they take up less space. Third, the process of typing them forces you to review the material.

Another alternative is to bypass handwriting altogether and take notes in class on a laptop computer. This solution has drawbacks: laptops are more expensive than PCs, and computer errors can wipe out your notes, leaving you with no backup.

Create summaries. Mind mapping is an excellent way to summarize large sections of your course notes or reading assignments. Create one map that shows all the main topics you want to remember. Then create another map about each main topic. After drawing your maps, look at your original notes and fill in anything you missed. This system is fun and quick.

Another option is to create a "cheat sheet." There's only one guideline: fit all your review notes on a single sheet of paper. Use any note-taking format that you want—mind map, outline, Cornell, or a combination of all of them. The beauty of this technique is that it forces you to pick out main ideas and key details. There's not enough room for anything else!

If you're feeling adventurous, create your cheat sheet on a single index card. Start with the larger sizes (5 × 7 or 4 × 6) and then work down to a 3 × 5 card.

Some instructors might let you use a summary sheet during an exam. But even if you can't, you'll benefit from creating one while you study for the test. Summarizing is a powerful way to review.

journal entry 14

Discovery Statement

Think about the way you have conducted reviews of your notes in the past. Respond to the following statements by checking "Always," "Often," "Sometimes," "Seldom," or "Never" after each.

I review my notes immediately after class.

_____ Always _____ Often _____ Sometimes

_____ Seldom _____ Never

I conduct weekly reviews of my notes.

_____ Always _____ Often _____ Sometimes

_____ Seldom _____ Never

I make summary sheets of my notes.

_____ Always _____ Often _____ Sometimes

_____ Seldom _____ Never

I edit my notes within 24 hours.

_____ Always _____ Often _____ Sometimes

_____ Seldom _____ Never

Before class, I conduct a brief review of the notes I took in the previous class.

_____ Always _____ Often _____ Sometimes

_____ Seldom _____ Never

Name _____ Date ____/____/____

1. What are the three major steps of effective note taking as explained in this chapter? Summarize each step in one sentence.

2. According to the text, neat handwriting and a knowledge of outlining are requirements for effective notes. True or False? Explain your answer.

3. What are some advantages of sitting in the front and center of the classroom?

4. Instructors sometimes give clues that the material they are presenting is important. List at least three of these clues.

5. Postponing judgment while taking notes means that you have to agree with everything that the instructor says. True or False? Explain your answer.

6. Graphic signals include:
   (a) Brackets and parentheses.
   (b) Stars and arrows.
   (c) Underlining and connecting lines.
   (d) Equal signs and greater- and less-than signs.
   (e) All of the above.

7. Describe the two types of key words. Then write down at least five key words from this chapter.

8. Describe at least three ways to apply the Power Process: "Be here now" to the job of taking notes in class.

9. Describe at least three strategies for reviewing notes.

10. According to the text, the Power Process: "I create it all" means that:
    (a) We control everything that happens to us.
    (b) We can choose our thoughts about what happens to us.
    (c) We can choose our behaviors as we respond to what happens to us.
    (d) Both b and c.
    (e) None of the above.

Chapter 7

Listening and Memory

CONVERSATIONS

i have just
wandered back
into our conversation
and find
that you
are still
rattling on
about something
or other
i think i must
have been gone
at least
twenty minutes
and you
never missed me
now this might say
something
about my acting ability
or it might say
something about
your sensitivity
one thing
troubles me tho
when it
is my turn
to rattle on
for twenty minutes
which i
have been known to do
have you
been missing too

Ric Masten

Do not speak, my son, unless you can improve on silence.

Irving Layton,
"Advice for David"

As Ric Masten's poem on the opposite page shows, there's more to listening than gazing politely at a speaker and nodding your head every so often. As you will soon learn, listening is a demanding and complex activity–and just as important as speaking in the communication process.

If frequency is a measure of importance, then listening easily qualifies as the most prominent kind of communication. We spend more time listening to others than in any other type of communication. One study (summarized in Figure 7.1) revealed that post-secondary students spent an average of 14 percent of their communicating time writing, 16 percent speaking, 17 percent reading, and a whopping 53 percent listening. Listening was broken down further into listening to mass communication media, such as radio and television, and listening to face-to-face messages. The former category accounted for 21 percent of the students' communication time, and the latter accounted for 32 percent–more than any other type of communication.[1] Canadians spend about 12.7 hours a week (up by 46% since 2002) on the Internet, and younger people spend more time surfing, scanning materials, and chatting with friends on line than they do watching television. If this activity is considered a form of writing, then increased use of the Internet will likely be reflected in future studies on the percentages of time we engage in each activity.[2]

Listening is still the most frequent form of communication, however, and is arguably just as important as speaking in making relationships work. In committed relationships, listening to personal information in everyday conversations is considered an important ingredient of satisfaction.[3] In one survey, marital counsellors identified "failing to take the other's perspective when listening" as one of the most frequent communication problems in the couples with whom they work.[4] When a group of adults was asked what communication skills were most important in family and social settings, listening was ranked first.[5] And listening well is just as important in the job as in personal relationships. A study examining the link between listening and career success revealed that better listeners rose to higher levels in their organizations.[6] When 1000 human resource executives were asked to identify skills of the ideal manager, the ability to listen effectively ranked at the top of the list.[7] In problem-solving groups, effective listeners are judged as having the most leadership skills.[8] When a diverse group of senior executives was asked what skills were most important on the job, listening was identified more often than any other skill, including technical competence, computer knowledge, creativity, and administrative talent.[9]

This chapter will explore the nature of listening. After looking at all the elements that make up the process of listening, we will take a look at a variety of poor listening habits and their causes. After reviewing this gloomy picture, you will learn some ways to improve your listening skills so that your chances of understanding others are better. Finally, we'll explore listening and responding skills that can help others solve their problems.

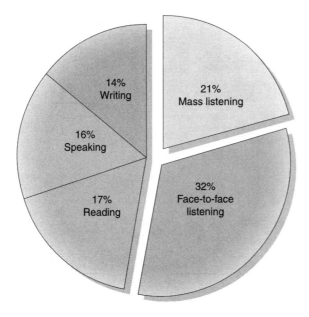

FIGURE 7.1
Types of Listening Activities

ELEMENTS IN THE LISTENING PROCESS

Before we go any further, it's important to offer a clear definition of listening. There's more to this activity than passively absorbing a speaker's words. See, for instance, Figure 7.2, the Chinese characters that are used to make up the verb *to listen*. In truth, **listening** is a process that consists of five elements: hearing, attending, understanding, responding, and remembering.

Hearing

Hearing is the physiological dimension of listening. It occurs when sound waves strike the ear at a certain frequency and loudness. Hearing is also influenced by background noise. If there are other loud noises, especially at the same frequency as the message we are trying to hear, it becomes difficult to sort out the important signals from the background. Hearing is also influenced by continuous exposure to the same tone or loudness. Marshall Chasin, an audiologist at the University of Toronto who also runs the Musicians' Clinics of Canada in Toronto, notes that prolonged exposure to sounds above 85 decibels (dB) can cause permanent hearing loss. Eighty-five dB would be the equivalent of the sound of a dial tone. Rock concerts register about 110 dB, and many of us have experienced hearing loss after attending one. Such losses are referred to as temporary threshold shifts (TTS), and, generally, hearing returns to normal within 16 to

Listening
A process that consists of hearing, attending to, understanding, responding to, and remembering an aural message.

Hearing
The physiological dimension of listening.

All speech . . . is a dead language until it finds a willing and prepared hearer.

Robert Louis Stevenson

FIGURE 7.2
The Chinese Characters in the Verb *to Listen*

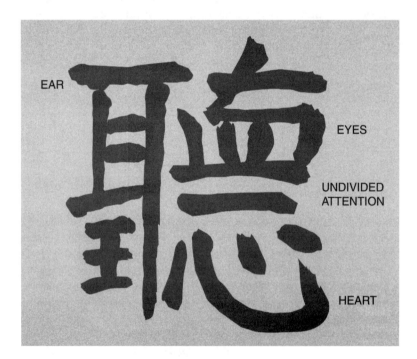

18 hours. Chasin recommends that rock groups take precautions like wearing custom earplugs, positioning speakers so as to minimize hearing loss, and spending time in quiet environments.[10] To preserve our hearing, we listeners should consider taking similar precautions and even reduce the volume of our CD and MP3 players.

As competent communicators, you need to recognize the likelihood that you may be speaking to someone with a hearing loss and adjust your approach accordingly. Speaking slowly, loudly, and clearly can be helpful. Making sure that the other person can see your face is also important. And if you don't understand what people with a hearing loss are saying to you, don't be embarrassed about asking them to repeat the statement.

Attending

Whereas hearing is a physiological process, **attending** is a psychological one and is part of the process of selection that we described in Chapter 4. We would go crazy if we attended to every sound we hear, so we filter out some messages and focus on others. Needs, wants, desires, and interests determine what is attended to. Not surprisingly, research shows that we attend most carefully to messages when there's a payoff for doing so.[11] If you're planning to see a movie, you'll listen to a friend's description more carefully than you otherwise would have. And when you want to get better acquainted with others, you'll pay careful attention to almost anything they say, in hopes of improving the relationship.

Surprisingly, attending doesn't help just the listener; it also helps the message sender. Participants in one study viewed brief movie segments and then described them to listeners who varied in their degree of attentiveness to the speakers. Later on, the researchers tested the speakers' long-term recall of details from the movie segments. Those who had recounted the movie to attentive listeners remembered more details of the film.[12]

Attending
The process of filtering out some messages and focusing on others.

Not comprehending, they hear like the deaf.

Heraclitus

Understanding

Understanding occurs when we make sense of a message. It is possible to hear and attend to a message without understanding it at all. And, of course, it's possible to *misunderstand* a message. This chapter describes the many reasons why we misunderstand others–and why they misunderstand us. It also outlines skills that will help you improve your own understanding of others.

Understanding
Occurs when sense is made of a message.

Responding

Responding to a message consists of giving observable feedback to the speaker. Listeners don't always respond visibly to a speaker–but research suggests that they should do so more often. One study of

Responding
Giving observable feedback to a speaker.

"I'm sorry, dear. I wasn't listening. Could you repeat what you've said since we've been married?"

© *The New Yorker* Collection, 2000 Robert Mankoff from cartoonbank.com. All rights reserved.

195 critical incidents in banking and medical settings showed that a major difference between effective and ineffective listening was the kind of feedback offered.[13] Good listeners showed that they were attentive by such nonverbal behaviours as keeping eye contact and reacting with appropriate facial expressions. Their verbal behaviour–answering questions and exchanging ideas, for example–also demonstrated their attention. It's easy to imagine how other responses would signal less effective listening. A slumped posture, bored expression, and yawning send a clear message that you are not tuned in to the speaker.

Adding responsiveness to our listening model demonstrates the fact we discussed in Chapter 1, that communication is *transactional* in nature. Listening isn't just a passive activity. As listeners, we are active participants in a communication transaction. At the same time that we receive messages, we also send them.

Remembering
The ability to recall information.

Remembering

Remembering is the ability to recall information. Research suggests that people remember only about 50 percent of what they hear *immediately* after hearing it. They forget half even if they work hard at listening. Within eight hours, the 50 percent remembered drops to 35 percent. After two months, the average recall is only about 25 percent of the original message. Given the amount of information we

Elements in the Listening Process

One of the most striking things about the human species is the fluidity of our memory and our capacity to forget.

Wade David, anthropologist, quoted in *Saturday Night*

process every day—from teachers, friends, the radio, the Internet, TV, and other sources—the *residual message* (what we remember) is a small fraction of what we hear. Although the tendency to forget information is common, there are ways to improve your attention and recall. You can begin to get a sense of how tough it is to listen effectively by trying the exercise below.

INVITATION TO INSIGHT

LISTENING BREAKDOWNS

You can overcome believing in some common myths about listening by recalling specific instances when
   a. you heard another person's message but did not attend to it.
   b. you attended to a message but forgot it almost immediately.
   c. you attended to and remembered a message but did not understand it accurately.
   d. you understood a message but did not respond sufficiently to convey your understanding to the sender.
   e. you failed to remember some or all of an important message.

SKILL BUILDER

HOW GOOD ARE YOUR LISTENING SKILLS?

Assess your listening skills by taking the listening test below.

Instructions
The following statements reflect various habits we use when listening to others. For each statement, indicate the extent to which you agree or disagree by selecting one number from the scale provided. Circle your response for each statement. Remember, there are no right or wrong answers.

Listening Skills Survey
- 1 = Strongly disagree
- 2 = Disagree
- 3 = Neither agree or disagree
- 4 = Agree
- 5 = Strongly Agree

1. I daydream or think about other things when listening to others.
   1   2   3   4   5
2. I do not summarize the ideas being communicated by a speaker.
   1   2   3   4   5
3. I do not use a speaker's tone of voice or body language to help interpret what he or she is saying.
   1   2   3   4   5
4. I listen more for facts than overall ideas during classroom lectures.
   1   2   3   4   5
5. I tune out dry speakers.
   1   2   3   4   5
6. I have a hard time paying attention to boring people.
   1   2   3   4   5
7. I can tell whether someone has anything useful to say before he or she finishes communicating a message.
   1   2   3   4   5
8. I quit listening to a speaker when I think he or she has nothing interesting to say.
   1   2   3   4   5
9. I get emotional or upset when speakers make jokes about issues or things that are important to me.
   1   2   3   4   5
10. I get angry or offensive when speakers use offensive words.
    1   2   3   4   5
11. I do not expend a lot of energy when listening to others.
    1   2   3   4   5
12. I pretend to listen to others even when I'm not really listening.
    1   2   3   4   5
13. I get distracted when listening to others.
    1   2   3   4   5
14. I deny or ignore information and comments that go against my thoughts and feelings.
    1   2   3   4   5

15. I do not seek opportunities to challenge my listening skills.
    1   2   3   4   5
16. I do not pay attention to the visual aids used during lectures.
    1   2   3   4   5
17. I do not take notes on handouts when they are provided.
    1   2   3   4   5

Now add up your total score for the 17 items and record it in the space provided. Refer to the norms below to evaluate your listening skills.

Total Score = _____

Norms

Use the following norms to evaluate your listening skills:

   17–34 = Good listening skills
   35–53 = Moderately good listening skills
   54–85 = Poor listening skills

How would you evaluate your listening skills?

Adapted from R. Kreitner, A. Kinicki, and N. Cole, *Fundamentals of Organizational Behaviour* (Toronto: McGraw-Hill Ryerson, 2003), p. 219.

THE CHALLENGE OF LISTENING

While listening may not always be easy, one way to become a better listener is to recognize areas that need improvement.

Types of Ineffective Listening

The preceding exercise demonstrated some of the most common types of poor listening. As you read on, you'll begin to recognize them as behaviours that you and those around you probably use quite often. Although you'll soon learn that a certain amount of ineffective listening is inevitable, and sometimes even understandable, it's important to be aware of these types so that you can avoid them when understanding others is important to you. Table 7.1 shows some of the types.

TABLE 7.1 Types of Ineffective Listening	
Pseudolistening	Defensive listening
Stage-hogging	Ambushing
Selective listening	Insensitive listening
Insulated listening	

310 Chapter 7 Listening: More Than Meets the Ear

Pseudolistening
An imitation of true listening in which the receiver's mind is elsewhere.

You may as well tell people the truth because they don't listen anyway.

Earl Work, sales motivator, quoting "a friend from Prince Albert"

Stage-hogging
A listening style in which the receiver is more concerned with making a point than with understanding the speaker.

Selective listening
A listening style in which receivers respond only to the messages that interest them.

Insulated listening
A style in which the receiver ignores undesirable information.

Defensive listening
A response style in which the receiver perceives a speaker's comments as an attack.

Pseudolistening Pseudolistening is an imitation of the real thing. Pseudolisteners give the appearance of being attentive: They look you in the eye, nod and smile at the right times, and may even answer you occasionally. Behind that appearance of interest, however, something entirely different is going on, for pseudolisteners use a polite façade to mask thoughts that have nothing to do with what the speaker is saying. Often pseudolisteners ignore you because of something on their minds that's more important to them than your remarks. Other times they may simply be bored or think that they've heard what you have to say before and so tune out your remarks. Whatever the reasons, the significant fact is that pseudolistening is really counterfeit communication.

Stage-Hogging Stage-hogs (sometimes called "conversational narcissists") try to turn the topic of conversations to themselves instead of showing interest in the speaker.[14] One **stage-hogging** strategy is a "shift-response"–changing the focus of the conversation from the speaker to the narcissist:

A: "I had a great time mountain-biking last weekend!"

B: "Mountain-biking's OK, but I'd rather go running."

A: "My math class is really tough."

B: "You think math is tough? You ought to try my physics class!"

Interruptions are another hallmark of stage-hogging. Besides preventing the listener from learning potentially valuable information, they can damage the relationship between the interrupter and the speaker. For example, applicants who interrupt the questions in an employment interview are likely to be rated less favourably than job seekers who wait until the interviewer has finished speaking before they respond.[15]

Selective Listening Selective listeners respond only to the parts of your remarks that interest them, rejecting everything else. Sometimes **selective listening** is legitimate, as when we screen out radio commercials and keep an ear cocked for our favourite song. Selective listening is less appropriate in personal settings, when your obvious inattention can insult or hurt the other person.

Insulated Listening Insulated listeners are almost the opposite of their selective cousins just mentioned. Instead of looking for something, such individuals avoid it. Whenever a topic arises that they'd rather not deal with, **insulated listening** means they can simply fail to hear or acknowledge it. You remind them about a problem, perhaps an unfinished job, poor grades, or the like, and they'll nod or answer you, and then promptly forget what you've just said.

Defensive Listening Defensive listening means taking others' remarks as personal attacks. The teenager who perceives her parents' questions about her friends and activities as distrustful snooping is a

Looking at Diversity

The Challenges of Hearing Disabilities

Bruce C. Anderson is studying to become a teacher of students who are deaf and hard of hearing. He is committed to making sure that nobody is deprived of an education or successful career because of her or his physical condition.

I grew up with a mild hearing disability. The word "mild" doesn't begin to describe how this affected my life. I couldn't hear many of the sounds or tones that are part of most peoples' voices. You can get an idea what this is like by imagining how hard it would be to listen to a muffled, quiet voice that is being drowned out by loud TV and radio playing at the same time, or trying to understand somebody whispering words while your ears are covered and your head is turned away.

When I flunked the school hearing tests in elementary school, I was put in a "special education" program. The other kids saw us as being different, and we were called the very worst names. I'm not perfect, so I fought back when I was picked on. I knew that I needed to escape this situation, so I devised a plan. In the next hearing test, I just followed the other students. When they heard a tone and raised their hands, I raised mine too. Believe it or not, this satisfied whoever was in charge and I got back into the regular classes. This didn't change the trouble I had hearing and understanding speech.

Back in the regular classes I would sit next to people who I knew, and they would let me copy their work. I changed it just enough so it wouldn't look identical. I watched how to do the assignments and either handed them in late or not at all. I also taught myself to read lips. I took all of the shop classes that I could, and I watched the demonstrations carefully so I could follow along. Many of my teachers let me slide by so I could either continue to play on the school athletic teams, or just to move me out of their classroom. The service sector of society needed workers and I (and people like me) would be filling those jobs.

I was very lucky in some ways: I'm mechanically inclined, and I have been working since I was 14 years old in the maintenance field. Since high school I have been a maintenance engineer, a welder on the railroad, and a service engineer for a commercial laundry equipment company. I have always had to learn things through a hands-on approach because I have never been able to understand completely what a person says to me unless it is in an environment that is quiet.

I chose to become a teacher because I don't want anybody to go through what I did in school. I want to expose hard of hearing and deaf students to options that they may never have considered because of their disabilities. I also want to educate hearing people that the hard of hearing and deaf are able to communicate, but as in all communication it must be a two-way process to be successful.

If you're communicating with someone who has a hearing disability, here are a few tips. Have patience when asked to repeat something over once, twice or even three times. Remember: the deaf and hard of hearing are doing the best they can. Help is very hard to ask for and it is very difficult to draw attention to yourself by asking others what was said. If this still has not solved the problem try another avenue such as using different words or moving to a more quiet location to talk. Even writing something down may be necessary. Hard of hearing and deaf people listen with our eyes, so make sure you're standing or sitting so that the other person can see your face and your gestures.

If you make efforts like these, you will help people with hearing disabilities. And you might also get a new appreciation and respect for their world.

---

defensive listener, as is the insecure breadwinner who explodes any time his mate mentions money, or the touchy parent who views any questioning by her children as a threat to her authority and parental wisdom. As your reading in Chapter 9 will suggest, it's fair to assume that many defensive listeners are suffering from shaky presenting images and avoid admitting it by projecting their own insecurities onto others.

International Listening Association

http://www.listen.org

Fellows who have no tongues are often all eyes and ears.

Thomas C. Haliburton, *Sam Slick's Wise Saws*

"Ear, Nose and Throat."

HERMAN: © Jim Unger/Dist. by Newspaper Enterprise Association, Inc.

Ambushing
A style in which the receiver listens carefully in order to gather information to use in an attack on the speaker.

Insensitive listening
Failure to recognize the thoughts or feelings that are not directly expressed by a speaker; instead, accepting the speaker's words at face value.

Ambushing Ambushers listen carefully to you, but only because they're collecting information they'll use to attack what you say. The cross-examining prosecution lawyer is a good example of **ambushing**. Needless to say, using this kind of strategy will justifiably initiate defensiveness in the other person.

Insensitive Listening Insensitive listening offers the final example of people who don't receive another person's messages clearly. As we've said before, people often don't express their thoughts or feelings openly but instead communicate them through a subtle and unconscious choice of words or nonverbal clues, or both. Insensitive listeners aren't able to look beyond the words and behaviour to understand their hidden meanings. Instead, they take a speaker's remarks at face value.

WHY WE DON'T LISTEN BETTER

After thinking about the styles of ineffective listening described in the previous pages, most people begin to see that they listen carefully only a small percentage of the time. Sad as it may be, it's impossible to listen *all* the time, for several reasons. Table 7.2 lays out some of those reasons.

Most conversations are simply monologues delivered in the presence of a witness.

Margaret Millar, *The Weak-Eyed Bat*

Message Overload The amount of speech most of us encounter every day makes careful listening to everything we hear impossible. As you have already read, many of us spend almost half the time we're

20 memory techniques

Experiment with these techniques to develop a flexible, custom-made memory system that fits your style of learning.

The 20 techniques are divided into four categories, each of which represents a general principle for improving memory:

Organize it. Organized information is easier to find.

Use your body. Learning is an active process; get all of your senses involved.

Use your brain. Work *with* your memory, not *against* it.

Recall it. Regularly retrieve and apply key information.

Read this article with application in mind. Mark the techniques you like best and use them. Also look for ways to combine techniques.

Organize it

1 Be selective. There's a difference between gaining understanding and drowning in information. During your stay in higher education, you will be exposed to thousands of facts and ideas. No one expects you to memorize all of them. To a large degree, the art of memory is the art of selecting what to remember in the first place.

As you dig into your textbooks and notes, make choices about what is most important to learn. Imagine that you are going to create a test on the material and consider the questions you would ask.

When reading, look for chapter previews, summaries, and review questions. Pay attention to anything printed in bold type. Also notice visual elements—tables, charts, graphs, and illustrations. All of these are clues pointing to what's important. During lectures, notice what the instructor emphasizes. Anything that's presented visually—on the board, on overheads, or with slides—is probably key.

2 Make it meaningful. One way to create meaning is to learn from the general to the specific. Before you begin your next reading assignment, skim it to locate the main idea. You can use the same techniques you learned in Exercise #1: "Textbook reconnaissance" on page 2. If you're ever lost, step back and look at the big picture. The details might make more sense.

You can organize any list of items—even random ones—in a meaningful way to make them easier to remember. In his book *Information Anxiety*, Richard Saul Wurman proposes five principles for organizing any body of ideas, facts, or objects:[4]

Principle	Example
Organize by **time**	Events in history or in a novel flow in chronological order.
Organize by **location**	Addresses for a large company's regional offices are grouped by state and city.
Organize by **category**	Nonfiction library materials are organized by subject categories.
Organize by **continuum**	Products rated in *Consumers Guide* are grouped from highest in price to lowest in price, or highest in quality to lowest in quality.
Organize by **alphabet**	Entries in a book index are listed in ABC order.

3 Create associations. The data already encoded in your neural networks is arranged according to a scheme that makes sense to you. When you introduce new data, you can remember it more effectively if you associate it with similar or related data.

Think about your favorite courses. They probably relate to subjects that you already know something about. If you know a lot about the history of twentieth-century music, for example, then you'll find it easier to remember facts about twenty-first century music.

Even when you're tackling a new subject, you can build a mental store of basic background information—the raw material for creating associations. Preview reading assignments, and complete those readings before you attend lectures. Before taking upper-level courses, master the prerequisites.

Use your body

4 Learn actively. Action is a great memory enhancer. Test this theory by studying your assignments with the same energy that you bring to the dance floor or the basketball court.

You can use simple, direct methods to infuse your learning with action. When you sit at your desk, sit up straight. Sit on the edge of your chair, as if you were about to spring out of it and sprint across the room.

Also experiment with standing up when you study. It's harder to fall asleep in this position. Some people insist that their brains work better when they stand. Pace back and forth and gesture as you recite material out loud. Use your hands. Get your body moving.

This includes your mouth. During a lecture, ask questions. With your textbooks, read key passages out loud. Use a louder voice for the main points.

Active learning also involves a variety of learning styles. In Chapter One, the article "Learning styles: Discovering how you learn" explains four aspects of learning: concrete experience, abstract conceptualization, active experimentation, and reflective observation. Many courses in higher education lean heavily toward abstract conceptualization—lectures, papers, and reading. These courses might not offer chances to actively experiment with ideas or test them in concrete experience.

Create those opportunities yourself. For example, your introductory psychology book probably offers some theories about how people remember information. Choose one of those theories and test it on yourself. See if you can discover a new memory technique.

Your sociology class might include a discussion about how groups of people resolve conflict. See if you can apply any of these ideas to resolving conflict in your own family.

The point behind each of these examples is the same: To remember an idea, go beyond thinking about it. *Do* something with it.

5 Relax. When you're relaxed, you absorb new information quickly and recall it with greater ease and accuracy. Students who can't recall information under the stress of a final exam can often recite the same facts later when they are relaxed.

Relaxing might seem to contradict the idea of active learning as explained in technique #4, but it doesn't. Being relaxed is not the same as being drowsy, zoned out, or asleep. Relaxation is a state of alertness, free of tension, during which your mind can play with new information, roll it around, create associations with it, and apply many of the other memory techniques. You can be active *and* relaxed. See Exercise #14: "Relax" for some tips on how to relax.

6 Create pictures. Draw diagrams. Make cartoons. Use these images to connect facts and illustrate relationships. Associations within and among abstract concepts can be "seen" and recalled more easily when they are visualized. The key is to use your imagination.

For example, Boyle's law states that at a constant temperature, the volume of a confined ideal gas varies inversely with its pressure. Simply put, cutting the volume in half doubles the pressure. To remember this concept, you might picture someone "doubled over" using a bicycle pump. As she increases the pressure in the pump by decreasing the volume in the pump cylinder, she seems to be getting angrier. By the time she has doubled the pressure (and halved the volume), she is boiling ("Boyle-ing") mad.

Another reason to create pictures is that visual information is associated with a part of the brain that is different from the part that processes verbal information. When you create a picture of a concept, you are anchoring the information in a second part of your brain. This increases your chances of recalling that information.

To visualize abstract relationships effectively, create an action-oriented image, such as the person using the pump. Make the picture vivid, too. The person's face could be bright red. And involve all of your senses.

Imagine how the cold metal of the pump would feel and how the person would grunt as she struggled with it. (Most of us would have to struggle. It would take incredible strength to double the pressure in a bicycle pump, not to mention a darn sturdy pump.)

7 Recite and repeat. When you repeat something out loud, you anchor the concept in two different senses. First, you get the physical sensation in your throat, tongue, and lips when voicing the concept. Second, you hear it. The combined result is synergistic, just as it is when you create pictures. That is, the effect of using two different senses is greater than the sum of their individual effects.

The "out loud" part is important. Reciting silently in your head can be useful—in the library, for example—but it is not as effective as making noise. Your mind can trick itself into thinking it knows something when it doesn't. Your ears are harder to fool.

The repetition part is important, too. Repetition is a common memory device because it works. Repetition blazes a trail through the pathways of your brain, making the information easier to find. Repeat a concept out loud until you know it, then say it five more times.

Recitation works best when you recite concepts in your own words. For example, if you want to remember that the acceleration of a falling body due to gravity at sea level equals 32 feet per second per second, you might say, "Gravity makes an object accelerate 32 feet per second faster for each second that it's in the air at sea level." Putting it in your own words forces you to think about it.

Have some fun with this technique. Recite by writing a song about what you're learning. Sing it in the shower. Use any style you want ("Country, jazz, rock, or rap—when you sing out loud, learning's a snap!").

Or imitate someone. Imagine your textbook being read by Will Ferrell, Madonna, or Clint Eastwood ("Go ahead, punk. Make my density equal mass over volume").

8 Write it down. This technique is obvious, yet easy to forget. Writing a note to yourself helps you remember an idea, even if you never look at the note again.

You can extend this technique by writing down an idea not just once, but many times. Let go of the old image of being forced to write "I will not throw paper wads" 100 times on the chalkboard after school. When you choose to remember something, repetitive writing is a powerful tool.

Writing engages a different kind of memory than speaking. Writing prompts us to be more logical, coherent, and complete. Written reviews reveal gaps in knowledge that oral reviews miss, just as oral reviews reveal gaps that written reviews miss.

Another advantage of written reviews is that they more closely match the way you're asked to remember materials in school. During your academic career, you'll probably take far more written exams than oral exams. Writing can be an effective way to prepare for such tests.

Finally, writing is physical. Your arm, your hand, and your fingers join in. Remember, learning is an active process—you remember what you *do*.

Use your brain

9 Engage your emotions. One powerful way to enhance your memory is to make friends with your amygdala. This is an area of your brain that lights up with extra neural activity each time you feel a strong emotion. When a topic excites love, laughter, or fear, the amygdala sends a flurry of chemical messages that say, in effect: *This information is important and useful. Don't forget it.*

You're more likely to remember course material when you relate it to a goal—whether academic, personal, or career—that you feel strongly about. This is one reason why it pays to be specific about what you want. The more goals you have and the more clearly they are defined, the more channels you create for incoming information.

You can use this strategy even when a subject seems boring at first. If you're not naturally interested in a topic, then create interest. Find a study partner in the class—if possible, someone you know and like—or form a study group. Also consider getting to know the instructor personally. When a course creates a bridge to human relationships, you engage the content in a more emotional way.

10 Overlearn. One way to fight mental fuzziness is to learn more than you need to know about a subject simply to pass a test. You can pick a subject apart, examine it, add to it, and go over it until it becomes second nature.

This technique is especially effective for problem solving. Do the assigned problems, and then do more problems. Find another textbook and work similar problems. Then make up your own problems and solve them. When you pretest yourself in this way, the potential rewards are speed, accuracy, and greater confidence at exam time.

11 Escape the short-term memory trap. Short-term memory is different from the kind of memory you'll need during exam week. For example, most of us can look at an unfamiliar seven-digit phone number once and remember it long enough to dial it. See if you can recall that number the next day.

Short-term memory can fade after a few minutes, and it rarely lasts more than several hours. A short review within minutes or hours of a study session can move material from short-term memory into long-term memory. That quick minireview can save you hours of study time when exams roll around.

12 Use your times of peak energy. Study your most difficult subjects during the times when your energy peaks. Many people can concentrate more effectively during daylight hours. The early morning hours can be especially productive, even for those who hate to get up with the sun. Observe the peaks and valleys in your energy flow during the day and adjust study times accordingly. Perhaps you will experience surges in memory power during the late afternoon or evening.

13 Distribute learning. As an alternative to marathon study sessions, experiment with shorter, spaced-out sessions. You might find that you can get far more done in three two-hour sessions than in one six-hour session.

For example, when you are studying for your American history exam, study for an hour or two and then wash the dishes. While you are washing the dishes, part of your mind will be reviewing what you studied. Return to American history for a while, then call a friend. Even when you are deep in conversation, part of your mind will be reviewing history.

You can get more done if you take regular breaks. You can even use the breaks as minirewards. After a productive study session, give yourself permission to log on and check your e-mail, listen to a song, or play 10 minutes of hide-and-seek with your kids.

Distributing your learning is a brain-friendly thing to do. You cannot absorb new information and ideas during all of your waking hours. If you overload your brain, it will find a way to shut down for a rest—whether you plan for it or not. By taking periodic breaks while studying, you allow information to sink in. During these breaks, your brain is taking the time to rewire itself by growing new connections between cells. Psychologists call this process *consolidation*.[5]

There is an exception to this idea of allowing time for consolidation. When you are so engrossed in a textbook that you cannot put it down, when you are consumed by an idea for a term paper and cannot think of anything else—keep going. The master student within you has taken over. Enjoy the ride.

14 Be aware of attitudes. People who think history is boring tend to have trouble remembering dates and historical events. People who believe math is difficult often have a hard time recalling mathematical equations and formulas. All of us can forget information that contradicts our opinions.

If you think a subject is boring, remind yourself that everything is related to everything else. Look for connections that relate to your own interests.

For example, consider a person who is fanatical about cars. She can rebuild a motor in a weekend and has a good time doing so. From this apparently specialized interest, she can explore a wide realm of knowledge. She can relate the workings of an engine to principles of physics, math, and chemistry. Computerized parts in newer cars can lead her to the study of data processing. She can research how the automobile industry has changed our cities and helped create suburbs, a topic that includes urban planning, sociology, business, economics, psychology, and history. Being aware of attitudes is not the same as fighting them or struggling to give them up. Just notice attitudes and be willing to put them on hold.

15 Elaborate. According to Harvard psychologist Daniel Schacter, all courses in memory improvement are based on this single technique. *Elaboration* means consciously encoding new information. Repetition is a basic way to elaborate. However, current brain research indicates that other types of elaboration are more effective for long-term memory.[6]

One technique is to ask questions about incoming information: Does this remind me of something or someone I already know? Is this similar to a technique that I already use? Where and when can I use this information?

When you learned to recognize Italy on a world map, your teacher probably pointed out that the country is shaped like a boot. This is a simple form of elaboration.

The same idea applies to more complex material. When you meet someone new, for example, ask yourself: Does she remind me of someone else? Or when doing the Learning Styles Applications in this book, ask how they relate to the Master Student Map that opens each chapter.

16 Intend to remember. To instantly enhance your memory, form the simple intention to *learn it now* rather than later. The intention to remember can be more powerful than any single memory technique.

You can build on your intention with simple tricks. During a lecture, for example, pretend that you'll be quizzed on the key points at the end of the period. Imagine that you'll get a $5 reward for every correct answer.

Also pay attention to your attention. Each time that your mind wanders during class, make a tick mark in the margins of your notes. The act of writing re-engages your attention.

If your mind keeps returning to an urgent or incomplete task, then write an Intention Statement about how you will handle it. With your intention safely recorded, return to what's important in the present moment.

Recall it

17 Remember something else. When you are stuck and can't remember something that you're sure you know, remember something else that is related to it.

If you can't remember your great-aunt's name, remember your great-uncle's name. During an economics exam, if you can't remember anything about the aggregate demand curve, recall what you do know about the aggregate supply curve. If you cannot recall specific facts, remember the example that the instructor used during her lecture. Information is encoded in the same area of the brain as similar information. You can unblock your recall by stimulating that area of your memory.

A brainstorm is a good memory jog. If you are stumped when taking a test, start writing down lots of answers to related questions, and—pop!—the answer you need is likely to appear.

18 Notice when you do remember. Everyone has a different memory style. Some people are best at recalling information they've read. Others have an easier time remembering what they've heard, seen, or done.

To develop your memory, notice when you recall information easily and ask yourself what memory techniques you're using naturally. Also notice when it's difficult to recall information. Be a reporter. Get the facts and then adjust your learning techniques. And remember to congratulate yourself when you remember.

19 Use it before you lose it. Even information encoded in long-term memory becomes difficult to recall when we don't use it regularly. The pathways to the information become faint with disuse. For example, you can probably remember your current phone number. What was your phone number 10 years ago?

This example points to a powerful memory technique. To remember something, access it a lot. Read it, write it, speak it, listen to it, apply it—find some way to make contact with the material regularly. Each time you do so, you widen the neural pathway to the material and make it easier to recall the next time.

Another way to make contact with the material is to teach it. Teaching demands mastery. When you explain the function of the pancreas to a fellow student, you discover quickly whether you really understand it yourself.

Study groups are especially effective because they put you on stage. The friendly pressure of knowing that you'll teach the group helps focus your attention.

20 Adopt the attitude that you never forget. You might not believe that an idea or a thought never leaves your memory. That's OK. In fact, it doesn't matter whether you agree with the idea or not. It can work for you anyway.

Test the concept. Instead of saying, "I don't remember," you can say, "It will come to me." The latter statement implies that the information you want is encoded in your brain and that you can retrieve it—just not right now.

People who use the flip side of this technique often get the opposite results. "I never remember anything," they say over and over again. "I've always had a poor memory. I'm such a scatterbrain." That kind of negative talk is self-fulfilling.

Instead, use positive affirmations that support you in developing your memory: "I recall information easily and accurately." "At any time I choose, I will be able to recall key facts and ideas." "My memory serves me well." Or even "I never forget!"

Power Process | Put It to Work | **Quiz** | Learning Styles Application | Master Student Profile

Name _____ Date _____/_____/_____

quiz

1. In the article about the memory jungle, the meadow:
   (a) Is a place that every animal (thought or perception) must pass through.
   (b) Represents short-term memory.
   (c) Represents the idea that one type of memory has a limited capacity.
   (d) All of the above.

2. Give a specific example of "setting a trap" for your memory.

3. Give two examples of ways that you can organize a long list of items.

4. Define *acronym* and give an example.

5. Memorization on a deep level can take place if you:
   (a) Repeat the idea.
   (b) Repeat the idea.
   (c) Repeat the idea.
   (d) All of the above.

6. Mnemonic devices are the most efficient ways to memorize facts and ideas. True or False? Explain your answer.

7. Briefly describe at least three memory techniques.

8. Thinking about three specific classmates or others you've met recently, explain which of the "remembering names" techniques you could use to remember their names.

9. Loving a problem means enjoying it. True or False? Explain your answer.

10. According to the text, "One powerful way to enhance your memory is to make friends with your amygdala." Briefly explain the meaning of this sentence.

Chapter 8

Test-Taking

What to do *before* the test

Do daily reviews. Daily reviews include short pre- and post-class reviews of lecture notes. Also conduct brief daily reviews with textbooks: Before reading a new assignment, scan your notes and the sections you underlined in the previous assignment. In addition, use the time you spend waiting for the bus or doing the laundry to conduct short reviews.

Concentrate daily reviews on two kinds of material. One is material you have just learned, either in class or in your reading. Second is material that involves simple memorization— equations, formulas, dates, definitions.

Begin to review on the first day of class. Most instructors outline the whole course at that time. You can even start reviewing within seconds after learning. During a lull in class, go over the notes you just took. Immediately after class, review your notes again.

Do weekly reviews. Review each subject at least once a week, allowing about one hour per subject. Include reviews of assigned reading and lecture notes. Look over any mind map summaries or flash cards you have created. Also practice working on sample problems.

Do major reviews. Major reviews are usually conducted the week before finals or other critical exams. They help integrate concepts and deepen understanding of material presented throughout the term. These are longer review periods—two to five hours at a stretch with sufficient breaks. Remember that the effectiveness of your review begins to drop after an hour or so unless you give yourself a short rest.

After a certain point, short breaks every hour might not be enough to refresh you. That's when it's time to quit. Learn your limits by being conscious of the quality of your concentration.

During long sessions, study the most difficult subjects when you are the most alert: at the beginning of the session.

Schedule reviews. Schedule specific times in your calendar for reviews. Start reviewing key topics at least five days before you'll be tested on them. This allows plenty of time to find the answers to questions and close any gaps in your understanding.

Create study checklists. Study checklists are used the way a pilot uses a preflight checklist. Pilots go through a standard routine before they take off. They physically mark off each item: test flaps, check magnetos, check fuel tanks, adjust instruments, check rudder. A written list helps them to be sure they don't miss anything. Once they are in the air, it's too late. Taking an exam is like flying a plane. Once the test begins, it's too late to memorize that one equation you forgot to include in your review.

Make a checklist for each subject. List reading assignments by chapters or page numbers. List dates of lecture notes. Write down various types of problems you will need to solve. Write down other skills to master. Include major ideas, definitions, theories, formulas, and equations. For math and science tests, choose some problems and do them over again as a way to review for the test.

Remember that a study checklist is not a review sheet; it is a to-do list. Checklists contain the briefest possible description of each item to study,

Create mind map summary sheets. There are several ways to make a mind map as you study for tests. Start by creating a map totally from memory. You might be surprised by how much you already know. After you have gone as far as you can using recall alone, go over your notes and text and fill in the rest of the map. Another option is to go through your notes and pick out key words. Then, without looking at your notes, create a mind map of everything you can recall about each key word. Finally, go back to your notes and fill in material you left out.

Create flash cards. Three-by-five flash cards are like portable test questions. On one side of the cards, write the questions. On the other, write the answers. It's that simple. Always carry a pack of flash cards with you, and review them whenever you have a minute to spare. Use flash cards for formulas, definitions, theories, key words from your notes, axioms, dates, foreign language phrases, hypotheses, and sample problems. Create flash cards regularly as the term progresses. Buy an inexpensive card file to keep your flash cards arranged by subject.

Monitor your reviews. Each day that you prepare for a test, assess what you have learned and what you still want to learn. See how many items you've covered from your study checklist. Look at the tables of contents in your textbooks and write an X next to the sections that you've summarized. This helps you gauge the thoroughness of your reviews and alert you to areas that still need attention.

Take a practice test. Write up your own questions and take this practice test several times before the actual exam. You might type this "test" so that it looks like the real thing. If possible, take your practice test in the same room where you will take the actual test.

Also meet with your instructor to go over your practice test. Ask whether your questions focus on appropriate topics and represent the kind of items you can expect to see. The instructor might decline to give you any of this information. More often, instructors will answer some or all of your questions about the test.

Get copies of old exams. Copies of previous exams for the class might be available from the instructor, the instructor's department, the library, or the counseling office. Old tests can help you plan a review strategy. One caution: If you rely on old tests exclusively, you might gloss over material the instructor has added since the last test. Also check your school's policy about making past tests available to students. Some might not allow it.

How to cram (even though you shouldn't)

Know the limitations of cramming and be aware of its costs. Cramming won't work if you've neglected all of the reading assignments, or if you've skipped most of the lectures and daydreamed through the rest. The more courses you have to cram for, the less effective cramming will be. Also, cramming is not the same as learning: You won't remember what you cram. The purpose of cramming is only to make the best of the situation.

Make choices. Pick out a *few* of the most important elements of the course and learn those backward, forward, and upside down. For example, devote most of your attention to the topic sentences, tables, and charts in a long reading assignment.

Make a plan. After you've chosen what elements you want to study, determine how much time to spend on each one.

Recite and recite again. The key to cramming is repetition. Go over your material again and again.

Don't "should" yourself. Avoid telling yourself that you *should* have studied earlier, you *should* have read the assignments, or you *should* have been more conscientious. Instead, write an Intention Statement about how you plan to change your study habits. Lighten up. Our brains work better when we aren't criticizing ourselves. Give yourself permission to be the fallible human being you are.

Ways to predict test questions

Predicting test questions can do more than get you a better grade. It can also keep you focused on the purpose of a course and help you design your learning strategies. Making predictions can be fun, too—especially when they turn out to be accurate.

Ask about the nature of the test. Eliminate as much guesswork as possible. Ask your instructor to describe upcoming tests. Do this early in the term so you can be alert for possible test questions throughout the course. Some questions to ask are:

- What course material will the test cover—readings, lectures, lab sessions, or a combination?
- Will the test be cumulative, or will it cover just the most recent material you've studied?
- Will the test focus on facts and details or major themes and relationships?
- Will the test call on you to solve problems or apply concepts?
- Will you have choices about which questions to answer?
- What types of questions will be on the test—true/false, multiple choice, short-answer, essay?

Note: In order to study appropriately for essay tests, find out how much detail the instructor wants in your answers. Ask how much time you'll be allowed for the test and how long the essay answers should be (number of pages, blue books, or word limit). Having that information before you begin studying will help you gauge your depth for learning the material.

Put yourself in your instructor's shoes. If you were teaching the course, what kinds of questions would you put on an exam? You can also brainstorm test questions with other students—a great activity for study groups.

Look for possible test questions in your notes and readings. Have a separate section in your notebook labeled "Test questions." Add several questions to this section after every lecture and assignment. You can also create your own code or graphic signal—such as a *T!* in a circle—to flag possible test questions in your notes. Use the same symbol to flag review questions and problems in your textbooks that could appear on a test.

Look for clues to possible questions during class. During lectures, you can predict test questions by observing what an instructor says and how he says it. Instructors often give clues. They might repeat important points several times, write them on the board, or return to them in later classes.

Gestures can indicate critical points. For example, your instructor might pause, look at notes, or read passages word for word.

Notice whether your teacher has any strong points of view on certain issues. Questions on those issues are likely to appear on a test. Also pay attention to questions the instructor poses to students, and note questions that other students ask.

When material from reading assignments is covered extensively in class, it is likely to be on a test. For science courses and other courses involving problem solving, work on sample problems using different variables.

Save all quizzes, papers, lab sheets, and graded materials of any kind. Quiz questions have a way of reappearing, in slightly altered form, on final exams. If copies of previous exams and other graded materials are available, use them to predict test questions.

Apply your predictions. To get the most value from your predictions, use them to guide your review sessions.

Remember the obvious. Be on the lookout for these words: *This material will be on the test.*[1]

For suggestions on ways to predict a variety of test questions, go to the *Becoming a Master Student* Website.

Cooperative *learning*

Working in groups

Education often seems like competition. We compete for entrance to school, for scholarships and grades while we're in school, and for jobs when we leave school. In that climate, it's easy to overlook the power of cooperation.

As social animals, humans draw strength from groups. In addition to offering camaraderie, study groups can lift your mood on days when you just don't feel like working. If you skip a solo study session, no one else will know. If you declare your intention to study with others who are depending on you, your intention gains strength.

Study groups are especially important if going to school has thrown you into a new culture. Joining a study group with people you already know can help ease the transition. To multiply the benefits of working with study groups, seek out people of other cultures, races, and ethnic groups. You can get a whole new perspective on the world, along with some valued new friends. And you can experience what it's like to be part of a diverse team—an important asset in today's job market.

Form a study group

Choose a focus for your group. Many students assume that the purpose of a study group is to help its members prepare for a test. That's one valid purpose—and there are others.

Through his research on cooperative learning, psychologist Joe Cuseo has identified several kinds of study groups.[2] For instance, *test review* groups compare answers and help each other discover sources of errors. *Note-taking* groups focus on comparing and editing notes, often meeting directly after the day's class. *Research* groups meet to help each other find, evaluate, and take notes on background materials for papers and presentations. *Reading* groups can be useful for courses in which test questions are based largely on textbooks. Meet with classmates to compare the passages you highlighted and the notes you made in the margins of your books.

Look for dedicated students. Find people you are comfortable with and who share your academic goals. Look for students who pay attention, participate in class, and actively take notes. Invite them to join your group.

Of course, there are other ways to recruit members. One is to make an announcement during class. Another option is to post signs asking interested students to contact you. Or pass around a sign-up sheet before class. While these methods can reach many people, they take more time to achieve results. And you have less control over who applies to join the group.

Limit groups to four people. Research on cooperative learning indicates that four people is an ideal group size.[3] Larger ones can be unwieldy.

Balance common interests with diversity. Studying with friends is fine, but if your common interests are pizza and jokes, beware of getting together to study.

Include people in your group who face academic or personal challenges similar to your own. For example, if you are divorced and have two toddlers at home, you might look for other single parents who have returned to school.

Also include people who face challenges that are different from your own. Choose people with similar educational goals who have different backgrounds and methods of learning. Each of you can gain by seeing the material from a new perspective.

Hold a planning session. Ask two or three people to get together for a snack and talk about group goals, meeting times, and other logistics. You don't have to make an immediate commitment.

As you brainstorm about places to meet, aim for a quiet meeting room with plenty of room to spread out materials. Also set clear starting and stopping times for meetings. Knowing that you only have an hour or two to get something done can help you be more productive.

Do a trial run. Test the group first by planning a one-time session. If that session works, plan another. After a few successful sessions, you can schedule regular meetings.

Conduct your group

Set an agenda for each meeting. At the beginning of each meeting, reach agreement on what you intend to do. Set a time limit for each agenda item and determine a quitting time. End each meeting with assignments for all members to complete before the next meeting.

Assign roles. To make the most of your time, ask one member to lead each group meeting. The leader's role is to keep the discussion focused on the agenda and ask for contributions from all members. Assign another person to act as recorder. This person will take notes on the meeting, recording possible test questions, answers, and main points from group discussions. Rotate both of these roles so that every group member takes a turn.

Teach each other. Teaching is a great way to learn something. Turn the material you're studying into a list of topics and assign a specific topic to each person, who will then teach it to the group.

When you're done presenting your topic, ask for questions or comments. Prompt each other to explain ideas more clearly, find gaps in understanding, consider other points of view, and apply concepts to settings outside the classroom. Here's where you tap into the power of cooperative learning. This kind of freewheeling conversation doesn't happen when you study by yourself.

Test each other. During your meeting, take a practice test created from questions contributed by group members. When you're finished, compare answers. Or turn testing into a game by pretending you're on a television game show. Use sample test questions to quiz each other.

Compare notes. Make sure that you all heard the same thing in class and that you all recorded the important information. Ask others to help explain material in your notes that is confusing to you.

Work in groups of two at a computer to review a course. One person can operate the keyboard while the other person dictates summaries of lectures and assigned readings. Together, both group members can check facts by consulting textbooks, lecture notes, and class handouts.

Create wall-size mind maps or concept maps to summarize a textbook or series of lectures. Work on large sheets of butcher paper, or tape together pieces of construction paper. When doing a mind map, assign one branch of the mind map to each member of the study group. Use a different colored pen or marker for each branch. (For more information on concept maps and mind maps, see Chapter Five: Notes.)

Pair off to do "book reports." One person can summarize a reading assignment. The other person can act as an interviewer on a talk show, posing questions and asking for further clarification.

Monitor effectiveness. On your meeting agenda, include an occasional discussion about your group's effectiveness. Are you meeting consistently? Is the group helping members succeed in class?

As a group, brainstorm ways to get unprepared members involved in the group. Reel in a dominating member by reminding him that everyone's voice needs to be heard.

To resolve conflict among group members, keep the conversation constructive. Focus on solutions. Move from vague complaints ("You're never prepared") to specific requests ("Will you commit to bring 10 sample test questions next time?"). Asking a "problem" member to lead the next meeting might make an immediate difference.

Ask for group support in personal areas. Other people might have insight into problems such as transportation, childcare, finances, and time management. Study groups can support you in getting what you want in many areas of life. Promote your success in school by refusing to go it alone.

---

journal entry 16

Intention Statement

In the space below, outline a plan to form a study group. Explain the steps you will take to get the group organized and set a first meeting date. Also describe the reward you anticipate for acting on this intention.

I intend to . . .

_____
_____
_____
_____
_____

What to do during the test

Prepare yourself for the test by arriving early. That often leaves time to do a relaxation exercise. While you're waiting for the test to begin and talking with classmates, avoid the question "How much did you study for the test?" This question might fuel anxious thoughts that you didn't study enough.

As you begin

Ask the teacher or test administrator if you can use scratch paper during the test. (If you use a separate sheet of paper without permission, you might appear to be cheating.) If you *do* get permission, use this paper to jot down memory aids, formulas, equations, facts, or other material you know you'll need and might forget. An alternative is to make quick notes in the margins of the test sheet.

Pay attention to verbal directions given as a test is distributed. Then scan the whole test immediately. Evaluate the importance of each section. Notice how many points each part of the test is worth and estimate how much time you'll need for each section, using its point value as your guide. For example, don't budget 20 percent of your time for a section that is worth only 10 percent of the points.

Read the directions slowly. Then reread them. It can be agonizing to discover that you lost points on a test merely because you failed to follow the directions. When the directions are confusing, ask to have them clarified.

Now you are ready to begin the test. If necessary, allow yourself a minute or two of "panic" time. Notice any tension you feel, and apply one of the techniques explained in the article "Let go of test anxiety" later in this chapter.

Answer the easiest, shortest questions first. This gives you the experience of success. It also stimulates associations and prepares you for more difficult questions. Pace yourself and watch the time. If you can't think of an answer, move on. Follow your time plan.

If you are unable to determine the answer to a test question, keep an eye out throughout the text for context clues that may remind you of the correct answer, or provide you with evidence to eliminate wrong answers.

Multiple choice questions

- *Answer each question in your head first.* Do this before you look at the possible answers. If you come up with an answer that you're confident is right, look for that answer in the list of choices.

- *Read all possible answers before selecting one.* Sometimes two answers will be similar and only one will be correct.

- *Test each possible answer.* Remember that multiple choice questions consist of two parts: the stem (an incomplete statement at the beginning) and a list of possible answers. Each answer, when combined with the stem, makes a complete statement that is either true or false. When you combine the stem with each possible answer, you are turning each multiple choice question into a small series of true/false questions. Choose the answer that makes a true statement.

- *Eliminate incorrect answers.* Cross off the answers that are clearly not correct. The answer you cannot eliminate is probably the best choice.

True/false questions

- *Read the entire question.* Separate the statement into its grammatical parts—individual clauses and

> **F is for feedback, not failure**
>
> When some students get an F on an assignment, they interpret that letter as a message: "You are a failure." That interpretation is not accurate. Getting an F means only that you failed a test—not that you failed your life.
>
> From now on, imagine that the letter *F* when used as a grade represents another word: *feedback*. An F is an indication that you didn't understand the material well enough. It's a message to do something differently before the next test or assignment.
>
> If you interpret F as *failure*, you don't get to change anything. But if you interpret F as *feedback*, you can change your thinking and behavior in ways that promote your success.

phrases—and then test each one. If any part is false, the entire statement is false.

- *Look for qualifiers.* These include words such as *all, most, sometimes,* or *rarely.* Absolute qualifiers such as *always* or *never* generally indicate a false statement.

- *Find the devil in the details.* Double-check each number, fact, and date in a true/false statement. Look for numbers that have been transposed or facts that have been slightly altered. These are signals of a false statement.

- *Watch for negatives.* Look for words such as *not* and *cannot.* Read the sentence without these words and see if you come up with a true or false statement. Then reinsert the negative words and see if the statement makes more sense. Watch especially for sentences with two negative words. As in math operations, two negatives cancel each other out: *We cannot say that Chekhov never succeeded at short story writing* means the same as *Chekhov succeeded at short story writing.*

Computer-graded tests

- Make sure that the answer you mark corresponds to the question you are answering.

- Check the test booklet against the answer sheet whenever you switch sections and whenever you come to the top of a column.

- Watch for stray marks; they can look like answers.

- If you change an answer, be sure to erase the wrong answer completely, removing all pencil marking completely.

Open-book tests

- Carefully organize your notes, readings, and any other materials you plan to consult when writing answers.

- Write down any formulas you will need on a separate sheet of paper.

- Bookmark the table of contents and index in each of your textbooks. Place Post-it Notes and Index Flags or paper clips on other important pages of books (pages with tables, for instance).

- Create an informal table of contents or index for the notes you took in class.

- Predict which material will be covered on the test and highlight relevant sections in your readings and notes.

Short-answer/fill-in-the-blank tests

- Concentrate on key words and facts. Be brief.

- Overlearning material can really pay off. When you know a subject backward and forward, you can answer this type of question almost as fast as you can write.

Matching tests

- Begin by reading through each column, starting with the one with fewer items. Check the number of items in each column to see if they're equal. If they're not, look for an item in one column that you can match with two or more items in the other column.

- Look for any items with similar wording and make special note of the differences between these items.

- Match words that are similar grammatically. For example, match verbs with verbs and nouns with nouns.

- When matching individual words with phrases, first read a phrase. Then look for the word that logically completes the phrase.

- Cross out items in each column when you are through with them.

Essay questions

Managing your time is crucial to answering essay questions. Note how many questions you have to answer and monitor your progress during the test period. Writing shorter answers and completing all of the questions on an essay test will probably yield a better score than leaving some questions blank.

Find out what an essay question is asking—precisely. If a question asks you to *compare* the ideas of Sigmund Freud and Karl Marx, no matter how eloquently you *explain* them, you are on a one-way trip to No Credit City.

Before you write, make a quick outline. An outline can help speed up the writing of your detailed answer, you're less likely to leave out important facts, and if you don't have time to finish your answer, your outline could win you some points. To use test time efficiently, keep your outline brief. Focus on key words to use in your answer.

Introduce your answer by getting to the point. General statements such as "There are many interesting facets to this difficult question" can cause acute irritation for teachers grading dozens of tests.

One way to get to the point is to begin your answer with part of the question. Suppose the question is "Discuss how increasing the city police budget might or might not contribute to a decrease in street crime." Your first sentence might be "An increase in police expenditures will not have a significant effect on street crime for the following reasons." Your position is clear. You are on your way to an answer.

When you expand your answer with supporting ideas and facts, start out with the most solid points. Be brief and avoid filler sentences.

Write legibly. Grading essay questions is in large part a subjective process. Sloppy, difficult-to-read handwriting might actually lower your grade.

Write on one side of the paper only. If you write on both sides of the paper, writing will show through and obscure the writing on the other side. If necessary, use the blank side to add points you missed. Leave a generous left-hand margin and plenty of space between your answers, in case you want to add to them later.

Finally, if you have time, review your answers for grammar and spelling errors, clarity, and legibility.

Words to watch for in essay questions

The following words are commonly found in essay test questions. They give you precise directions about what to include in your answer. Get to know these words well. When you see them on a test, underline them. Also look for them in your notes. Locating such key words can help you predict test questions.

Analyze: Break into separate parts and discuss, examine, or interpret each part. Then give your opinion.

Compare: Examine two or more items. Identify similarities and differences.

Contrast: Show differences. Set in opposition.

Criticize: Make judgments. Evaluate comparative worth. Criticism often involves analysis.

Define: Explain the exact meaning—usually, a meaning specific to the course or subject. Definitions are usually short.

Describe: Give a detailed account. Make a picture with words. List characteristics, qualities, and parts.

Discuss: Consider and debate or argue the pros and cons of an issue. Write about any conflict. Compare and contrast.

Explain: Make an idea clear. Show logically how a concept is developed. Give the reasons for an event.

Prove: Support with facts (especially facts presented in class or in the text).

Relate: Show the connections between ideas or events. Provide a larger context for seeing the big picture.

State: Explain precisely.

Summarize: Give a brief, condensed account. Include conclusions. Avoid unnecessary details.

Trace: Show the order of events or the progress of a subject or event.

Notice how these words differ. For example, *compare* asks you to do something different than *contrast*. Likewise, *criticize* and *explain* call for different responses. If any of these terms are still unclear to you, look them up in an unabridged dictionary.

Review these key words and other helpful vocabulary terms by using the online flash cards on the *Becoming a Master Student* Website.

Student Website

The test isn't over until...

Many students believe that a test is over as soon as they turn in the answer sheet. Consider another point of view: You're not done with a test until you know the answer to any question that you missed—and why you missed it.

This point of view offers major benefits. Tests in many courses are cumulative. In other words, the content included on the first test is assumed to be working knowledge for the second test, mid-term, or final exam. When you discover what questions you missed and understand the reasons for lost points, you learn something—and you greatly increase your odds of achieving better scores later in the course.

To get the most value from any test, take control of what you do at two critical points: the time immediately following the test, and the time when the test is returned to you.

Immediately following the test. After finishing a test, your first thought might be to nap, snack, or go out with friends to celebrate. Restrain those impulses for a short while so that you can reflect on the test. The time you invest now carries the potential to raise your grades in the future.

To begin with, sit down in a quiet place and take a few minutes to write some Discovery Statements related to your experience of taking the test. Describe how you felt about taking the test, how effective your review strategies were, and whether you accurately predicted the questions that appeared on the test.

Follow up with an Intention Statement or two. State what, if anything, you will do differently to prepare for the next test. The more specific you are, the better.

When the test is returned. When a returned test includes a teacher's comments, view this document as a treasure-trove of intellectual gold.

First, make sure that the point totals add up correctly and double-check for any other errors in grading. Even the best teachers make an occasional mistake.

Next, ask these questions:

- On what material did the teacher base test questions—readings, lectures, discussions, or other class activities?
- What types of questions appeared in the test—objective (such as matching items, true/false questions, or multiple choice), short-answer, or essay?
- What types of questions did you miss?
- Can you learn anything from the instructor's comments that will help you prepare for the next test?

Also see if you can correct any answers that lost points. To do this, carefully analyze the source of your errors and find a solution. Consult the chart for help.

Source of test error	Possible solutions
Study errors–studying material that was not included on the test, or spending too little time on material that *did* appear on the test	• Ask your teacher about specific topics that will be included on a test. • Practice predicting test questions. • Form a study group with class members to create mock tests.
Careless errors, such as skipping or misreading directions	• Read and follow directions more carefully–especially when tests are divided into several sections with different directions. • Set aside time during the next test to proofread your answers.
Concept errors–mistakes made when you do not understand the underlying principles needed to answer a question or solve a problem	• Look for patterns in the questions you missed. • Make sure that you complete all assigned readings, attend all lectures, and show up for laboratory sessions. • Ask your teacher for help with specific questions.
Application errors–mistakes made when you understand underlying principles but fail to apply them correctly	• Rewrite your answers correctly. • When studying, spend more time on solving sample problems. • Predict application questions that will appear in future tests and practice answering them.
Test mechanics errors–missing more questions in certain parts of the test than others, changing correct answers to incorrect ones at the last minute, leaving items blank, miscopying answers from scratch paper to the answer sheet	• Set time limits for taking each section of a test and stick to them. • Proofread your test answers carefully. • Look for patterns in the kind of answers you change at the last minute. • Change answers only if you can state a clear and compelling reason to do so.

The high costs of cheating

Cheating on tests can be a tempting choice. One benefit is that we might get a good grade without having to study.

Instead of studying, we could spend more time watching TV, partying, sleeping, or doing anything that seems like more fun. Another benefit is that we could avoid the risk of doing poorly on a test—which could happen even if we *do* study.

Also remember that cheating carries costs. Here are some to consider.

Risk of failing the course or expulsion from college. The consequences for cheating are serious. Cheating can result in failing the assignment, failing the entire course, getting suspended, or getting expelled from college entirely. Documentation of cheating may also prevent you from being accepted to other colleges.

We learn less. While we might think that some courses offer little or no value, it is more likely that we can create value from any course. If we look deeply enough, we can discover some idea or acquire some skill to prepare us for future courses or a career after graduation.

We lose time and money. Getting an education costs a lot of money. It also calls for years of sustained effort. Cheating sabotages our purchase. We pay full tuition and invest our energy without getting full value for it.

Fear of getting caught promotes stress. When we're fully aware of our emotions about cheating, we might discover intense stress. Even if we're not fully aware of our emotions, we're likely to feel some level of discomfort about getting caught.

Violating our values promotes stress. Even if we don't get caught cheating, we can feel stress about violating our own ethical standards. Stress can compromise our physical health and overall quality of life.

Cheating on tests can make it easier to violate our integrity again. Human beings become comfortable with behaviors that they repeat. Cheating is no exception.

Think about the first time you drove a car. You might have felt excited—even a little frightened. Now driving is probably second nature, and you don't give it much thought. Repeated experience with driving creates familiarity, which lessens the intense feelings you had during your first time at the wheel.

We can experience the same process with almost any behavior. Cheating once will make it easier to cheat again. And if we become comfortable with compromising our integrity in one area of life, we might find it easier to compromise in other areas.

Cheating lowers our self-concept. Whether or not we are fully aware of it, cheating sends us the message that we are not smart enough or responsible enough to make it on our own. We deny ourselves the celebration and satisfaction of authentic success.

An alternative to cheating is to become a master student. Ways to do this are described on every page of this book.

mastering technology

PERILS OF HIGH-TECH CHEATING

While digital technology offers many blessings, it also expands the options for cheating during a test. For example, one student loaded class notes into a Sidekick (a handheld device) and tried to read them. Another student dictated his class notes into files stored on his iPod and tried to listen to them. At another school, students used cell phones to take photos of test questions. They sent the photos to classmates outside the testing room, who responded by text-messaging the answers.[4]

All of these students were caught. Schools are becoming sophisticated about detecting high-tech cheating. Some install cameras in exam rooms. Others use software that monitors the programs running on students' computers during tests. And some schools simply ban all digital devices during tests.

There's no need to learn the hard way—through painful consequences—about the high costs of high-tech cheating. Using the suggestions in this chapter can help you succeed on tests *and* preserve your academic integrity.

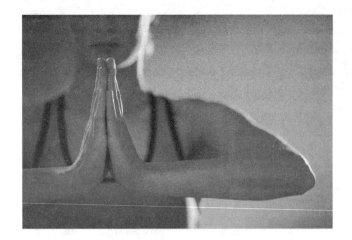

If you freeze during tests and flub questions when you know the answers, you might be suffering from test anxiety.

Let go of *test anxiety*

A little tension before a test is good. That tingly, butterflies-in-the-stomach feeling you get from extra adrenaline can sharpen your awareness and keep you alert. You can enjoy the benefits of a little tension while you stay confident and relaxed. Sometimes, however, tension is persistent and extreme. It causes loss of sleep, appetite, and sometimes even hair. That kind of tension is damaging. It is a symptom of test anxiety, and it can prevent you from doing your best on exams.

Other symptoms include nervousness, fear, dread, irritability, and a sense of hopelessness. Boredom also can be a symptom of test anxiety. Frequent yawning immediately before a test is a common reaction. Though it suggests boredom, yawning is often a sign of tension. It means that oxygen is not getting to the brain because the body is tense. A yawn is one way the body increases its supply of oxygen.

You might experience headaches, an inability to concentrate, or a craving for food. For some people, test anxiety makes asthma or high blood pressure worse. During an exam, symptoms can include confusion, panic, mental blocks, fainting, sweaty palms, and nausea.

Symptoms after a test include the following.

> *Mock indifference:* "I answered all the multiple choice questions as 'none of the above' because I was bored."
> *Guilt:* "Why didn't I study more?"
> *Anger:* "The teacher never wanted me to pass this stupid course anyway."
> *Blame:* "If only the textbook weren't so dull."
> *Depression:* "After that test, I don't see any point in staying in school."

Test anxiety can be serious—students have committed suicide over test scores. This anxiety can also be managed.

Test anxiety has two components: mental and physical. The mental component of stress includes all of your thoughts and worries about tests. The physical component includes bodily sensations and tension.

The following techniques can help you deal with the mental and physical components of stress in any situation, from test anxiety to stage fright.

Dealing with thoughts

Yell "Stop!" When you notice that your mind is consumed with worries and fears, that your thoughts are spinning out of control, mentally yell "Stop!" If you're in a situation that allows it, yell it out loud.

This action is likely to bring your focus back to the present moment and allow you to redirect your thoughts. Once you've broken the cycle of worry or panic, you can use any of the following techniques.

Daydream. When you fill your mind with pleasant thoughts, there is no room left for anxiety. If you notice yourself worrying about an upcoming test, replace visions of doom with images of something you like to do.

Visualize success. Most of us live up—or down—to our own expectations. If we spend a lot of time mentally rehearsing what it will be like to fail a test, our chances of doing so increase. Instead, you can take time to rehearse what it will be like to succeed. Be specific. Create detailed pictures, actions, and even sounds as part of your visualization.

Focus. Focus your attention on a specific object. Examine details of a painting, study the branches on a tree, or observe the face of your watch (right down to the tiny scratches in the glass). During an exam, take a few seconds to listen to the sounds of concentration—the squeaking of chairs, the scratching of pencils, the muted coughs. Touch the surface of your desk and notice the texture. Concentrate all of your attention on one point. Don't leave room in your mind for anxiety-related thoughts.

Praise yourself. Talk to yourself in a positive way. Many of us take the first opportunity to belittle ourselves: "Way to go, dummy! You don't even know the answer to the first question on the test." We wouldn't dream of treating a friend this way, yet we do it to ourselves.

An alternative is to give yourself some encouragement. Treat yourself as if you were your own best friend. Consider telling yourself, "I am very relaxed. I am doing a great job on this test."

Consider the worst. Rather than trying to put a stop to your worrying, consider the very worst thing that could happen. Take your fear to the limit of absurdity.

Imagine the catastrophic problems that might occur if you were to fail the test. You might say to yourself, "Well, if I fail this test, I might fail the course, lose my financial aid, and get kicked out of school. Then I won't be able to get a job, so the bank will repossess my car, and I'll start drinking." Keep going until you see the absurdity of your predictions. After you stop chuckling, you can backtrack to discover a reasonable level of concern. Your worry about failing the entire course if you fail the test might be justified. At that point ask yourself, "Can I live with that?" Unless you are taking a test in parachute packing and the final question involves jumping out of a plane, the answer will almost always be yes. (If the answer is no, use another technique. In fact, use several other techniques.)

The cold facts are hardly ever as bad as our worst fears. Shine a light on your fears, and they become more manageable.

Dealing with the physical sensations of anxiety

Breathe. You can calm physical sensations within your body by focusing your attention on your breathing. Concentrate on the air going in and out of your lungs. Experience it as it passes through your nose and mouth.

Do this for two to five minutes. If you notice that you are taking short, shallow breaths, begin to take longer and deeper breaths. Imagine your lungs to be a pair of bagpipes. Expand your chest to bring in as much air as possible. Then listen to the plaintive chords as you slowly release the air.

Scan your body. Simple awareness is an effective technique to reduce the tension in your body.

Sit comfortably and close your eyes. Focus your attention on the muscles in your feet and notice if they are relaxed. Tell the muscles in your feet that they can relax.

Move up to your ankles and repeat the procedure. Next go to your calves and thighs and buttocks, telling each group of muscles to relax.

Do the same for your lower back, diaphragm, chest, upper back, neck, shoulders, jaw, face, upper arms, lower arms, fingers, and scalp.

Tense and relax. If you are aware of a particularly tense part of your body or if you discover tension when you're scanning your body, you can release this tension with the tense-relax method.

To do this, find a muscle that is tense and make it even more tense. If your shoulders are tense, pull them back, arch your back, and tense your shoulder muscles even more tightly. Then relax. The net result is that you can be aware of the relaxation and allow yourself to relax even more.

You can use the same procedure with your legs, arms, abdomen, chest, face, and neck. Clench your fists, tighten your jaw, straighten your legs, and tense your abdomen all at once. Then relax and pay close attention to the sensations of relaxation. By paying attention, you can learn to re-create these sensations whenever you choose.

Use guided imagery. Relax completely and take a quick fantasy trip. Close your eyes, free your body of tension, and imagine yourself in a beautiful, peaceful, natural setting. Create as much of the scene as you can. Be specific. Use all of your senses.

For example, you might imagine yourself at a beach. Hear the surf rolling in and the seagulls calling to each other. Feel the sun on your face and the hot sand between your toes. Smell the sea breeze. Taste the salty mist from the surf. Notice the ships on the horizon and the rolling sand dunes. Use all of your senses to create a vivid imaginary trip.

Find a place that works for you and practice getting there. When you become proficient, you can return to it quickly for trips that might last only a few seconds.

With practice, you can use this technique even while you are taking a test.

Be with it. As you describe your anxiety in detail, don't resist it. When you completely experience a physical sensation, it will often disappear. People suffering from severe and chronic pain have used this technique successfully.

Exercise aerobically. This is one technique that won't work in the classroom or while you're taking a test. Yet it is an excellent way to reduce body tension. Exercise regularly during the days that you review for a test. See what effect this has on your ability to focus and relax during the test.

college.hmco.com/pic/bams12e

Do some kind of exercise that will get your heart beating at twice your normal rate and keep it beating at that rate for 15 or 20 minutes. Aerobic exercises include rapid walking, jogging, swimming, bicycling, basketball, and anything else that elevates your heart rate and keeps it elevated.

Get help. When these techniques don't work, when anxiety is serious, get help. If you become withdrawn, have frequent thoughts about death or suicide, get depressed and stay depressed for more than a few days, or have prolonged feelings of hopelessness, see a counselor.

Depression and anxiety are common among students. Suicide is the third leading cause of death among young adults between the ages of 15 and 24.[5] This is tragic and unnecessary. Many schools have counselors available. If not, the student health service or another office can refer you to community agencies that provide free or inexpensive counseling. You can also get emergency assistance over the phone. Most phone books contain listings for suicide prevention hot lines and other emergency services.

Have some FUN!

Contrary to popular belief, finals week does not have to be a drag.

In fact, if you have used techniques in this chapter, exam week can be fun. You will have done most of your studying long before finals arrive.

When you are well prepared for tests, you can even use fun as a technique to enhance your performance. The day before a final, go for a run or play a game of basketball. Take in a movie or a concert. A relaxed brain is a more effective brain. If you have studied for a test, your mind will continue to prepare itself even while you're at the movies.

Get plenty of rest, too. There's no need to cram until 3 a.m. when you have reviewed material throughout the term.

On the first day of finals, you can wake up refreshed, have a good breakfast, and walk into the exam room with a smile on your face. You can also leave with a smile on your face, knowing that you are going to have a fun week. It's your reward for studying regularly throughout the term.

exercise 18

TWENTY THINGS I LIKE TO DO

One way to relieve tension is to mentally yell "Stop!" and substitute a pleasant daydream for the stressful thoughts and emotions you are experiencing.

In order to create a supply of pleasant images to recall during times of stress, conduct an eight-minute brainstorm about things you like to do. Your goal is to generate at least 20 ideas. Time yourself and write as fast as you can in the space below.

When you have completed your list, study it. Pick out two activities that seem especially pleasant and elaborate on them by creating a mind map. Write down all of the memories you have about that activity.

You can use these images to calm yourself in stressful situations.

journal entry 17

Discovery/Intention Statement

Do a timed, four-minute brainstorm of all the reasons, rationalizations, justifications, and excuses you have used to avoid studying. Be creative. List your thoughts in the space below by completing the following Discovery Statement.

I discovered that I . . .

_____

Next, review your list, pick the excuse that you use the most, and circle it. In the space below, write an Intention Statement about what you will do to begin eliminating your favorite excuse. Make this Intention Statement one that you can keep, with a timeline and a reward.

I intend to . . .

_____

journal entry 18

Discovery Statement

Explore your feelings about tests. Complete the following sentences.

As exam time gets closer, one thing I notice that I do is . . .

_____

When it comes to taking tests, I have trouble . . .

_____

The night before a test, I usually feel . . .

_____

The morning of a test, I usually feel . . .

_____

During a test, I usually feel . . .

_____

After a test, I usually feel . . .

_____

When I get a test score, I usually feel . . .

_____

An online version of this exercise is available on the *Becoming a Master Student* Website.

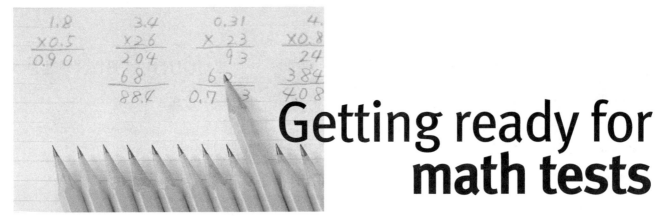

Getting ready for math tests

Many students who could succeed in math shy away from the subject. Some had negative experiences in past courses. Others believe that math is only for gifted students.

At some level, however, math is open to all students. There's more to this subject than memorizing formulas and manipulating numbers. Imagination, creativity, and problem-solving skills are important, too.

Consider a three-part program for math success. Begin with strategies for overcoming math anxiety. Next, boost your study skills. Finally, let your knowledge shine during tests.

Overcome math anxiety

Many schools offer courses in overcoming math anxiety. Ask your advisor about resources on your campus. Also experiment with the following suggestions.

Connect math to life. Think of the benefits of mastering math courses. You'll have more options for choosing a major and career. Math skills can also put you at ease in everyday situations—calculating the tip for a waiter, balancing your checkbook, working with a spreadsheet on a computer. If you follow baseball statistics, cook, do construction work, or snap pictures with a digital camera, you'll use math. And speaking the language of math can help you feel at home in a world driven by technology.

Pause occasionally to get an overview of the branch of math that you're studying. What's it all about? What basic problems is it designed to solve? How is this knowledge applied in daily life? For example, many architects, engineers, and space scientists use calculus daily.

Take a First Step. Math is cumulative. Concepts build upon each other in a certain order. If you struggled with algebra, you may have trouble with trigonometry or calculus.

To ensure that you have an adequate base of knowledge, tell the truth about your current level of knowledge and skill. Before you register for a math course, locate assigned texts for the prerequisite courses. If that material seems new or difficult for you, see the instructor. Ask for suggestions on ways to prepare for the course.

Remember that it's OK to continue your study of math from your current level of ability, whatever that level might be.

Notice your pictures about math. Sometimes what keeps people from succeeding at math is their mental picture of mathematicians. They see a man dressed in a baggy plaid shirt and brown wingtip shoes. He's got a calculator on his belt and six pencils jammed in his shirt pocket.

These pictures are far from the truth. Succeeding in math won't turn you into a nerd. Actually, you'll be able to enjoy school more, and your friends will still like you.

Mental pictures about math can be funny, and they can have serious effects. If math is seen as a field for white males, then women and people of color get excluded. Promoting math success for all students helps to overcome racism and sexism.

Change your conversation about math. When students fear math, they often say negative things to themselves about their abilities in these subjects. Many times this self-talk includes statements such as *I'll never be fast enough at solving math problems.* Or *I'm good with words, so I can't be good with numbers.*

Get such statements out in the open and apply some emergency critical thinking. You'll find two self-defeating assumptions lurking there: *Everybody else is better at math and science than I am.* And *Since I don't understand a math concept right now, I'll never understand it.* Both of these are illogical.

Replace negative beliefs with logical, realistic statements that affirm your ability to succeed in math: *Any confusion I feel now can be resolved. I learn math without comparing myself to others.* And *I ask whatever questions are needed to aid my understanding.*

Choose your response to stress. Math anxiety is seldom just "in your head." It can also register as sweaty palms, shallow breathing, tightness in the chest, or a mild headache. Instead of trying to ignore these sensations, just notice them without judgment. Over time, simple awareness decreases their power.

In addition, use stress management techniques. "Let go of test anxiety" on page 188 offers a bundle of them.

No matter what you do, remember to breathe. You can relax in any moment just by making your breath slower and deeper. Practice doing this while you study math. It will come in handy at test time.

Boost study skills for math

Choose teachers with care. Whenever possible, find a math teacher whose approach to math matches your learning style. Try several teachers until you find one whom you enjoy.

Another option is to ask around. Maybe your academic advisor can recommend math teachers. Also ask classmates to name their favorite math teachers—and to explain the reasons for their choices.

Perhaps only one teacher is offering the math course you'll need. Use the following suggestions to learn from this teacher regardless of her teaching style.

Take math courses back to back. Approach math in the same way that you learn a foreign language. If you take a year off in between Spanish I and Spanish II, you won't gain much fluency. To master a language, you take courses back to back. It works the same way with math, which is a language in itself.

Form a study group. During the first week of each math course, organize a study group. Ask each member to bring five problems to group meetings, along with solutions. Also exchange contact information so that you can stay in touch via e-mail, phone, and instant messaging.

Avoid short courses. Courses that you take during summer school or another shortened term are condensed. You might find yourself doing far more reading and homework each week than you do in longer courses. If you enjoy math, the extra intensity can provide a stimulus to learn. But if math is not your favorite subject, then give yourself extra time. Enroll in courses with more calendar days.

Participate in class. Success in math depends on your active involvement. Attend class regularly. Complete homework assignments *when they're due*—not just before the test. If you're confused, get help right away

▶ Succeeding in science courses

Many of the strategies that help you prepare for math tests can also help you succeed in science courses. For example, forming small study groups can be a fun way to learn these subjects.

Relating science to your career interests and daily life is also important. People in many professions—from dentists to gardeners—rely on sciences to do their job. And even if you don't choose a science-driven career, you will live in a world that's driven by technology. Understanding how scientists observe, collect data, and arrive at conclusions can help you feel more at home in this world.

More strategies for succeeding in science are available on the *Becoming a Master Student* Website.

In addition, use some strategies that are unique to succeeding in science courses.

Prepare for variety. Remember that the word *science* refers to a vast range of subjects—astronomy, biology, chemistry, physics, physiology, geology, ecology, geography, and more. Most of these subjects include math as one of their tools. Beyond that, however, are key differences.

You can take advantage of this variety. Choose courses in a science that matches your personal interests and comfort level for technical subjects.

Prepare for lab sessions. Laboratory work is crucial to many science classes. To get the most out of these sessions, be prepared. Complete required reading before you enter the lab. Also gather the materials you'll need.

Prepare for several types of tests. Math tests often involve lists of problems to solve. Science tests can involve matching, multiple choice, and essay items as well. Ask your instructor about what type of tests to expect. Then prepare for the tests using strategies from this chapter.

from an instructor, tutor, or study group. Instructor's office hours, free on-campus tutoring, and classmates are just a few of the resources available to you. Also support class participation with time for homework. Make daily contact with math.

Ask questions fearlessly. It's a cliché, and it's true: In math, there are no dumb questions. Ask whatever questions will aid your understanding. Keep a running list of them and bring the list to class.

Make your text top priority. Math courses are often text-driven. Class activities closely follow the book. This makes it important to complete your reading assignments. Master one concept before going on to the next, and stay current with your reading. Be willing to read slowly and reread sections as needed.

Read actively. To get the most out of your math texts, read with paper and pencil in hand. Work out examples. Copy diagrams, formulas, and equations. Use chapter summaries and introductory outlines to organize your learning.

From time to time, stop, close your book, and mentally reconstruct the steps in solving a problem. Before you memorize a formula, understand the basic concepts behind it.

Practice solving problems. To get ready for math tests, work *lots* of problems. Find out if practice problems or previous tests are on file in the library, in the math department, or with your math teacher.

Isolate the types of problems that you find the most difficult. Practice them more often. Be sure to get help with these *before* exhaustion or frustration sets in.

To prepare for tests, practice working problems fast. Time yourself. This is a great activity for math study groups.

Approach problem solving with a three-step process. During each step, apply an appropriate strategy. For ideas, see the chart on this page.

Use tests to show what you know

Practice test taking. Part of preparing for any math test is rehearsal. Instead of passively reading through your text or scanning class notes, do a practice test:

- Print out a set of practice problems and set a timer for the same length of time as your testing period.

- Whenever possible, work these problems in the same room where you will take the actual test.

- Use only the kinds of supporting materials—such as scratch paper or lists of formulas—that will be allowed during the test.

- As you work problems, use deep breathing or another technique to enter a more relaxed state.

Ask appropriate questions. If you don't understand a test item, ask for clarification. The worst that can happen is that an instructor or proctor will politely decline to answer your question.

Write legibly. Put yourself in the instructor's place and imagine the prospect of grading stacks of illegible answer

---

1: Prepare

- Read each problem two or three times, slowly and out loud whenever possible.
- Consider creating a chart with three columns labeled *What I already know*, *What I want to find out*, and *What connects the two*. This third column is the place to record a formula that can help you solve the problem.
- Determine which arithmetic operations (addition, subtraction, multiplication, division) or formulas you will use to solve the problem.
- See if you can estimate the answer before you compute it.

2: Compute

- Reduce the number of unknowns as much as you can. Consider creating a separate equation to solve each unknown.
- When solving equations, carry out the algebra as far as you can before plugging in the actual numbers.
- Cancel and combine. For example, if the same term appears in both dividend and divisor, they will cancel each other out.
- Remember that it's OK to make several attempts at solving the problem before you find an answer.

3: Check

- Plug your answer back into the original equation or problem and see if it works out correctly.
- Ask yourself if your answer seems likely when compared to your estimate. For example, if you're asked to apply a discount to an item, that item should cost less in your solution.
- Perform opposite operations. If a problem involves multiplication, check your work by division; add, then subtract; factor, then multiply; find the square root, then the square; differentiate, then integrate.
- Keep units of measurement clear. Say that you're calculating the velocity of an object. If you're measuring distance in meters and time in seconds, the final velocity should be in meters per second.

sheets. Make your answers easy to read. If you show your work, underline key sections and circle your answer.

Do your best. There are no secrets involved in getting ready for math tests. Master some stress management techniques, do your homework, get answers to your questions, and work sample problems. If you've done those things, you're ready for the test and deserve to do well. If you haven't done all those things, just do the best you can.

Remember that your personal best can vary from test to test, and even day to day. Even if you don't answer all test questions correctly, you can demonstrate what you *do* know right now.

During the test, notice when solutions come easily. Savor the times when you feel relaxed and confident. If you ever feel math anxiety in the future, these are the times to remember. [6]

journal entry 19

Discovery/Intention Statement

Most of us can recall a time when learning became associated with anxiety. For many of us, this happened early in math courses.

One step toward getting past this anxiety is to write a math autobiography. Recall specific experiences in which you first felt stress related to this subject. Where were you? How old were you? What were you doing, thinking, and feeling? Who else was with you? What did those people say or do?

Describe one of these experiences in the space below.

_____
_____
_____
_____

Now recall any incidents in your life that gave you *positive* feelings about math. Describe one of these incidents briefly in the space below.

_____
_____
_____
_____

Now sum up any discoveries you made while describing these two sets of experiences.

I discovered that my biggest barrier to learning math is . . .

_____
_____
_____

I discovered that the most satisfying aspect of doing math is . . .

_____
_____
_____

Finally, prepare to take positive action. List three things you can do to succeed more consistently with math. Include a specific time frame for taking each action.

Action 1: I intend to . . .

_____
_____

Action 2: I intend to . . .

_____
_____

Action 3: I intend to . . .

_____
_____

Power Process | Put It to Work | **Quiz** | Learning Styles Application | Master Student Profile

Name _____ Date _____/_____/_____

quiz

1. According to the text, test scores measure your accomplishments in a course. True or False? Explain your answer.

2. When answering multiple choice questions, it is better to read all of the possible answers before answering the question in your head. True or False? Explain your answer.

3. The presence of absolute qualifiers, such as *always* or *never*, generally indicates a false statement. True or False? Explain your answer.

4. Briefly explain the differences between a daily review and a major review.

5. Define the term *study checklist* and give three examples of what to include on such checklists.

6. Describe how *detachment* differs from *denial*.

7. Study groups can focus on:
    (a) Comparing and editing class notes.
    (b) Doing research to prepare for papers and presentations.
    (c) Finding and understanding key passages in assigned readings.
    (d) Creating and taking practice tests.
    (e) All of the above.

8. The text offers a three-step process for solving math problems. Name these steps and list a strategy related to each one.

9. Describe at least three techniques for dealing with the thoughts connected to test anxiety.

10. Describe at least three techniques for dealing with the physical feelings connected to test anxiety.

201   college.hmco.com/pic/bams12e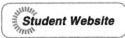

Chapter 9

Critical and Creative Thinking

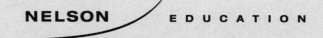

Becoming a critical thinker

Critical thinking is a path to intellectual adventure. Though there are dozens of possible approaches, the process boils down to *asking and answering questions*.

The four basic questions in the Learning Styles Applications in this book—*Why? What? How?* and *What if?*—are powerful guides to thinking. As they take you through the cycle of learning, they can also guide you in becoming a critical thinker. This article offers a variety of tools for answering those questions. For more handy implements, see *Becoming a Critical Thinker* by Vincent Ryan Ruggiero.

1 *Why* am I considering this issue? Critical thinking and personal passion go together. Begin critical thinking with a question that matters to you. Seek a rationale for your learning. Understand why it is important for you to think about a specific topic. You might want to arrive at a new conclusion, make a prediction, or solve a problem. By finding a personal connection with an issue, your interest in acquiring and retaining new information increases.

2 *What* are various points of view on this issue? Imagine Karl Marx, Cesar Chavez, and Donald Trump assembled in one room to choose the most desirable economic system. Picture Mahatma Gandhi, Winnie Mandela, and General George Patton lecturing at a United Nations conference on conflict resolution. Visualize Fidel Castro, George W. Bush, and Mother Teresa in a discussion about distributing the world's resources equitably. When seeking out alternative points of view, let such events unfold in your mind.

Dozens of viewpoints exist on every important issue—reducing crime, ending world hunger, preventing war, educating our children, and countless other concerns. In fact, few problems have any single, permanent solution. Each generation produces its own answers to critical questions, based on current conditions. Our search for answers is a conversation that spans centuries. On each question, many voices are waiting to be heard.

You can take advantage of this diversity by seeking out alternative views with an open mind. When talking to another person, be willing to walk away with a new point of view—even if it's the one you brought to the table, supported with new evidence.

Examining different points of view is an exercise in analysis, which you can do with the suggestions that follow.

Define terms. Imagine two people arguing about whether an employer should limit health care benefits to members of a family. To one person, the word *family* means a mother, father, and children; to the other person, the word *family* applies to any long-term, supportive relationship between people who live together. Chances are, the debate will go nowhere until these people realize that they're defining the same word in different ways.

Conflicts of opinion can often be resolved—or at least clarified—when we define our key terms up front. This is especially true with abstract, emotion-laden terms such as *freedom, peace, progress,* or *justice.* Blood has been shed over the meaning of these words. Define them with care.

Look for assertions. A speaker's or writer's key terms occur in a larger context called an assertion. An *assertion* is a complete sentence that directly answers a key question. For example, consider this sentence from the article "The Master Student" in Chapter One: "A master is a person who has attained a level of skill that goes beyond technique." This sentence is an assertion that answers an important question: How do we recognize a master?

Look for at least three viewpoints. When asking questions, let go of the temptation to settle for just a single answer. Once you have come up with an answer, say to yourself, "Yes, that is one answer. Now what's another?" Using this approach can sustain honest inquiry, fuel creativity, and lead to conceptual breakthroughs. Be prepared: The world is complicated, and critical thinking is a complex business. Some of your answers might contradict others. Resist the temptation to have all of your ideas in a neat, orderly bundle.

Practice tolerance. One path to critical thinking is tolerance for a wide range of opinions. Taking a position on important issues is natural. When we stop having an opinion on things, we've probably stopped breathing.

The problem occurs when we become so attached to our current viewpoints that we refuse to consider alternatives. Many ideas that are widely accepted in western cultures—for example, civil liberties for people of color and the right of women to vote—were once considered dangerous. Viewpoints that seem outlandish today might become widely accepted a century, a decade, or even a year from now. Remembering this can help us practice tolerance for differing beliefs and, in doing so, make room for new ideas that might alter our lives.

3 *How* **well is each point of view supported?** Uncritical thinkers shield themselves from new information and ideas. As an alternative, you can follow the example of scientists, who constantly search for evidence that contradicts their theories. The following suggestions can help.

Look for logic and evidence. The aim of using logic is to make statements that are clear, consistent, and coherent. As you examine a speaker's or writer's assertions, you might find errors in logic—assertions that contradict each other or assumptions that are unfounded.

Also assess the evidence used to support points of view. Evidence comes in several forms, including facts, expert testimony, and examples. To think critically about evidence, ask questions such as:

- Are all or most of the relevant facts presented?
- Are the facts consistent with each other?
- Are facts presented accurately—or in a misleading way?
- Are enough examples included to make a solid case for the viewpoint?
- Do the examples truly support the viewpoint?
- Are the examples typical? That is, could the author or speaker support the assertion with other examples that are similar?
- Is the expert credible—truly knowledgeable about the topic?

Consider the source. Look again at that article on the problems of manufacturing cars powered by natural gas. It might have been written by an executive from an oil company. Check out the expert who disputes the connection between smoking and lung cancer. That "expert" might be the president of a tobacco company.

This is not to say that we should dismiss the ideas of people who have a vested interest in stating their opinions. Rather, we can take their self-interest into account as we consider their ideas.

Understand before criticizing. Polished debaters can sum up their opponents' viewpoints—often better than the people who support those viewpoints themselves. Likewise, critical thinkers take the time to understand a statement of opinion before agreeing or disagreeing with it.

Effective understanding calls for listening without judgment. Enter another person's world by expressing her viewpoint in your own words. If you're conversing with that person, keep revising your summary until she agrees that you've stated her position accurately. If you're reading an article, write a short summary of it. Then scan the article again, checking to see if your synopsis is on target.

Watch for hot spots. Many people have mental "hot spots"—topics that provoke strong opinions and feelings. Examples are abortion, homosexuality, gun control, and the death penalty.

To become more skilled at examining various points of view, notice your own particular hot spots. Make a clear intention to accept your feelings about these topics and to continue using critical thinking techniques.

One way to cool down our hot spots is to remember that we can change or even give up our current opinions without giving up ourselves. That's a key message behind the articles "Ideas are tools" and "Detach." These Power Processes remind us that human beings are much more than the sum of their current opinions.

Be willing to be uncertain. Some of the most profound thinkers have practiced the art of thinking by using a magic sentence: "I'm not sure yet."

Those are words that many people do not like to hear. Our society rewards quick answers and quotable sound bites. We're under considerable pressure to utter the truth in 10 seconds or less.

In such a society, it is courageous and unusual to take the time to pause, to look, to examine, to be thoughtful, to consider many points of view—and to be unsure. When a society adopts half-truths in a blind rush for certainty, a willingness to embrace uncertainty can move us forward.

4 What if I could combine various points of view or create a new one? Finding the truth is like painting a barn door by tossing an open can of paint at it. Few people who throw at the door miss it entirely. Yet no one can cover the whole door in a single toss.

People who express a viewpoint are seeking the truth. And no reasonable person claims to cover the whole barn door—to understand the whole truth about anything. Instead, each viewpoint can be seen as one approach among many possible alternatives. If you don't think that any one opinion is complete, combine different perspectives on the issue. Experiment with the following strategies.

Create a critical thinking "spreadsheet." When you consult authorities with different stands on an issue, you might feel confused about how to sort, evaluate, and combine their points of view. To overcome confusion, create a critical thinking "spreadsheet." List the authorities across the top of a page and key questions down the left side. Then indicate each authority's answer to each question, along with your own answers.

For example, the following spreadsheet clarifies different points of view on the issue of whether to outlaw boxing.

You could state your own viewpoint by combining your answers to the questions in the above spreadsheet: "I favor legalized boxing. While boxing poses dangers, so do other sports. And like other sports, the risk of injury can be reduced when boxers get proper training."

Write about it. Thoughts can move at blinding speed. Writing slows down that process. Gaps in logic that slip by us in thought or speech are often exposed when we commit the same ideas to paper. Writing down our thoughts allows us to compare, contrast, and combine points of view more clearly—and therefore to think more thoroughly.

Accept your changing perspectives. Researcher William Perry found that students in higher education move through stages of intellectual development.[2] In earlier stages, students tend to think there is only one correct viewpoint on each issue, and they look to their instructors to reveal that truth. Later, students acknowledge a variety of opinions on issues and construct their own viewpoints.

	Medical doctor	Former boxer	Sports journalist	Me
Is boxing a sport?	No	Yes	Yes	Yes
Is boxing dangerous?	Yes	Yes	Yes	Yes
Is boxing more dangerous than other sports?	Yes	No	Yes	No
Can the risk of injury be overcome by proper training?	No	No	No	Yes

Source: Vincent Ryan Ruggiero, *Becoming a Critical Thinker,* Fifth Edition. Copyright © 2006 by Houghton Mifflin Company. Reprinted with permission.

Monitor changes in your thinking processes as you combine viewpoints. Distinguish between opinions that you accept from authorities and opinions that are based on your own use of logic and your search for evidence. Also look for opinions that result from objective procedures (such as using the *Why? What? How?* and *What if?* questions in this article) and personal sources (using intuition or "gut feelings").

Remember that the process of becoming a critical thinker will take you through a variety of stages. Give yourself time, and celebrate your growing mastery.

Attitudes of a critical thinker

The American Philosophical Association invited a panel of 46 scholars from the United States and Canada to come up with answers to the following two questions: "What is college-level critical thinking?" and "What leads us to conclude that a person is an effective critical thinker?"[3] After two years of work, this panel concluded that critical thinkers share the attitudes summarized in the following chart.

Attitude	Sample statement
Truth-seeking	"Let's follow this idea and see where it leads, even if we feel uncomfortable with what we find out."
Open-minded	"I have a point of view on this subject, and I'm anxious to hear yours as well."
Analytical	"Taking a stand on the issue commits me to take some new action."
Systematic	"The speaker made several interesting points, and I'd like to hear some more evidence to support each one."
Self-confident	"After reading the book for the first time, I was confused. I'll be able to understand it after studying the book some more."
Inquisitive	"When I first saw that painting, I wanted to know what was going on in the artist's life when she painted it."
Mature	"I'll wait until I gather some more facts before reaching a conclusion on this issue."

Finding "aha!"
Creativity fuels critical thinking

This chapter offers you a chance to practice two types of critical thinking: convergent thinking and divergent thinking.

Convergent thinking involves a narrowing-down process. Out of all the possible viewpoints on an issue or alternative solutions to a problem, you choose the one that is the most reasonable or that provides the most logical basis for action.

Some people see convergent thinking and critical thinking as the same thing. However, there's more to critical thinking. Before you choose among viewpoints, generate as many of them as possible. Open up alternatives and consider all of your options. Define problems in different ways. Keep asking questions and looking for answers. This opening-up process is called *divergent* or *creative thinking*.

Creative thinking provides the basis for convergent thinking. In other words, one path toward having good ideas is to have *lots* of ideas. Then you can pick and choose from among them, combining and refining them as you see fit.

Choose when to think creatively. The key is to make conscious choices about what kind of thinking to do in any given moment. Generally speaking, creative thinking is more appropriate in the early stages of planning and problem solving. Feel free to dwell in this domain for a while. If you narrow down your options too soon, you run the risk of missing an exciting solution or of neglecting a novel viewpoint.

Remember that creative thinking and convergent thinking take place in a continuous cycle. After you've used convergent thinking to narrow down your options, you can return to creative thinking at any time to generate new ones.

Cultivate "aha!" Central to creative thinking is something called the "aha!" experience. Nineteenth-century poet Emily Dickinson described aha! this way: "If I feel physically as if the top of my head were taken off, I know that is poetry." Aha! is the burst of creative energy heralded by the arrival of a new, original idea. It is the sudden emergence of an unfamiliar pattern, a previously undetected relationship, or an unusual combination of familiar elements. It is an exhilarating experience.

Aha! does not always result in a timeless poem or a Nobel Prize. It can be inspired by anything from playing a new riff on a guitar to figuring out why your car's fuel pump doesn't work. A nurse might notice a patient's symptom that everyone else missed. That's an aha! An accountant might discover a tax break for a client. That's an aha! A teacher might devise a way to reach a difficult student. Aha!

Follow through. The flip side of aha! is following through. Thinking is both fun and work. It is effortless and uncomfortable. It's the result of luck and persistence. It involves spontaneity and step-by-step procedures, planning and action, convergent and creative thinking.

Companies that depend on developing new products and services need people who can find aha! and do something with it. The necessary skills include the ability to spot assumptions, weigh evidence, separate fact from opinion, organize thoughts, and avoid errors in logic. All of this can be demanding work. Just as often, it can be energizing and fun.

▶ Tangram

A tangram is an ancient Chinese puzzle game that stimulates the "play instinct" so critical to creative thinking. The cat figure here was created by rearranging seven sections of a square. Hundreds of images can be devised in this manner. Playing

with tangrams allows us to see relationships we didn't notice before.

The rules of the game are simple: Use these seven pieces to create something that wasn't there before. Be sure to use all seven. You might start by mixing up the pieces and seeing whether you can put them back together to form a square.

Make your own tangram by cutting pieces like those above out of poster board. When you come up with a pattern you like, trace around the outside edges of it and see if a friend can discover how you did it.

Ways to *create ideas*

Anyone can think creatively. Use the following techniques to generate ideas about everything, whether you're studying math problems, remodeling a house, or writing a bestseller. With practice, you can set the stage for creative leaps, jump with style, and land on your feet with brand-new ideas in hand.

Conduct a brainstorm. Brainstorming is a technique for finding solutions, creating plans, and discovering new ideas. When you are stuck on a problem, brainstorming can break the logjam. For example, if you run out of money two days before payday every week, you can brainstorm ways to make your money last longer. You can brainstorm ways to pay for your education. You can brainstorm ways to find a job.

The purpose of brainstorming is to generate as many solutions as possible. Sometimes the craziest, most outlandish ideas, while unworkable in themselves, can lead to new ways to solve problems. Use the following steps to try out the brainstorming process.[4]

- *Focus on a single problem or issue.* State your focus as a question. Open-ended questions that start with the words *what, how, who, where*, and *when* often make effective focusing questions.

- *Relax.* Creativity is enhanced by a state of relaxed alertness. If you are tense or anxious, use relaxation techniques such as those described in "Let go of test anxiety" in Chapter Six.

- *Set a quota or goal for the number of solutions you want to generate.* Goals give your subconscious mind something to aim for.

- *Set a time limit.* Use a clock to time it to the minute. Digital sports watches with built-in stopwatches work well. Experiment with various lengths of time. Both short and long brainstorms can be powerful.

- *Allow all answers.* Brainstorming is based on attitudes of permissiveness and patience. Accept every idea. If it pops into your head, put it down on paper. Quantity, not quality, is the goal. Avoid making judgments and evaluations during the brainstorming session. If you get stuck, think of an outlandish idea and write it down. One crazy idea can unleash a flood of other, more workable solutions.

- *Brainstorm with others.* This is a powerful technique. Group brainstorms take on lives of their own. Assign one member of the group to write down solutions. Feed off the ideas of others, and remember to avoid evaluating or judging anyone's idea during the brainstorm.

After your brainstorming session, evaluate the results. Toss out any truly nutty ideas, but not before you give them a chance.

Focus and let go. Focusing and letting go are alternating parts of the same process. Intense focus taps the resources of your conscious mind. Letting go gives your subconscious mind time to work. When you focus for intense periods and then let go for a while, the conscious and subconscious parts of your brain work in harmony.

Focusing attention means being in the here and now. To focus your attention on a project, notice when you pay attention and when your mind starts to wander. And involve all of your senses. For example, if you are having difficulty writing a paper at a computer, practice focusing by listening to the sounds as you type. Notice the feel of the keys as you strike them. When you know the sights, sounds, and sensations you associate with being truly in focus, you'll be able to repeat the experience and return to your paper more easily.

Be willing to recognize conflict, tension, and discomfort. Notice them and fully accept them rather than fight against them. Look for the specific thoughts and body sensations that make up the discomfort. Allow them to come fully into your awareness, and then let them pass.

You might not be focused all of the time. Periods of inspiration might last only seconds. Be gentle with yourself when you notice that your concentration has lapsed. In fact, that might be a time to let go. "Letting go" means not forcing yourself to be creative. Practice focusing for short periods at first, then give yourself a break. Take a nap when you are tired. Thomas Edison took frequent naps. Then the light bulb clicked on.

Cultivate creative serendipity. The word *serendipity* was coined by the English author Horace Walpole from the title of an ancient Persian fairy tale, "The Three Princes of Serendip." The princes had a knack for making lucky discoveries. Serendipity is that knack, and it involves more than luck. It is the ability to see something valuable that you weren't looking for.

History is full of serendipitous people. Country doctor Edward Jenner noticed "by accident" that milkmaids seldom got smallpox. The result was his discovery that mild cases of cowpox immunized them. Penicillin was also discovered "by accident." Scottish scientist Alexander Fleming was growing bacteria in a laboratory petri dish. A spore of *Penicillium notatum,* a kind of mold, blew in the window and landed in the dish, killing the bacteria. Fleming isolated the active ingredient. A few years later, during World War II, it saved thousands of lives. Had Fleming not been alert to the possibility, the discovery might never have been made.

You can train yourself in the art of serendipity. Keep your eyes open. You might find a solution to an accounting problem in a Saturday morning cartoon. You might discover a topic for your term paper at the corner convenience store. Multiply your contacts with the world. Resolve to meet new people. Join a study or discussion group. Read. Go to plays, concerts, art shows, lectures, and movies. Watch television programs you normally wouldn't watch.

Also expect discoveries. One secret for success is being prepared to recognize "luck" when you see it.

Keep idea files. We all have ideas. People who treat their ideas with care are often labeled "creative." They not only recognize ideas but also record them and follow up on them.

One way to keep track of ideas is to write them down on 3 × 5 cards. Invent your own categories and number the cards so you can cross-reference them. For example, if you have an idea about making a new kind of bookshelf, you might file a card under "Remodeling." A second card might also be filed under "Marketable Ideas." On the first card, you can write down your ideas, and on the second, you can write "See card #321—Remodeling."

Include in your files powerful quotations, random insights, notes on your reading, and useful ideas that you encounter in class. Collect jokes, too.

Keep a journal. Journals don't have to be exclusively about your own thoughts and feelings. You can record observations about the world around you, conversations with friends, important or offbeat ideas—anything.

To fuel your creativity, read voraciously, including newspapers and magazines. Keep a clip file of interesting articles. Explore beyond mainstream journalism. There are hundreds of low-circulation specialty magazines and online news journals that cover almost any subject you can imagine.

Keep letter-size file folders of important correspondence, magazine and news articles, and other material. You can also create idea files on a computer using word processing, outlining, or database software.

Safeguard your ideas, even if you're pressed for time. Jotting down four or five words is enough to capture the essence of an idea. You can write down one quotation in a minute or two. And if you carry 3 × 5 cards in a pocket or purse, you can record ideas while standing in line or sitting in a waiting room.

Review your files regularly. Some amusing thought that came to you in November might be the perfect solution to a problem in March.

Collect and play with data. Look from all sides at the data you collect. Switch your attention from one aspect to another. Examine each fact, and avoid getting stuck on one particular part of a problem. Turn a problem upside down by picking a solution first and then working backward. Ask other people to look at the data. Solicit opinions.

Living with the problem invites a solution. Write down data, possible solutions, or a formulation of the problem on 3 × 5 cards and carry them with you. Look at them before you go to bed at night. Review them when you are waiting for the bus. Make them part of your life and think about them frequently.

Look for the obvious solutions or the obvious "truths" about the problem—then toss them out. Ask yourself: "Well, I know X is true, but if X were *not* true, what would happen?" Or ask the reverse: "If that *were* true, what would follow next?"

Put unrelated facts next to each other and invent a relationship between them, even if it seems absurd at first. In *The Act of Creation,* novelist Arthur Koestler says that finding a context in which to combine opposites is the essence of creativity.[5]

Make imaginary pictures with the data. Condense it. Categorize it. Put it in chronological order. Put it in alphabetical order. Put it in random order. Order it from most to least complex. Reverse all of those orders. Look for opposites.

It has been said that there are no new ideas—only new ways to combine old ideas. Creativity is the ability to discover those new combinations.

Create while you sleep. A part of our mind works as we sleep. You've experienced this directly if you've ever fallen asleep with a problem on your mind and awakened the next morning with a solution. For some of us, the solution appears in a dream or just before falling asleep or waking up.

You can experiment with this process. Ask yourself a question as you fall asleep. Keep pencil and paper or a recorder near your bed. The moment you wake up, begin writing or speaking and see if an answer to your question emerges.

Many of us have awakened from a dream with a great idea, only to fall asleep and lose it forever. To capture your ideas, keep a notebook by your bed at all times. Put the notebook where you can find it easily.

There is a story about how Benjamin Franklin used this suggestion. Late in the evenings, as he was becoming drowsy, he would sit in his rocking chair with a rock in his right hand and a metal bucket on the floor beneath the rock. The moment he fell asleep, the rock would fall from his grip into the bottom of the bucket, making a loud noise that awakened him. Having placed a pen and paper nearby, he immediately wrote down what he was thinking. Experience taught him that his thoughts at this moment were often insightful and creative.

Refine ideas and follow through. Many of us ignore this part of the creative process. How many great moneymaking schemes have we had that we never pursued? How many good ideas have we had for short stories that we never wrote? How many times have we said to ourselves, "You know, what they ought to do is attach two handles to one of those things, paint it orange, and sell it to police departments. They'd make a fortune." And we never realize that we are "they."

Genius resides in the follow-through—the application of perspiration to inspiration. One powerful tool you can use to follow through is the Discovery and Intention Journal Entry system. First write down your idea in a Discovery Statement, and then write what you intend to do about it in an Intention Statement. You also can explore the writing techniques discussed in Chapter Eight: Communicating as a guide for refining your ideas.

Another way to refine an idea is to simplify it. And if that doesn't work, mess it up. Make it more complex.

Finally, keep a separate file in your ideas folder for your own inspirations. Return to it regularly to see if there is anything you can use. Today's defunct term paper idea could be next year's A in speech class.

Create success strategies. Use creative thinking techniques to go beyond the pages of this book and create your own ways to succeed in school. Read other books on success. Interview successful people. Reflect on any of your current behaviors that help you do well in school. Change any habits that fail to serve you.

If you have created a study group with people from one of your classes, set aside time to talk about ways to succeed in any class. Challenge each other to practice your powers of invention. Test any new strategies you create and report to the group on how well they're working for you.

Trust the process. Learn to trust the creative process—even when no answers are in sight. We are often reluctant to look at problems if no immediate solution is at hand. Trust that a solution will show up. Frustration and a feeling of being stuck are often signals that a solution is imminent.

Sometimes solutions break through in a giant AHA! More often they come in a series of little aha!s. Be aware of what your aha!s look, feel, and sound like. That sets the stage for even more flights of creative thinking.

> ### ▶ Create on your feet
>
> A popular trend in executive offices is the "stand-up" desk—a raised working surface at which you stand rather than sit.
>
> Standing has advantages over sitting for long periods. You can stay more alert and creative when you're on your feet. One theory is that our problem-solving ability improves when we stand, due to increased heart rate and blood flow to the brain.
>
> Standing can ease lower-back pain, too. Sitting for too long aggravates the spine and its supporting muscles.
>
> This is a technique with tradition. If you search the Web for stand-up desks, you'll find models based on desks used by Thomas Jefferson, Winston Churchill, and writer Virginia Woolf. Consider setting your desk up on blocks or putting a box on top of your desk so that you can stand while writing, preparing speeches, or studying. Discover how long you can stand comfortably while working, and whether this approach works for you.
>
>

Power Process | Put It to Work | **Quiz** | Learning Styles Application | Master Student Profile

Name _____ Date _____/_____/_____

quiz

1. List four questions that can guide you on your path to becoming a critical thinker.

2. Briefly describe one strategy for answering each question you listed in your response to #1.

3. Briefly explain the difference between convergent and divergent thinking.

4. Explain what is meant in this chapter by *aha!*

5. Briefly describe three strategies for creative thinking.

6. Summarize the main steps in the process of choosing a major, as explained in this chapter.

7. List three types of logical fallacies and give an example of each one.

8. List an assumption that underlies the following statement: "Why save money? I want to enjoy life today."

9. Name at least one logical fallacy involved in this statement: "Everyone who's ever visited this school agrees that it's the best in the state."

10. According to the text, the words *choose* and *decide* are synonyms. True or False? Explain your answer.

college.hmco.com/pic/bams12e

Chapter 10

Diversity

Diversity is real—and valuable

We have always lived with people of different races and cultures. Many of us come from families who immigrated to Canada just recently or one or two generations ago. The things we eat, the tools we use, and the words we speak are a cultural tapestry woven by many different peoples.

Think about a common daily routine. A typical Canadian citizen awakens in a bed (an invention from the Near East). After dressing in clothes (often designed in Italy), she slices a banana (grown in Honduras) on her bowl (made in China) of cereal, and brews coffee (shipped from Nicaragua). After breakfast, she reads the morning newspaper (printed by a process invented in Germany on paper, which was first made in China). Then she flips on a CD player (made in Japan) and listens to music (possibly performed by a band from Cuba). Multiculturalism refers to ethnic diversity—and many other kinds of diversity as well. As anthropologist Dorothy Lee reminds us, culture is simply one society's solutions to perennial human problems, such as how to worship, celebrate, resolve conflict, work, think, and learn.[2] Culture is a set of learned behaviours—a broader concept than race, which refers to the biological make-up of people. From this standpoint, we can speak of the culture of large corporations or the culture of the fine arts.

Multiculturalism refers to racial and ethnic diversity—and many other kinds of diversity as well.

There are the cultures of men and women; heterosexual, homosexual, and bisexual people; and older and younger people. There are differences between urban and rural dwellers, between able-bodied people and those with disabilities, and between people from two-parent families, people from single-parent families, and people from same-sex families. There are social classes based on differences in standards of living. And diversity in religion is a factor, too. This can be especially difficult to accept, since many people identify strongly with their religious faith. In some respects, culture can be compared to an iceberg. Only parts of any given culture—such as language patterns or distinctive apparel—exist on a visible level. Just as most of an iceberg lies under water and out of sight, many aspects of culture lie beneath our conscious awareness. This invisible realm includes assumptions about the meanings of beauty and friendship, the concepts of sin and justice, approaches to problem solving, interpretations of eye contact and body language, and patterns of supervisor and employee relationships.

People can differ in countless ways—race, gender, ethnic group, sexual orientation, and more. The suggestions offered in this chapter can help you respond effectively to the many kinds of diversity you'll encounter. Higher education can help reinforce an attitude of tolerance, open-mindedness, and respect for individual differences.

Discrimination is also real. The ability to live with diversity is now more critical than ever. Racism, sexism, homophobia, and other forms of discrimination still exist, even in educational settings. The Canadian Human Rights Commission investigates complaints of discrimination and fosters public understanding and adherence to the principles of the Human Rights Act.

Consider how you would respond to these situations:

- Members of a sociology class are debating the merits of social welfare in Canada. The instructor calls on a student from the Six Nations Reserve and says, "Tell us. What's the First Nations perspective on this issue anyway?" Here the student is being stereotyped as a spokesperson for her entire ethnic group.

- Students in a mass media communications class are learning to think critically about television programs. They're talking about a situation comedy set in an urban high school. "Man, they really whitewashed that show," says one student. "It's mostly about inner-city kids, but they didn't show anybody getting into trouble, doing drugs, or joining gangs." The student's comment perpetuates common racial stereotypes.

- On the first day of the term, students taking English composition enter a class taught by a professor from India. One of the students asks the professor, "Am I in the right class? Maybe there's been a mistake. I thought this was supposed to be an English class." The student assumed that only people with white skins are qualified to teach English courses.

Forrest Toms of Training Research and Development defines racism as "prejudice plus power"—the power to define reality, to enshrine one set of biases. The operating assumption behind racism is that differences mean deficits.

When racism lives, we all lose—even those groups with social and political power. We lose the ability to make friends and to function effectively on teams. We crush human potential. People without the skills to bridge cultures are already at a disadvantage.

Higher education offers a chance to change this. Academic environments can become cultural laboratories—places where people of diverse races and cultures can meet in an atmosphere of tolerance. Students who create alliances outside their immediate group are preparing to succeed in both school and work.

Diversity is valuable. Synergy is the idea that the whole is more than the sum of its parts. Consider some examples: A symphony orchestra consists of many different instruments; when played together, their effect is multiplied many times. A football team has members with different specialties; when their talents are combined, they can win a league championship.

Diversity in a society offers another example of synergy. It takes no more energy to believe that differences enrich us than it does to believe that differences endanger us. Embracing diversity adds value to any organization and can be far more exciting than just meeting the minimum requirements for affirmative action.

Today we are waking up not only to the *fact* of diversity but also to the *value* of diversity. Biologists tell us that diversity of animal species benefits our ecology. The same idea applies to the human species. Through education our goal can be to see that we are all part of a complex world—that our own culture is different from, not better than, others. Knowing this, we can stop saying, "This is the way to work, learn, relate to others, and view the world." Instead, we can say, "Here is the way I have been doing it. I would also like to see your way."

The fact of diversity also represents opportunity in the workplace. Understanding cultural differences—local and international—will help you to embrace others' viewpoints that can lead to profitable solutions. Organizations that are attuned to diversity are more likely to prosper in the global marketplace.

Higher education can help reinforce an attitude of tolerance, open-mindedness, and respect for individual differences.

Accepting diversity does not mean ignoring the differences among cultures so that we all become the same. Instead, we can become more like a mosaic—a piece of art in which each element maintains its individuality and blends with others to form a harmonious whole.

Learning to live with diversity is a process of returning to "beginner's mind"—a place where we question our biases and assumptions. This is a magical place, a place of new beginnings and options. It takes courage to dwell in beginner's mind—courage to go outside the confines of our own culture and world view. It can feel uncomfortable at first. Yet there are lasting rewards to gain.

As you read the following articles, look to yourself. This chapter aims to help you examine your own biases. With self-awareness, you can go beyond them.

student voices

A master student tries on other people's skin, and it is not judgmental. We are all different and a master student accepts that diversity.

—LYNN LINEBERGER

Communicating across cultures

Communicating with people of other cultures is a learned skill—a habit. According to Stephen R. Covey, author of *The Seven Habits of Highly Effective People*, a habit is the point at which desire, knowledge, and skill meet.[3] Desire is about wanting to do something. Knowledge is understanding what to do. And skill is the ability to do it.

Desire, knowledge, and skill are equally important for bridging gaps in cultural understanding. This article speaks to the first two factors—*desire* and *knowledge*—and also provides suggestions for gaining *skill*.

Desire to communicate. When our actions are grounded in a sincere desire to understand others, we can be much more effective. Knowing techniques for communicating across cultures is valuable. At the same time, this cannot take the place of the sincere desire and commitment to create understanding. If you truly value cultural diversity, you can discover and create ways to build bridges between people.

Know about other cultures. Back up your desire with knowledge. People from different cultures read differently, write differently, think differently, eat differently, and learn differently than you. Knowing this, you can be more effective with your classmates, co-workers, and neighbours.

Cultures also differ in a variety of dimensions. One of the most important dimensions is *style*. We can also speak of learning styles, communication styles, relationship styles, and other styles.

Educator James Anderson speaks of the relationship between analytical and relational styles.[4] Most of our schools favour students with an analytical style. These students learn abstract concepts easily and are adept at reading, writing, and discussing ideas. They can learn parts of a subject even if they don't have a view of the whole. Often these students are self-directed, and their performance is not affected by the opinions of others.

A bias toward the analytical style tends to exclude students with a relational style—students who learn by getting the big picture of a subject before the details. They learn better initially by speaking, listening, and doing rather than by reading or writing. These students prefer to learn about subjects that relate to their concerns or are presented in a lively, humourous way. In addition, they are influenced by the opinions of people they value and respect. All of these things point to a unique learning style.

Differing styles exist in every aspect of life—family structure, religion, relationships with authority, and more. First Nations people might avoid conflict and seek mediators. People from some Asian cultures might feel that it's rude to ask questions. Knowing about such differences can help avoid misunderstandings.

Today there is a wealth of material about cultural diversity. The greater our knowledge of other cultures, the easier it is for us to be tolerant. The more we explore our differences, the more we can discover our similarities.

Begin with an intention to increase your sensitivity toward other cultures. Be willing to ask questions and share ideas with all kinds of people. Just get the conversation started. You can learn something valuable from anyone when you reach out.

Develop skills. With the desire to communicate and gain knowledge of other cultures, you can develop specific skills on three levels. The first is personal—becoming aware of your own biases. The second is interpersonal—forming alliances with people of other races and cultures. The third is institutional—pointing out the discrimination and racism that you observe in organizations. Be an advocate for change.

Be active. Learning implies activity. Learning ways to communicate across cultures is no exception. It's ineffective to assume that this skill will come to you merely by sharing the same classroom with people from other races and ethnic groups. It's not the responsibility of others to raise your cultural awareness. That job is yours, and it calls for energy.

Look for common ground. Some goals cross culture lines. Most people want health, physical safety, economic security, and education.

Most students want to succeed in post-secondary education and prepare for a career. They often share the same instructors. They have access to many of the same resources at school. They meet in the classroom, on the athletic field, and at cultural events. To promote cultural understanding, we can become aware of and celebrate our differences.

The greater our knowledge of other cultures, the easier it is for us to be tolerant.

We can also practise looking for common ground. You can cultivate friends from other cultures. Do this through volunteering, serving on committees, or joining study groups—any activity in which people from other cultures are also involved. Then your understanding of other people unfolds in a natural, spontaneous way.

The key is to honour the differences among people while remembering what we have in common.

Assume differences in meaning. Each day we can make an intention to act and speak with the awareness that cultures differ. One option is to look for several possible meanings of our words and actions.

Assume that differences in meaning exist, even if you don't know what they are. After first speaking to someone from another culture, don't assume that you've been understood or that you fully understand the other person. The same action can have different meanings at different times, even for members of the same culture. Check it out. Verify what you think you have heard. Listen to see if what you spoke is what the other person received.

If you're speaking to someone who doesn't understand English well, keep the following ideas in mind:

- Speak slowly and distinctly.

- To clarify your statement, don't repeat individual words over and over again. Restate your entire message in simple, direct language. Avoid slang.

- Use gestures to accompany your words.

- Since English courses for non-native speakers often emphasize written English, write down what you're saying. Print your message in capitalized block letters.

- Stay calm and avoid sending non-verbal messages that you're frustrated.

Look for individuals, not group representatives. Sometimes the way we speak glosses over differences among individuals and reinforces stereotypes. For example, a student worried about her mark in math expresses concern over "all those Asian students who are skewing the class curve." Or a music major assumes that her Caribbean classmate knows a lot about reggae. We can avoid such errors by seeing people as individuals—not spokespersons for an entire group.

Get inside another culture. You might find yourself fascinated by one particular culture. Consider learning as much about it as possible. Immerse yourself in that culture. Read novels, see plays, go to concerts, listen to music, look at art, take courses, learn the language. Find opportunities to speak with members of that culture. Your quest for knowledge will be an opening to new conversations.

Celebrate your own culture. Learning about other cultures does not mean abandoning your own. You could gain new appreciation for it. You might even find out that members of your ethnic group have suffered discrimination. In the process of celebrating your own culture, you can gain valuable insights into the experiences of other people.

Find a translator, mediator, or model. People who move with ease in two or more cultures can help us greatly. Professor Diane de Anda speaks of three kinds of people who can communicate across cultures. She calls them *translators, mediators,* and *models.*[5]

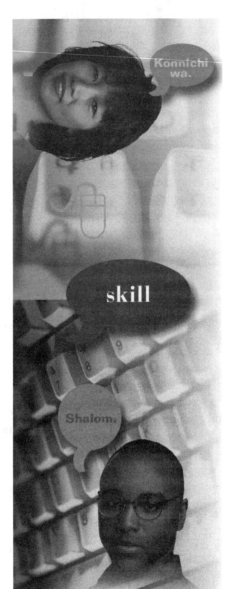

A *translator* is someone who is truly bicultural—a person who relates skilfully to people in a mainstream culture and people from a contrasting culture. This person can share her own experiences in overcoming discrimination, learning another language or dialect, and coping with stress. She can point out differences in meaning between cultures and help resolve conflict.

Mediators are people who belong to the dominant or mainstream culture. Unlike translators, they might not be bicultural. However, mediators value diversity and are committed to cultural understanding. Often they are teachers, counsellors, tutors, mentors, or social workers.

Models are members of a culture who are positive examples. Models include students from any nationality or cultural group who participate in class and demonstrate effective study habits. Models can also include entertainers, athletes, and community leaders.

Your institution might have people who serve these functions, even if they're not labelled translators, mediators, or models. Some educational institutions have mentor or "bridge" programs that pair new students with instructors of the same race or culture. Students in these programs get coaching in study and life skills; they also develop friendships with possible role models. Ask your student counselling service about such programs.

Develop support systems. Many students find that their social adjustment affects their academic performance. Students with strong support systems—such as families, friends, places of worship, self-help groups, and mentors—are using a powerful strategy for success in school. As an exercise, list the support systems that you rely on right now. Also list new support systems you could develop.

Support systems can help you bridge culture gaps. With a strong base of support in your own group, you can feel more confident in meeting people outside that group.

Ask for help. If you're unsure about how well you're communicating, ask questions: "I don't know how to make this idea clear for you. How might I communicate better?" "When you look away from me during our conversation, I feel uneasy. Is there something else we

The key is to honour the differences among people while remembering what we have in common.

need to talk about?" "When you don't ask questions, I wonder if I am being clear. Do you want any more explanation?" Questions such as these can get cultural differences out in the open in a constructive way.

Remember diversity when managing conflict. While in school or on the job, you might come into conflict with a person from another culture. Conflict is challenging enough to manage when it occurs between members of the same culture. When conflict gets enmeshed with cultural or ethnic differences, the situation can become even more difficult.

Fortunately, many of the guidelines for managing conflict offered in Chapter Eight: Communicating apply across cultures. Also keep the following suggestions in mind:

- *Keep your temper in check.* People from other cultures might shrink from displays of sudden, negative emotion—for example, shouting or pointing.

- *Deliver your criticisms in private.* People in many Asian and Middle Eastern cultures place value on "saving face" in public.

- *Give the other person space.* Standing too close can be seen as a gesture of intimidation.

- *Address people as equals.* For example, don't offer the other person a chair so that she can sit while you stand and talk.

- *Stick to the point.* When feeling angry or afraid, you might talk more than usual. A person from another culture—especially one who's learning your language—might find it hard to take in everything you're saying. Pause from time to time so that others can ask clarifying questions.

- *Focus on actions, not personalities.* People are less likely to feel personally attacked when you request specific changes in behaviour. "Please show up for work right at 9 a.m." is often more effective than "You're irresponsible."

- *Be patient.* This guideline applies especially when you're a manager or supervisor. People from other cultures might find it difficult to speak candidly with someone they view as an authority figure. Encourage others to speak. Allowing periods of silence might help.

- *Take time to comment when others do well.* However, avoid excessive compliments. People from other cultures might be uncomfortable with public praise and even question your sincerity.

Change the institution. None of us are individuals living in isolation. We live in systems that can be racist. As a student, you might see people of colour ignored in class. You might see people of a certain ethnic group passed over in job hiring or underrepresented in school organizations. And you might see gay, lesbian, and transgendered students ridiculed or even threatened with violence. One way to stop these actions is to point them out.

The Constitution as well as the written policies of most educational institutions ban racial and ethnic discrimination. Many institutions have formal procedures that protect students against such discrimination. Find out what those procedures are and use them, if necessary.

In recent history, students have fueled much social change. When it comes to ending discrimination, you are in an environment where you can make a difference. Run for student government. Write for school publications. Speak at rallies. Express your viewpoint. This is training for citizenship in a multicultural world.

Reap the rewards. The price we pay for failing to understand other cultures is fear and bigotry—the assumption that one group has the right to define all others. Attitudes such as these cannot withstand the light of knowledge, compassion, and common values.

Overcome stereotypes with critical thinking

Consider assertions such as "Students like to drink heavily," "People who speak English as a second language are hard to understand," and "Most of the people who live on the East Coast are on welfare."

These are examples of stereotyping—generalizing about a group of people based on the behaviour of isolated group members. Stereotypes are a potent source of intellectual error. They are signals to shift our thinking skills into high gear—to demand evidence, examine logic, and insist on accurate information.

The word *stereotype* originally referred to a method used by printers to produce duplicate pages of text. This usage still rings true. When we stereotype, we gloss over individual differences and assume that every member of a group is the same.

Stereotypes infiltrate every dimension of human individuality. People are stereotyped on the basis of their race, nationality, physical or mental abilities, ethnic group, religion, political affiliation, geographic location, job, age, gender, IQ, height, or hobby. We stereotype people based on everything from the colour of their hair to the year of their car.

Stereotypes have many possible sources: fear of the unknown, uncritical thinking, and negative encounters between individual members of different groups. Whatever their cause, stereotypes abound.

In themselves, generalizations are neither good nor bad. In fact, they are essential. Mentally sorting people, events, and objects into groups allows us to make sense of the world. But when we consciously or unconsciously make generalizations that rigidly divide the people of the world into "us" versus "them," we create stereotypes and put on the blinders of prejudice.

You can take several steps to free yourself from stereotypes.

Look for errors in thinking. Some of the most common errors are:

- *Selective perception.* Stereotypes can literally change the way we see the world. If we assume that homeless people are lazy, for instance, we tend to notice only the examples that support our opinion. Stories about homeless people who are too young or too ill to work will probably escape our attention.

- *Self-fulfilling prophecy.* When we interact with people based on stereotypes, we set them up in ways that confirm our thinking. For example, when people of colour were denied access to higher education based on stereotypes about their intelligence, they were deprived of opportunities to demonstrate their intellectual gifts.

- *Self-justification.* Stereotypes can allow people to assume the role of a victim and to avoid taking responsibility for their own lives. An unemployed white male might believe that affirmative action programs are making it impossible for him to get a job—even as he overlooks his own lack of experience or qualifications.

Create categories in a more flexible way. Stereotyping has been described as a case of "hardening of the categories." Avoid this problem by making your categories broader. Instead of seeing people based on their skin colour, you could look at them on the basis of their heredity. (People of all races share most of the same genes.) Or you could make your categories narrower. Instead of talking about "religious extremists," look for subgroups among the people who adopt a certain religion. Distinguish between groups that advocate violence and those that shun it.

Test your generalizations about people through action. You can do this by actually meeting people of other cultures. It's easy to believe almost anything about certain groups of people as long as we never deal directly with individuals. Inaccurate pictures tend to die when people from various cultures study together, work together, and live together. Consider joining a school or community organization that will put you in contact with people of other cultures. Your rewards will include a more global perspective and an ability to thrive in a multicultural world.

Be willing to see your own stereotypes. The Power Process: "Notice your pictures and let them go" can help. One belief about ourselves that many of us can shed is *I have no pictures about people from other cultures.* Even people with the best of intentions can harbour subtle biases. Admitting this possibility allows us to look inward even more deeply for stereotypes. Every time that we notice an inaccurate picture buried in our mind and let it go, we take a personal step toward embracing diversity.

Chapter 11

Making Presentations and Public Speaking

Mastering public speaking

Some people tune out during a speech. Just think of all the times you have listened to instructors, lecturers, and politicians. Remember all the wonderful daydreams you had during their speeches.

Your audiences are like you. The way you plan and present your speech can determine the number of audience members who will stay with you until the end. Polishing your speaking and presentation skills can also help you think on your feet and communicate clearly. These are skills that you can use in any course and in any career you choose.

Analyze your audience

Developing a speech is similar to writing a paper. Begin by writing out your topic, purpose, and thesis statement as described in "Phase 1: Getting ready to write" on page 251. Then carefully analyze your audience by using the strategies in the chart on page 260.

Organize your presentation

Consider the length of your presentation. Plan on delivering about 100 words per minute. This is only a general guideline, however, so time yourself as you practice your presentation.

Aim for a lean presentation—enough words to make your point but not so many as to make your audience restless. Leave your listeners wanting more. When you speak, be brief and then be seated.

Speeches are usually organized in three main parts: the introduction, the main body, and the conclusion.

Write the introduction. Rambling speeches with no clear point or organization put audiences to sleep. Solve this problem with your introduction. The following introduction, for example, reveals the thesis and exactly what's coming. The speech will have three distinct parts, each in logical order:

Dog fighting is a cruel sport. I intend to describe exactly what happens to the animals, tell you who is doing this, and show you how you can stop this inhumane practice.

Whenever possible, talk about things that hold your interest. Include your personal experiences and start with a bang! Consider this introduction to a speech on the subject of world hunger:

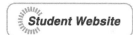

I'm very honored to be here with you today. I intend to talk about malnutrition and starvation. First, I want to outline the extent of these problems, then I will discuss some basic assumptions concerning world hunger, and finally I will propose some solutions.

If your topic is new to listeners...	• Explain why your topic matters to them. • Relate the topic to something that listeners already know and care about. • Define any terms that listeners might not know.
If listeners already know about your topic...	• Acknowledge this fact at the beginning of your speech. • Find a narrow aspect of the topic that may be new to listeners. • Offer a new perspective on the topic, or connect it to an unfamiliar topic.
If listeners disagree with your thesis...	• Tactfully admit your differences of opinion. • Reinforce points on which you and your audience agree. • Build credibility by explaining your qualifications to speak on your topic. • Quote expert figures that agree with your thesis—people whom your audience is likely to admire. • Explain that their current viewpoint has costs for them, and that a slight adjustment in their thinking will bring significant benefits.
If listeners may be uninterested in your topic...	• Explain how listening to your speech can help them gain something that matters deeply to them. • Explain ways to apply your ideas in daily life.

You can almost hear the snores from the audience. Following is a rewrite:

More people have died from hunger in the past five years than have been killed in all of the wars, revolutions, and murders in the past 150 years. Yet there is enough food to go around. I'm honored to be here with you today to discuss solutions to this problem.

Though some members of an audience begin to drift during any speech, most people pay attention for at least the first few seconds. Highlight your main points in the beginning sentences of your speech.

Draft your introduction and then come back to it after you've written the rest of your speech. In the process of creating the main body and conclusion, your thoughts about the purpose and main points of your speech might change. You might even want to write the introduction last.

Write the main body. The main body of your speech is the content, which accounts for 70 to 90 percent of most speeches. In the main body, you develop your ideas in much the same way that you develop a written paper.

Transitions are especially important. Give your audience a signal when you change points, using meaningful pauses and verbal emphasis as well as transitional phrases: "On the other hand, until the public realizes what is happening to children in these countries..." or "The second reason hunger persists is...."

In long speeches, recap from time to time. Also preview what's to come. Use facts, descriptions, expert opinions, and statistics to hold your audience's attention.

Write the conclusion. At the end of the speech, summarize your points and draw your conclusion. You started with a bang; now finish with drama. The first and last parts of a speech are the most important. Make it clear to your audience when you've reached the end. Avoid endings such as "This is the end of my speech." A simple standby is "So in conclusion, I want to reiterate three points: First...." When you are finished, stop talking.

Create speaking notes. Some professional speakers recommend writing out your speech in full, then putting key words or main points on a few 3 × 5 cards. Number the cards so that if you drop them, you can quickly put them in order again. As you finish the information on each card, move it to the back of the pile. Write information clearly and in letters large enough to be seen from a distance.

The disadvantage of the 3 × 5 card system is that it involves card shuffling. Some speakers prefer to use standard outlined notes. Another option is mind mapping. Even an hour-long speech can be mapped on one sheet of paper. You can also use memory techniques to memorize the outline of your speech.

Overcome fear of public speaking

While you may not be able to eliminate fear of public speaking, you can take steps to reduce and manage it.

Prepare thoroughly. Research your topic thoroughly. Knowing your topic inside and out can create a baseline of confidence.

Accept your physical sensations. You've probably experienced physical sensations that are commonly associated with stage fright: dry mouth, a pounding heart, sweaty hands, muscle jitters, shortness of breath, and a shaky voice. One immediate way to deal with such sensations is to simply notice them. Tell yourself, "Yes, my hands are clammy. Yes, my stomach is upset. Also, my face feels numb." Trying to deny or ignore such facts can increase your fear. When you fully accept sensations, however, they start to lose power.

Focus on content, not delivery. Michael Motley, a professor at the University of California—Davis, distinguishes between two orientations to speaking. People with a *performance orientation* believe that the speaker must captivate their audiences by using formal techniques that differ from normal conversation. In contrast, speakers with a *communication orientation* see public speaking simply as an extension of one-to-one conversation. The goal is not to perform but to communicate your ideas to an audience in the same ways that you would explain them to a friend.[11]

Adopting a communication orientation can reduce your fear of public speaking. Instead of thinking about yourself, focus on your message. Your audiences are more interested in *what* you have to say than *how* you say it. Give them valuable ideas and information that they can use.[12]

Practice your presentation

The key to successful public speaking is practice.

Use your "speaker's voice." When you practice, do so in a loud voice. Your voice sounds different when you talk loudly, and this can be unnerving. Get used to it early on.

Practice in the room in which you will deliver your speech. Hear what your voice sounds like over a sound system. If you can't practice your speech in the actual room, at least visit the site ahead of time. Also make sure that the materials you will need for your speech, such as an overhead projector and screen, will be available when you want them.

Make a recording. Many schools have recording equipment available for student use. Use it while you practice, then view the finished recording to evaluate your presentation.

Listen for repeated phrases. Examples include *you know, kind of, really*, plus any little *uh*'s, *umm*'s, and *ah*'s. To get rid of these, tell yourself that you intend to notice every time they pop up in your daily speech. When you hear them, remind yourself that you don't use those words anymore.

Keep practicing. Avoid speaking word for word, as if you were reading a script. When you know your material well, you can deliver it in a natural way. Practice your presentation until you could deliver it in your sleep. Then run through it a few more times.

Deliver your presentation

Before you begin, get the audience's attention. If people are still filing into the room or adjusting their seats, they're not ready to listen. When all eyes are on you, then begin.

Project your voice. When you speak, talk loudly enough to be heard. Avoid leaning over your notes or the podium.

Maintain eye contact. When you look at people, they become less frightening. Remember, too, that it is easier for the audience to listen to someone when that person is looking at them. Find a few friendly faces around the room and imagine that you are talking to each person individually.

Notice your nonverbal communication. Be aware of what your body is telling your audience. Contrived or staged gestures will look dishonest. Be natural. If you don't know what to do with your hands, notice that. Then don't do anything with them.

Notice the time. You can increase the impact of your words by keeping track of the time during your speech. Better to end early than run late.

Pause when appropriate. Beginners sometimes feel that they have to fill every moment with the sound of their voice. Release that expectation. Give your listeners a chance to make notes and absorb what you say.

Have fun. Chances are that if you lighten up and enjoy your presentation, so will your listeners.

Reflect on your presentation

Review and reflect on your performance. Did you finish on time? Did you cover all of the points you intended to cover? Was the audience attentive? Did you handle any nervousness effectively?

Welcome evaluation from others. Most of us find it difficult to hear criticism about our speaking. Be aware of resisting such criticism and then let go of your resistance. Listening to feedback will increase your skill.

▶ Making the grade in group presentations

When preparing group presentations, you can use three strategies for making a memorable impression.

Get organized. As soon as you get the assignment, select a group leader and exchange contact information. Schedule specific times and places for planning, researching, writing, and practicing your presentation.

At your first meeting, write a to-do list including all of the tasks involved in completing the assignment. Distribute tasks fairly, paying attention to the strengths of individuals in your group. For example, some people excel at brainstorming while others prefer researching.

As you get organized, remember how your presentation will be evaluated. If the instructor doesn't give grading criteria, create your own. One powerful way to get started is to define clearly the topic and thesis, or main point, of your presentation. Then support your thesis by looking for the most powerful facts, quotations, and anecdotes you can find.

Get coordinated. Coordinate your presentation so that you have transitions between individual speakers. Practice making those transitions smooth.

Also practice using visuals such as flip charts, posters, DVDs, videotapes, or slides. To give visuals their full impact, make them appropriate for the room where you will present. Make sure that text is large enough to be seen from the back of the room. For bigger rooms, consider using presentation software or making overhead transparencies.

Get cooperation. Presentations that get top scores take teamwork and planning—not egos. Communicate with group members in an open and sensitive way. Contribute your ideas and be responsive to the viewpoints of other members. When you cooperate, your group is on the way to scoring well.

Power Process | Put It to Work | **Quiz** | Learning Styles Application | Master Student Profile

Name _____ Date ____/____/____

quiz

1. According to the text, human communication is always flawed to some extent. True or False? Explain your answer.

2. During a conversation, if someone is trying to act as a sender when you want to be the sender, you can:
    (a) Stop sending and be the receiver.
    (b) Stop sending and leave the conversation.
    (c) Ask the other person to stop sending so that you can send.
    (d) Any of the above.

3. This chapter suggests techniques for nonverbal and verbal listening. Briefly explain the difference between these two approaches to listening, and give one example of each.

4. Reword the following complaint as a request: "You always interrupt when I talk!"

5. List the five parts of an "I" message (the five ways to say "I").

6. You can listen skillfully to a speaker even when you disagree with that person's viewpoint. True or False? Explain your answer.

7. Which of the following is an effective thesis statement? Explain your answer.
    (a) Two types of thinking.
    (b) Critical thinking and creative thinking go hand in hand.
    (c) The relationship between critical thinking and creative thinking.

8. Define *plagiarism* and explain ways to avoid it.

9. Describe at least three techniques for practicing and delivering a speech.

10. What characteristic distinguishes the top five rungs of the ladder of powerful speaking from the bottom rung?

Chapter 12

Financial Planning

Financial planning

Meeting your money goals

You've probably heard the saying, "Time is money." There's wisdom in that time-worn saying.

Many of the skills that help you plan—such as monitoring your behaviour and setting priorities—can also help you manage money. An important part of planning is setting and meeting financial goals.

Some people shy away from setting financial goals. They think that money is a complicated subject. Yet most money problems result from spending more than is available. It's that simple, even though often we do everything we can to make the problem much more complicated.

The solution also is simple: *Don't spend more than you have.* If you are spending more money than you have, increase your income, decrease your spending, or do both. This idea has never won a Nobel Prize in economics, but you won't go broke applying it.

Starting today, you can take three simple steps to financial independence:

- Tell the truth about how much money you have and how much you spend.

- Make a commitment to spend no more than you have.

- Begin saving money.

If you do these three things consistently, you could meet your monetary goals and even experience financial independence. This does not necessarily mean having all of the money you could ever desire. Rather, you can be free from money worries by living within your means. Soon you will control money instead of letting money control you.

Increase money in

For many of us, making more money is the most appealing way to fix a broken budget. This approach is reasonable—and it has a potential problem: When our income increases, most of us continue to spend more than we make. Our money problems persist, even at higher incomes. You can avoid this dilemma by managing your expenses no matter how much money you make.

There are several ways to increase your income while you go to school. One of the most obvious ways is to get a job. You could also apply for scholarships and grants. You might borrow money, inherit it, or receive it as a gift. You could sell property, collect income from investments, or use your savings. Other options—such as lotteries and gambling casinos—pose obvious risks. Stick to making money the old-fashioned way: Earn it.

Work while you're in school. If you work while you go to school, you can earn more than money. Working helps you gain experience, establish references, and expand your contacts in the community. Doing well at a co-op job or an internship while you're in school can also help you land a good job after you graduate.

Regular income, even at a lower wage scale, can make a big difference. Look at your monthly budget to see how it would be affected if you worked just 15 hours a week (times 4 weeks a month) for $10 an hour.

Find a job. Make a list of several places that you would like to work. Include places that have advertised job openings and those that haven't. Then go to each place on your list and tell someone that you would like a job. This will yield more results than depending on the want ads alone. The people you speak to might say that there isn't a job available, or that the job is filled. That's OK. Ask to see the person in charge of hiring and tell him that you want to be considered for future job openings. Then ask when you can check back.

Keep your job in perspective. If your job is in your career field, great. If it is meaningful and contributes to society, great. If it involves working with people you love and respect, fantastic. If none of these things—well, remember that almost any job can help you reach your educational goals.

It's also easy to let a job eat up time and energy that you need for your education. You can avoid this by managing your time effectively. If you are a full-time student, try to limit your work commitment to 20 hours per week. That leaves 148 hours to focus on your most important present goal—becoming a master student.

Decrease money out

You do not have to live like a miser, pinching pennies and saving used dental floss. There are many ways to decrease the amount of money you spend and still enjoy life. Consider the ideas that follow.

Look at the big-ticket items. Your choices about which school to attend, what car to buy, and where to live can save you tens of thousands of dollars. When you look for places to cut expenses, start with the items that cost the most. For example, there are several ways to keep your housing costs reasonable. Sometimes a place a little farther from your school or a smaller apartment will be much less expensive. You can cut your housing costs in half by finding a roommate. Also look for opportunities to house-sit rather than paying rent. Some homeowners will even pay a responsible person to live in their house when they are away.

Look at the small-ticket items. Decreasing the money you spend on small purchases can help you balance your budget. A three-dollar cappuccino is tasty, but the amount that some people spend on such treats over the course of a year could give anyone the jitters.

Monitor money out. Each month, review your chequing account, receipts, and other financial records. Sort your expenditures into major categories such as school expenses, housing, personal debt, groceries, eating out, and entertainment. At the end of the month, total up how much you spend in each category. You might be surprised. Once you discover the truth, it might be easier to decrease unnecessary spending.

Create a budget. When you have a budget and stick to it, you don't have to worry about whether you can pay your bills on time. The basic idea is to project how much money is coming in and how much is going out and to make sure that those two amounts balance.

Creating two kinds of budgets is even more useful. A monthly budget includes regularly recurring income and expense items such as your earnings, food costs, and housing. A long-range budget includes unusual monetary transactions such as annual dividends, bursaries, and tuition payments that occur only a few times a year. With an eye to the future, you can make realistic choices about money today.

Shop comparatively. Prices on just about anything you want to buy can vary dramatically. You can clip coupons and wait for sales or shop around at secondhand stores, discount outlets, or garage sales. When you first go shopping, leave your cheque book and debit and credit cards at home, a sure way to control impulse buying. Look at all of the possibilities. Then later when you don't feel pressured, make your decision. To save time, money, and gas, you can also search the Internet for sites that compare prices on items.

Use public transportation or car pools. Aside from tuition, a car can be the biggest financial burden in a student's budget. The purchase price is often only the tip of

the iceberg. Be sure to consider the cost of parking, insurance, repairs, gas, maintenance, and tires. When you add up all of those items, you might find it makes more sense to car-pool or to take the bus or a cab instead.

Notice what you spend on "fun." Blowing your money on fun is fun. It is also a quick way to ruin your budget. When you spend money on entertainment, ask yourself what the benefits will be and whether you could get the same benefits for less money. You can read or borrow magazines at the library. Most libraries also lend CDs, DVDs, and videotapes at no cost. Student councils often sponsor activities, such as dances and music performances, for which there is no fee. Schools with sports facilities set aside times when students can use them at no cost. Meeting your friends for a quick game of basketball at the gym can be more fun than meeting at a bar, where there is a cover charge.

Free entertainment is everywhere. However, it usually isn't advertised, so you'll have to search it out. Start with your school bulletin boards and local newspapers.

Redefine money. Reinforce all of the above ideas by understanding money in a new way. According to authors Joe Dominguez and Vicki Robin, money is what we accept in exchange for the time, passion, and effort that we put into our work.[6] When you take this view of money, you might naturally find yourself being more selective about how often you spend it and what you spend it on. It's not just cash you're putting on the line—it's your life energy.

Remember that education is worth it . . .

A college diploma or university degree is one of the safest and most worthwhile investments you can make. Money invested in land, gold, oil, or stocks can be lost, but your education will last a lifetime. It can't rust, corrode, break down, or wear out. Once you have an education, it becomes a permanent part of you.

Think about all of the services and resources that your tuition money buys: academic and personal counselling; health services; access to the student health centre; counselling career planning and job placement services; athletic, arts, and entertainment facilities and events; and often a student centre where you can meet people and socialize. If you live in residence, you get a place to stay, sometimes with meals provided. By the way, you also get to attend classes.

In the long run, education pays off in increased income, job promotions, career satisfaction, and more creative use of your leisure time. These are benefits that you can sustain for a lifetime.

. . . and you can pay for it

Most students in Canada can afford to pay for post-secondary education. Financial aid is available for those students who require more money than they have. Financial aid includes money you don't pay back (bursaries and scholarships), money you do pay back (loans), and co-op programs that land you a job while you're in school.

A great source of information in your college or university is your financial aid, financial assistance, or financial awards office. They can provide you with up-to-date information in three important areas: federal government assistance programs; provincial government assistance programs; and institutional awards, bursaries, scholarship, and loan programs. You can get more information about awards and loans from various publications at most public, college, and university libraries.

Create a master plan—a long-term budget listing how much you need to complete your education and where you plan to get the money. Having a plan for paying for your entire education makes completing your degree work a more realistic possibility.

Once you've lined up financial aid, keep it flowing. Find out the requirements for renewing your loans, bursaries, and scholarships.

Create money for the future

You don't have to wait until you finish school to begin saving and investing. You can start now, even if you are in debt and living on a diet of macaroni.

Start saving. Saving is one of the most effective ways to reach your money goals. Aim to save at least 10 percent of your monthly take-home pay. If you can save more, that's even better.

One possible goal is to have savings equal to at least six months of living expenses. Build this nest egg first as a cushion for financial emergencies. Then save for major, long-term expenses.

Put your money into insured savings accounts, money market funds, savings bonds, or guaranteed investment certificates (GICs). These are low-risk options that you can turn into cash immediately. Even a small amount of money set aside each month can grow rapidly. The sooner you begin to save, the more opportunity your money has to grow. Time allows you to take advantage of the power of compound interest.

Invest after you have a cushion. Remember that investing is risky. Invest only money that you can afford to lose. Consider something safe, such as bills, notes, and bonds backed by the federal or provincial governments; no-load mutual funds; or blue chip stocks.

Avoid taking a friend's advice on how to invest your hard-earned money. Be wary, too, of advice from someone who has something to sell, such as a stockbroker or a realtor. See your banker or an independent certified financial planner instead.

Save on insurance. Shop around for insurance. Benefits, premiums, exclusions, and terms vary considerably from policy to policy, so study each one carefully. Buy health, auto, and life insurance with high deductibles to save on premiums. Also ask about safe driver, non-smoker, or good student discounts.

Be careful with contracts. Before you sign anything, read the fine print. If you are confused, ask questions and keep asking until you are no longer confused. After you sign a contract, policy, or lease, read the entire document again. If you think you have signed something that you will regret, back out quickly and get your release in writing.

Use credit wisely. If you don't already have one, you can begin to establish a credit rating now. Borrow a small amount of money and pay it back on time. Also pay your bills on time. Avoid the temptation to let big companies wait for their money. Develop a good credit rating so that later on you can borrow large amounts of money if you need to.

Before you take out a loan to buy a big-ticket item, find out what that item will be worth *after* you buy it. A brand-new $20,000 car might be worth only $15,000 the minute you drive it off the lot. To maintain your net worth, don't borrow any more than $15,000 to buy the car.

If you're in trouble. If you find yourself in over your financial head, get specific data about your present situation. Find out exactly how much money you owe, earn, and spend on a monthly basis. If you can't pay your bills in full, be honest with creditors. Many will allow you to pay off a large debt in small installments. Also consider credit counselling with professional advisers who can help you straighten out your financial problems. You can locate these people through your campus or community phone directories.

Places to find money for your post-secondary education

- Federal government student loans and grants, such as the Canadian Student Loans Program (CSLP), for Canadians with a demonstrated financial need.
- Provincial loan plans, such as Ontario Student Assistance Program (OSAP) and the Nova Scotia Student Assistance.
- Canada Study Grants (CSG) for students with permanent disabilities, high-need part-time students, women in doctoral studies, and student with dependents.
- Financial assistance to First Nations students (through band councils) and to Protected Persons and Convention Refugees (through CSLP).
- Private student bank loans and lines of credit.
- Scholarships, bursaries, and awards from institutions, organizations, unions, and associations.
- Corporate or union assistance programs.
- Part-time or full-time jobs and co-op programs.
- Relatives
- Personal savings
- Selling a personal possession, such as a car, boat, piano, or house

Note: Award and loan programs change constantly. In some cases, money is limited and application deadlines are critical. Be sure to get the most current information from your educational institution.

voices

student

I made a goal to make it to college. And here I am, even though in high school I was told that it wouldn't happen and there wasn't enough money to go. I achieved my goal and am working to support myself as well as working hard at my grades to get a better education.

—TRICIA MILLS

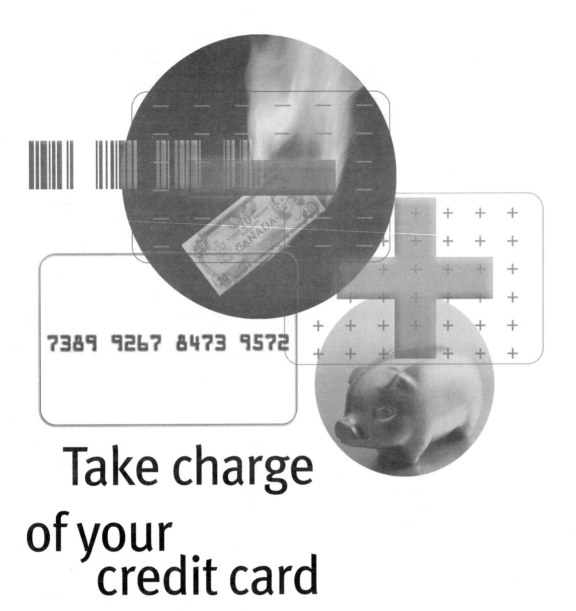

Take charge of your credit card

A credit card is compact and convenient. That piece of plastic seems to promise peace of mind. Low on cash this month? Just whip out your card, slide it across the counter, and relax. Your worries are over—that is, until you get the bill.

Credit cards often come with a hefty interest rate, sometimes as high as 27 percent. That can be over one-fifth of your credit card bill. Imagine working five days a week and getting paid for only four: You'd lose one-fifth of your income. Likewise, when people rely on high-interest credit cards to get by from month to month, they lose one-fifth of their monthly payments to interest charges. A recent survey showed that 78 percent of undergraduate students had credit cards. Their average credit card debt was $2,748. Suppose that a student with this debt used a card with an annual percentage rate of 18 percent. Also suppose that he pays only the minimum balance due each month. He'll be making payments for 15 years and will pay an additional $2,748 in interest fees.

Credit cards do offer potential benefits. Getting a card is one way to establish a credit record. Many cards offer rewards, such as frequent flier miles and car rental discounts. Your monthly statement also offers a way to keep track of your expenses.

Used wisely, credit cards can help us become conscious of what we spend. Used unwisely, they can leave us with a load of debt that takes decades to repay. That load can seriously delay other goals—paying off student loans, financing a new car, buying a home, or saving for retirement.

Use the following three steps to take control of your credit cards before they take control of you. Write these steps on an index card and don't leave home without it.

Do a First Step about money. See your credit card usage as an opportunity to take a financial First Step. If you rely on credit cards to make ends meet every month, tell the truth about that. If you typically charge up to the maximum limit and pay just the minimum balance due each month, tell the truth about that, too.

Write Discovery Statements focussing on what doesn't work—and what does work—about the way you use credit cards. Follow up with Intention Statements regarding steps you can take to use your cards differently. Then take action. Your bank account will benefit directly.

Scrutinize credit card offers. Beware of cards offering low interest rates. These rates are often only temporary. After a few months, they could double or triple. Also look for annual fees and other charges buried in the fine print.

To simplify your financial life and take charge of your credit, consider using only one card. Choose one with no annual fee and the lowest interest rate. Don't be swayed by offers of free T-shirts or coffee mugs. Consider the bottom line and be selective.

Pay off the balance each month. Keep track of how much you spend with credit cards each month. Then save an equal amount in cash. That way, you can pay off the card balance each month and avoid interest charges. Following this suggestion alone might transform your financial life.

If you do accumulate a large credit card balance, ask your bank about a "bill-payer" loan with a lower interest rate. You can use this loan to pay off your credit cards. Then promise yourself never to accumulate credit card debt again.

voices

student

The "Education by the hour" exercise made me realize that school is costing me a lot and everything counts when I don't attend class or do an assignment. I couldn't believe how much of my money I was wasting by not attending only one of my classes.

— LUZ LOPEZ

exercise 10

EDUCATION BY THE HOUR

Determine exactly what it costs you to go to school. Fill in the blanks below using totals for a semester, quarter, or whatever session system your school uses.

Note: Include only the costs that relate directly to going to school. For example, under "Transportation," list only the amount that you pay for gas to drive back and forth to school—not the total amount you spend on gas for a session.

Tuition	$_____
Books	$_____
Fees	$_____
Transportation	$_____
Clothing	$_____
Food	$_____
Housing	$_____
Entertainment	$_____
Other (such as insurance, medications, child care)	$_____
Subtotal	$_____
Salary you could earn per term if you weren't in school	$_____
Total (A)	$_____

Now figure out how many classes you attend in one term. This is the number of your scheduled class periods per week multiplied by the number of weeks in your school term. Put that figure below:

Total (B)   _____

Divide the **Total (B)** into the **Total (A)** and put that amount here:

$_____

This is what it costs you to go to one class one time.

On a separate sheet of paper, describe your responses to discovering this figure. Also list anything you will do differently as a result of knowing the hourly cost of your education.